ANTI-BLACK THOUGHT

1863 - 1925

"THE NEGRO PROBLEM"

AN ELEVEN –VOLUME ANTHOLOGY OF RACIST WRITINGS

edited and introduced by

JOHN DAVID SMITH

**Alumni Distinguished Professor of History
at North Carolina State University**

A GARLAND SERIES

VOLUME FOUR

THE "BENEFITS" OF SLAVERY

THE NEW PROSLAVERY ARGUMENT
PART II

edited with introductions by

JOHN DAVID SMITH

GARLAND PUBLISHING, INC.
NEW YORK & LONDON
1993

Library of Congress Cataloging-In-Publication Data

The "Benefits" of Slavery : the new proslavery argument / edited by John David Smith.
     p.   cm. — (Anti-Black thought, 1863–1925 ; v. 4)
    Includes bibliographical references.
    ISBN 0-8153-0976-7 (alk. paper)
    1. Slavery—United States—Justification. 2. Slavery—United States. 3. Afro-
Americans. 4. White supremacy movements—United States—History. 5. Racism—
United States—History. 6. United States—Race relations. I. Smith, John David,
1949– . II. Series.
E449.B4197 1993
305.896'073—dc20   92-27189
                                            CIP

Printed on acid-free, 250-year-life paper
Manufactured in the United States of America

FOR ALEX, LISA, AND LORENZ

CONTENTS

THE "BENEFITS" OF SLAVERY

ACKNOWLEDGMENTS

Anti-Black Thought 1863–1925 began in 1989 when Professor Paul Finkelman suggested to Leo F. Balk, Vice President of Garland Publishing, Inc., that I undertake an anthology of texts that documented late nineteenth-century American racism. I am grateful to Professor Finkelman for his endorsement and to Mr. Balk for his commitment to and enthusiasm for the project. My editors at Garland, Anita Vanca and Jonathan Oestreich, have been most helpful in locating texts, obtaining permissions to publish, and hammering out details. I very much appreciate their labors.

At North Carolina State University, I benefited from the research assistance of graduate students Eric Jackson, Paul Peterson, Michelle Justice, and Jo Frost. Eric and Paul helped me compile a data base of possible texts and verified citations. Michelle and Jo joined me in the appraisal process and Jo played an important role in deciding upon the final arrangement of the texts. Much of this work was tedious, and I value the care and precision with which these graduate students performed their tasks.

Professor Randall M. Miller offered keen advice regarding my use of the American Colonization Society texts. Dr. Jeffrey J. Crow and Professors David P. Gilmartin, William Kimler, and Linda O. McMurry subjected the "General Introduction" and the volume introductions to thoughtful criticism and thereby strengthened the entire project. I am especially indebted to Will Kimler for his painstaking analysis of the introductory section on "science" and race in Volumes V and VI, and for his help in revising this section. I hold in high regard the judgments of each of these colleagues and thank them for the time and effort they devoted to evaluating various drafts of my essay.

As the project neared completion, Alex Andrusyszyn assisted me in managing the extensive files. And finally, over the course of editing *Anti-Black Thought 1863–1925*, Sylvia A. Smith provided valuable insights into the nature of racial and sexual oppression and the role of law in social change.

When a man attempts to discuss the negro problem at the South, he may begin with the negro, but he really touches, with however light a hand, the whole bewildering problem of a civilization.

—Edgar Gardner Murphy (1904)[1]

The most formidable of all the ills which threaten the future existence of the Union arises from the presence of a black population upon its territory; and in contemplating the cause of the present embarrassments or of the future dangers of the United States, the observer is invariably led to consider this as a primary fact.

—Alexis de Tocqueville (1835)[2]

GENERAL INTRODUCTION

Writing in 1903, more than a half-century after Alexis de Tocqueville, W.E.B. Du Bois, the brilliant black historian, sociologist, and polemicist, viewed America's "ills" from a radically different perspective. Nonetheless, the two men concurred on the role that race played in defining America's character and destiny. Du Bois wrote in the shadow of Jim Crow race relations, American imperialism, and emerging Progressivism. As he looked back toward the nineteenth century, Du Bois found a legacy of slavery and racial oppression. He branded it a blot on the United States, which was then an emerging industrial and world power.

"The problem of the twentieth century," wrote Du Bois in *The Souls of Black Folk*, was "the problem of the color-line,—the relation of the darker to the lighter races of men in Asia and Africa, in America and the islands of the sea." Summarizing the history and cultural lives of African Americans, Du Bois underscored a question that ran as a leitmotif through white racial thought from the age of emancipation to the age of segregation. "What," he asked, "shall be *done* with Negroes?"[3] In his many writings Du Bois pounded away at the passive roles whites had always assigned to blacks— first as slaves—and later as freedmen, all too often caught in the web of neoslavery. From years of observing racial conditions in the North and South, Du Bois concluded that blacks and whites lived worlds and cultures apart—separated by a veil of racism. Years later, reflecting on the emancipation experience, Du Bois lamented that the freedman shared little of the progress and optimism that had marked white Victorian America. He wrote with elegant pathos: "The slave went free; stood a brief moment in the sun; then moved back again toward slavery."[4]

Though a propagandist for black rights, Du Bois in no way overstated the case. Most white Americans in the nineteenth century, north and south, before and after emancipation, did in fact view blacks as inferior "others." Though their attitudes toward blacks varied from place to place and over time, the vast majority of whites nevertheless held blacks, as a people and as a class, in contempt. To be sure there were exceptions. Whites always could identify "good Negroes," persons who conformed to their definition of acceptable behavior—deferential blacks who knew their "place." In the main, however, whites treated blacks as persons who differed in pejorative ways from themselves.

As so often in American history, whites defined "different" to mean "inferior." Not only their skin color, but their temperament, culture, and community, allegedly marked African Americans as "different." Such variances from the "normal"—the white ideal—were interpreted by the dominant caste as immutable characteristics. Yet, in what constituted just one of many contradictions in the ideology of white racism, whites lived in seemingly constant fear of racial mixing. If black "traits" were unalterable, why then were whites so apprehensive of miscegenation? The Old South's large mulatto population stood as a silent reminder that racial fears had not prevented racial mixing under slavery. After slavery whites continued to perceive blacks as marginal men and women—persons who mattered little, whose alleged childlike behavior and intellects deserved minimal respect. Blacks were to be acted upon. Decisions were to be made for them, not by them. During slavery's long history, various schools of racists trotted out a broad range of arguments—biblical, "scientific," historical, social, and economic—to bolster the idea of keeping blacks in chains.[5]

Following emancipation in 1865, whites, notably southerners, continued to describe blacks as degraded, certainly unprepared for the responsibilities and challenges of freedom. Many whites predicted that blacks could not survive as freedmen and women. Without the alleged paternalism of slavery, they reasoned, blacks would fall by the wayside, unable to compete in the class and racial struggle with whites. Some extreme racists even continued to define blacks as subhuman "beings," whose reported separate creation destined them to a perpetual servitude regardless of laws and legislation passed by civil authorities.

There was a direct relationship, of course, between the end of slavery and the determined search by whites for other means to regulate blacks. By the post-Civil War years, explains historian George M. Fredrickson, an "explicit or ideological racism" had taken root in the South. Social forces—"selfishness, greed, and the pursuit of privilege"—exacerbated the notion that blacks were natural inferiors. By the end of the century, social and economic tensions—as well as an upsurge of racism worldwide—led whites to campaign for the legal segregation and disfranchisement of their former slaves.[6]

At first white southerners settled on the Black Codes passed and then overthrown during Presidential Reconstruction. When other forms of racial control failed, post-Civil War whites eventually resorted to violent means.

From 1882, when statistics began to be collected systematically, until 1903, white mobs lynched 1,941 blacks.[7] Many other lynchings no doubt went unreported. Those blacks who were spared the barbarities of white racial "justice" faced a labyrinth of legal and extralegal barriers: *de jure* segregation under the Jim Crow laws and *de facto* segregation imposed by custom. Turn-of-the-century blacks had to fight to gain the most basic constitutional rights, minimally adequate schools, medical care, housing, and economic opportunities. As historian Nell Irvin Painter has delineated:

> At the turn of the twentieth century nine out of ten blacks lived in the South, and three-quarters of black farmers were tenants or sharecroppers. In the generation since emancipation, blacks, who constituted about 40 percent of the southern population, had bought one-eight [sic] of the region's farms. Even so, nearly all Afro-Americans, even the landowning minority, were poor. The most oppressed lived as peons, tied to planters by long-term contracts that deprived them of the right to change employers for as much as ten years, or as convicts, whom the states leased to planters and industrialists. In either situation, employers, who cared only about extracting a maximum of work from actual or virtual prisoners, provided wretched living and working conditions. These southern blacks, who earned bare subsistence and often died before earning their freedom, represented the worst-paid workers in this country.

Though African Americans never stood passively by acquiescing to white hegemony, theirs was a constant uphill struggle. Again, as before Appomattox, blacks confronted a maze of white arguments determined to keep them locked into inferior social, political, and economic status.[8]

Writing in 1908, the reform journalist Ray Stannard Baker analyzed the causes and consequences of America's race "problem," what whites generally termed "The Negro Problem." In *Following the Color Line* Baker identified "the most sinister phase of the race problem" as "instinctive race repulsion and competitive jealousy." Race relations, marred by "mutual fear and suspicion," led to the segregation of blacks and whites, what Baker described as "the rapid flying apart of the races." "More and more," he noted, "they are becoming a people wholly apart—separate in their churches, separate in their schools, separate in cars, conveyances, hotels, restaurants, with separate professional men. In short, we discover tendencies in this country toward the development of a caste system."[9]

This system of American apartheid marred the burgeoning industrial complex of the North as well as the agricultural South. Black northerners experienced *de facto* segregation while competing for jobs, housing, and social services with the "new" immigrants who populated the urban North. Racial violence often erupted in the North as persons with different cultural and ethnic backgrounds clashed. Race riots, for example, occurred in Springfield, Ohio, in March, 1904, and in August, 1906; in Springfield, Illinois, in August, 1908; in East St. Louis, Illinois, in July, 1917; and in

Chicago in July, 1919. To be sure, the northward migration of blacks after the turn of the century added diversity, texture, and power to the northern black community. Blacks challenged white discrimination at every turn. While Baker observed "comparatively little social and political prejudice" in the North, he nevertheless admitted that in the North "the Negro has a hard fight to get anything but the most subservient place in the economic machine." Black workers, in East St. Louis, for example, "had separate washrooms and dressing rooms, usually worked in segregated labor gangs, and ate meals in 'the colored section' of the lunchrooms." The African Americans lived in black ghettoes and their children attended "Negro schools."[10]

In the South, post-Civil War whites drew upon a two-hundred-year history of perceiving blacks as passive extensions of the master class. The old proslavery argument remained very much alive long after General Robert E. Lee's men stacked their guns at Appomattox, becoming a permanent fixture in the intellectual life and economic and legal world of the New South.[11] While few whites dreamed of reviving chattel slavery, conditions of neoslavery—modified serfdom, economic peonage, enticement laws, emigrant agent restrictions, contract laws, vagrancy statutes, the criminal-surety and convict labor systems—ensnared African Americans. After 1890 Jim Crow laws in one southern state after another locked blacks into a truly separate and unequal world.[12] Frightened by the thought of "social equality" and economic competition with blacks, white southerners employed all manner of racial violence to keep African Americans generally landless, undereducated, and powerless. Whites even conjured up the notion of black men as rapists of white women, thereby projecting their racial fantasies upon the sons of their ex-slaves. "Racial purity" became a catch-all phrase in the lexicon of the Jim Crow South. White southerners' determination to maintain absolute control over blacks amounted to what historian Joel Williamson has termed a "rage for order." "Uppity" blacks— men and women who demanded respect, fair treatment, and equal opportunities—threatened the very fabric of the South's biracial system.

Determined to maintain racial control, white Americans after the Civil War published widely on the causes and consequences of what they defined to be "The Negro Problem." As they struggled to find answers to the race question, whites flooded popular magazines, newspapers, scholarly journals, polemical tracts, monographs, and "scientific" treatises with writings on racial themes. Conferences, symposia, and public lectures underscored the sense of immediacy whites felt about the "race problem." By the turn of the century discussion of the "The Negro Problem" had virtually become a cottage industry. "Race thinkers" aplenty satisfied the seemingly insatiable demand in the white community for "experts" on just how to deal with the Negro.[13]

This eleven-volume anthology of writings on "The Negro Problem," written with only one exception by white authors, documents the various strains of racist thought in America from 1863 to 1925. The collection reproduces in facsimile format eighty-six texts that espoused a broad range of racist ideas—from relatively mild paternalistic remarks to extreme racialist diatribes—prevalent over the course of the post-emancipation age. It contains a microcosm of the various negative images whites held of blacks, including vulgar racist caricatures, genteel but condescending suggestions for black "uplift," and endorsements of black colonization. Many of the eighty-six texts are obscure racist pamphlets and speeches. To round out the collection, and to provide context, I have included several hard-to-find books, conference proceedings, and Ku Klux Klan items. The texts are drawn from the holdings of nineteen research libraries, and from the collections of the editor and the publisher.

In order to provide researchers with convenient topical access, the volumes are arranged thematically. Some themes (for example, the alleged backwardness of Africans, innate inferiority of blacks, slavery's "civilizing" influence, the horrors of emancipation and Reconstruction, fear of miscegenation among whites, the crucial importance of maintaining white supremacy, and the advantages of racial segregation) appear again and again throughout the collection. The topical format has eliminated much redundancy from volume to volume and serves to illustrate the breadth and depth of racist thought. Within the topical arrangement, each volume is arranged chronologically, suggesting the continuity and evolution of thought, as well as the subtle shift of racial themes over time. With no illusions of being "comprehensive" (the difficulties of locating texts and then gaining permission to publish them have been staggering), this edition is by design selective and eclectic. Nonetheless, it is hoped that *Anti-Black Thought 1863-1925* provides a representative sampling of conservative and reactionary racial thought from the era of the Civil War until the 1920s.

To be sure, these volumes tell only one side of the story—the white side of the discourse on race during the age of Jim Crow. They document the hurtful racial stereotypes and unfortunate images of blacks associated with that period. They illustrate how whites viewed the black presence as a "problem"—a menace—and how whites defined sources of the "problem" and identified solutions to it. For almost twenty years I have worked with these and similar materials and I am cognizant of just how painful and disturbing this sort of material is to African Americans. It is my determination, however, that the process of bringing such historical texts to light— and making them readily available for students and a general audience— will play some small role in battling racial injustice, bigotry, and class rule. An understanding of the pervasiveness and intensity of white racism is a key to comprehending the obstacles to true black freedom and equality.

This is not to suggest that blacks were passive and stood aimlessly by as whites acted upon them. Fortunately recent historical scholarship has uncovered how blacks actively fought slavery and the Jim Crow system that replaced it—a system with the cards consistently stacked against African

Americans. Blacks resisted nonetheless.[14] In different ways W.E.B. Du Bois, Booker T. Washington, Charles W. Chesnutt, Kelly Miller, and hundreds of other black leaders forcefully engaged their white critics and demanded racial justice throughout the period. With eloquent outrage they protested lynching, limited industrial education, disfranchisement, and segregation in every avenue of American life. Along with such white reformers as George Washington Cable, Lewis H. Blair, Albion W. Tourgée, and Franz Boas they challenged Jim Crow America. The overwhelming scale of the white racist barrage, however, had the effect of keeping blacks on the defensive. Just as whites controlled American society, so too did their racist dogma dominate the popular press. As a result, all too often blacks were forced to respond to whites on their terms. In other words, whites dictated the contours of the turn-of-the-century discourse on race. One of the tragedies of white racism is that the talents of many black scholars were diverted from more useful pursuits to defending what should have been obvious—the humanity of African Americans.

Even so, Du Bois and other African Americans remained ever hopeful that "out of the shame and oppression of the past" that "a new and broader humanity" might succor suffering blacks. As Frederick Douglass explained in 1886, the phrase "the negro problem" was itself "a misnomer." Eight years later Douglass referred to the "so-called but mis-called Negro problem." Responding to the common assumption among whites that they were civilized and blacks were uncivilized, Douglass charged "that there is nothing in the history of savages to surpass the blood-chilling horrors and fiendish excesses perpetrated against the coloured people of this country, by the so-called enlightened and Christian people of the South." "The Negro Problem" was, as Tocqueville, Du Bois, and Douglass had known all along, the white man's problem after all.[15]

Endnotes

[1]Murphy, *Problems of the Present South: A Discussion of Certain of the Educational, Industrial and Political Issues in the Southern States* (New York: Macmillan Company, 1904), 158.

[2]Tocqueville, *Democracy in America,* 2 vols. (1835; New York: Schocken Books, 1974), 1:424.

[3]Du Bois, *The Souls of Black Folk: Essays and Sketches* (1903; Greenwich: Fawcett Publications, 1961), 23, second quotation, emphasis added.

[4]Du Bois, *Black Reconstruction in America* (1934; New York: Atheneum, 1973), 30.

[5]George M. Fredrickson, *The Black Image in the White Mind: The Debate on Afro-American Character and Destiny, 1817–1914* (New York: Harper and

Row, 1971); Larry E. Tise, *Proslavery: A History of the Defense of Slavery in America, 1701–1840* (Athens: University of Georgia Press, 1987).

[6]Fredrickson, "Toward a Social Interpretation of the Development of American Racism," in Nathan I. Huggins, Martin Kilson, and Daniel M. Fox, eds., *Key Issues in the Afro-American Experience*, 2 vols. (New York: Harcourt Brace Jovanovich, 1971), 1:241, 254.

[7]Robert L. Zangranado, *The NAACP Crusade Against Lynching, 1909–1950* (Philadelphia: Temple University Press, 1980), 6. On the recent literature on racial violence, see W. Fitzhugh Brundage, "Mob Violence North and South, 1865–1940," *Georgia Historical Quarterly*, 75 (Winter, 1991): 748–770.

[8]I.A. Newby, *Jim Crow's Defense: Anti-Negro Thought in America, 1900–1930* (Baton Rouge: Louisiana State University Press, 1965); Lawrence J. Friedman, *The White Savage: Racial Fantasies in the Postbellum South* (Englewood Cliffs: Prentice-Hall, 1970); Joel Williamson, *The Crucible of Race: Black-White Relations in the American South Since Emancipation* (New York: Oxford University Press, 1984); Painter, *Standing at Armageddon: The United States, 1877–1919* (New York: W.W. Norton, 1987), xxi.

[9]Baker, *Following the Color Line: American Negro Citizenship in the Progressive Era* (New York: Doubleday, Page & Company, 1908), 298, 299, 300.

[10]Baker, *Following the Color Line*, 129; Elliott Rudwick, *Race Riot at East St. Louis, July 2, 1917* (New York: Atheneum, 1972), 6.

[11]John David Smith, *An Old Creed for the New South: Proslavery Ideology and Historiography, 1865–1918* (1985; Athens: University of Georgia Press, 1991).

[12]Pete Daniel, *The Shadow of Slavery: Peonage in the South, 1901–1969*(1972; New York: Oxford University Press, 1973); Daniel A. Novak, *The Wheel of Servitude: Black Forced Labor After Slavery* (Lexington: University Press of Kentucky, 1978); William Cohen, *At Freedom's Edge: Black Mobility and the Southern White Quest for Racial Control, 1861–1915* (Baton Rouge: Louisiana State University Press, 1991).

[13]See Alfred Holt Stone, "More Race Problem Literature," *Publications of the Southern History Association*, 10 (July, 1906): 218–227. "The great salient feature of the problem of race relations to-day," concluded Stone, "is the steadily increasing uniformity of ideas among white men all over the world,—as they come face to face with the negro." See p. 227.

[14]See, for example, Arnold H. Taylor, *Travail and Triumph: Black Life and Culture in the South Since the Civil War* (Westport: Greenwood Press, 1976); Leon F. Litwack, *Been in the Storm So Long: The Aftermath of Slavery* (New York: Alfred A. Knopf, 1979); Vincent Harding, *There Is a*

River: The Black Struggle for Freedom in America (New York: Harcourt Brace Jovanovich, 1981); Mary Frances Berry and John W. Blassingame, *Long Memory: The Black Experience in America* (New York: Oxford University Press, 1982); John Hope Franklin and August Meier, eds., *Black Leaders of the Twentieth Century* (Urbana: University of Illinois Press, 1982); Howard N. Rabinowitz, ed., *Southern Black Leaders of the Reconstruction Era* (Urbana: University of Illinois Press, 1982); Eric Foner, *Nothing But Freedom: Emancipation and Its Legacy* (Baton Rouge: Louisiana State University Press, 1983); Armstead L. Robinson, "The Difference Freedom Made: The Emancipation of Afro-Americans," in Darlene Clark Hine, ed., *The State of Afro-American History: Past, Present, Future* (Baton Rouge: Louisiana State University Press, 1986), 51–75; Leon Litwack and August Meier, eds., *Black Leaders of the Nineteenth Century* (Urbana: University of Illinois Press, 1988).

[15]Du Bois, "The Negro South and North," *Bibliotheca Sacra*, 62 (July, 1905), in Herbert Aptheker, ed., *The Complete Published Works of W.E.B. Du Bois: Volume I, 1891–1909* (Millwood, NY: Kraus-Thompson Organization, 1982), 256; Douglass to W.H. Thomas, July 16, 1886, Frederick Douglass Papers, Manuscript Division, Library of Congress; Douglass, *The Lessons of the Hour* (1894), in Philip S. Foner, ed., *The Life and Writings of Frederick Douglass*, 4 vols. (1955; New York International Publishers, 1975), 4:491, 492–493.

FURTHER READINGS[1]

Anderson, Eric. *Race and Politics in North Carolina, 1872–1901: The Black Second.* Baton Rouge: Louisiana State University Press, 1981.

Bauman, Mark K. "Race and Mastery: The Debate of 1903." In *From the Old South to the New: Essays on the Transitional South.* Edited by Walter J. Fraser, Jr., and Winfred B. Moore, Jr. Westport: Greenwood Press, 1981.

Berry, Mary Frances. "Repression of Blacks in the South, 1890–1945: Enforcing the System of Segregation." In *The Age of Segregation: Race Relations in the South, 1890–1945.* Edited by Robert Haws. Jackson: University Press of Mississippi, 1978.

Boskin, Joseph. *Sambo: The Rise & Demise of an American Jester.* New York: Oxford University Press, 1986.

Bowler, Peter J. *The Eclipse of Darwinism: Anti-Darwinian Evolution Theories in the Decades Around 1900.* Baltimore: The Johns Hopkins University Press, 1983.

————. *Theories of Human Evolution: A Century of Debate, 1844–1944.* Baltimore: The Johns Hopkins University Press, 1986.

Bruce, Dickson D., Jr. *Black American Writing From the Nadir: The Evolution of a Literary Tradition, 1877–1915.* Baton Rouge: Louisiana State University Press, 1989.

Burton, Orville Vernon. "'The Black Squint of the Law': Racism in South Carolina." In *The Meaning of South Carolina History: Essays in Honor of George C. Rogers, Jr.* Edited by David R. Chesnutt and Clyde N. Wilson. Columbia: University of South Carolina Press, 1991.

Cartwright, Joseph H. *The Triumph of Jim Crow: Tennessee Race Relations in the 1880s.* Knoxville: University of Tennessee Press, 1976.

Cassity, Michael J., editor. *Chains of Fear: American Race Relations Since Reconstruction.* Westport: Greenwood Press, 1984.

_____ , editor. *Legacy of Fear: American Race Relations to 1900.* Westport: Greenwood Press, 1985.

Cell, John W. *The Highest Stage of White Supremacy: The Origins of Segregation in South Africa and the American South.* Cambridge: Cambridge University Press, 1982.

Clayton, Bruce. *The Savage Ideal: Intolerance and Intellectual Leadership in the South, 1890–1914.* Baltimore: Johns Hopkins University Press, 1972.

Cooper, William J., Jr. *The Conservative Regime: South Carolina, 1877–1890.* Baltimore: The Johns Hopkins University Press, 1968.

Cortner, Richard C. *A Mob Intent on Death: The NAACP and the Arkansas Riot Cases.* Middletown: Wesleyan University Press, 1988.

Crow, Jeffrey J. "An Apartheid for the South: Clarence Poe's Crusade for Rural Segregation." In *Race, Class, and Politics in Southern History: Essays in Honor of Robert F. Durden.* Edited by Jeffrey J. Crow, Paul D. Escott, and Charles L. Flynn, Jr. Baton Rouge: Louisiana State University Press, 1989.

Dittmer, John. *Black Georgia in the Progressive Era, 1900–1920.* Urbana: University of Illinois Press, 1977.

Drago, Edmund L. *Initiative, Paternalism, and Race Relations: Charleston's Avery Normal Institute.* Athens: University of Georgia Press, 1990.

Ellsworth, Scott. *Death in a Promised Land: The Tulsa Race Riot of 1921.* Baton Rouge: Louisiana State University Press, 1982.

Fields, Barbara J. "Ideology and Race in American History." In *Region, Race, and Reconstruction: Essays in Honor of C. Vann Woodward.* New York: Oxford University Press, 1982.

Fischer, Roger A. *The Segregation Struggle in Louisiana, 1862–77.* Urbana: University of Illinois Press, 1974.

Flynn, Charles L., Jr. *White Land, Black Labor: Caste and Class in Late Nineteenth-Century Georgia.* Baton Rouge: Louisiana State University Press, 1983.

Fredrickson, George M. *The Arrogance of Race: Historical Perspectives on Slavery, Racism, and Social Inequality.* Middletown: Wesleyan University Press, 1988.

————."Black-White Relations Since Emancipation: The Search for a Comparative Perspective." In *What Made the South Different? Essays and Comments.* Edited by Kees Gispen. Jackson: University Press of Mississippi, 1990.

Gerber, David A. *Black Ohio and the Color Line, 1860–1915*. Urbana: University of Illinois Press, 1976.

Gossett, Thomas F. *Race: The History of an Idea in America*. Dallas: Southern Methodist University Press, 1963.

Graves, John William. *Town and Country: Race Relations in an Urban-Rural Context, Arkansas, 1865–1905*. Fayetteville: University of Arkansas Press, 1990.

Gutman, Herbert G. *The Black Family in Slavery and Freedom, 1750–1925*. New York: Pantheon Books, 1976.

Hair, William Ivy. *Carnival of Fury: Robert Charles and the New Orleans Race Riot of 1900*. Baton Rouge: Louisiana State University Press, 1976.

Harlan, Louis R. *Booker T. Washington: The Making of a Black Leader, 1856–1901*. New York: Oxford University Press, 1972.

———. *Booker T. Washington: The Wizard of Tuskegee, 1901–1915*. New York: Oxford University Press, 1983.

———. *Separate and Unequal: Public School Campaigns and Racism in the Southern Seaboard States, 1901–1915*. Chapel Hill: University of North Carolina Press, 1958.

Harrison, Alferdteen, editor. *Black Exodus: The Great Migration from the American South*. Jackson: University Press of Mississippi, 1991.

Hartzell, Lawrence L. "The Exploration of Freedom in Black Petersburg, Virginia, 1865–1902." In *The Edge of the South: Life in Nineteenth-Century Virginia*. Edited by Edward L. Ayers and John C. Willis. Charlottesville: University Press of Virginia, 1991.

Haynes, Robert V. *A Night of Violence: The Houston Riot of 1917*. Baton Rouge: Louisiana State University Press, 1976.

Horsman, Reginald. *Josiah Nott of Mobile: Southerner, Physician, and Racial Theorist*. Baton Rouge: Louisiana State University Press, 1987.

Ingalls, Robert P. *Urban Vigilantes in the New South: Tampa, 1882–1936*. Knoxville: University of Tennessee Press, 1988.

Lofgren, Charles A. *The Plessy Case: A Legal-Historical Interpretation*. New York: Oxford University Press, 1987.

Luker, Ralph E. "In Slavery's Shadow: North Carolina Methodism and Race Relations, 1885–1920." In *Methodism Alive in North Carolina*. Edited by O. Kelly Ingram. Durham: Duke Divinity School, 1976.

———. *The Social Gospel in Black & White: American Racial Reform, 1885–1912.* Chapel Hill: University of North Carolina Press, 1991.

McGovern, James R. *Anatomy of a Lynching: The Killing of Claude Neal.* Baton Rouge: Louisiana State University Press, 1982.

McMillen, Neil R. *Dark Journey: Black Mississippians in the Age of Jim Crow.* Urbana: University of Illinois Press, 1989.

Mandle, Jay R. *Not Slave, Not Free: The African American Experience Since the Civil War.* Durham: Duke University Press, 1992.

Newby, I. A., editor. *The Development of Segregationist Thought.* Homewood: The Dorsey Press, 1968.

Nieman, Donald G. *Promises to Keep: African–Americans and the Constitutional Order, 1776 to the Present.* New York: Oxford University Press, 1991.

Olsen, Otto H., editor. *The Negro Question: From Slavery to Caste, 1863–1910.* New York: Pitman Publishing Corporation, 1971.

———, editor. *The Thin Disguise: Turning Point in Negro History, Plessy v. Ferguson, A Documentary Presentation (1864–1896).* New York: Humanities Press, 1967.

Painter, Nell Irvin. "'Social Equality,' Miscegenation, Labor, and Power." In *The Evolution of Southern Culture.* Edited by Numan V. Bartley. Athens: University of Georgia Press, 1988.

Perman, Michael. "Counter Reconstruction: The Role of Violence in Southern Redemption." In *The Facts of Reconstruction: Essays in Honor of John Hope Franklin.* Edited by Eric Anderson and Alfred A. Moss, Jr. Baton Rouge: Louisiana State University Press, 1991.

Rabinowitz, Howard N. "A Comparative Perspective on Race Relations in Southern and Northern Cities, 1860–1900, with Special Emphasis on Raleigh." In *Black Americans in North Carolina and the South.* Edited by Jeffrey J. Crow and Flora J. Hatley. Chapel Hill: University of North Carolina Press, 1984.

———. *Race Relations in the Urban South, 1865–1890.* New York: Oxford University Press, 1978.

———. "Segregation and Reconstruction." In *The Facts of Reconstruction: Essays in Honor of John Hope Franklin.* Edited by Eric Anderson and Alfred A. Moss, Jr. Baton Rouge: Louisiana State University Press, 1991.

———. "The Weight of the Past Versus the Promise of the Future: Southern Race Relations in Historical Perspective." In *The Future South: A Historical Perspective for the Twenty-first Century.* Edited by Joe P. Dunn and Howard L. Preston. Urbana: University of Illinois Press, 1991.

Rable, George C. *But There Was No Peace: The Role of Violence in the Politics of Reconstruction.* Athens: University of Georgia Press, 1984.

Rogers, William Warren and Robert David Ward. *August Reckoning: Jack Turner and Racism in Post-Civil War Alabama.* Baton Rouge: Louisiana State University Press, 1973.

Shapiro, Herbert. *White Violence and Black Response: From Reconstruction to Montgomery.* Amherst: University of Massachusetts Press, 1988.

Smith, H. Shelton. *In His Image, But . . . Racism in Southern Religion, 1780–1910.* Durham: Duke University Press, 1972.

Stanfield, John H. *Philanthropy and Jim Crow in American Social Science.* Westport: Greenwood Press, 1985.

Takaki, Ronald T. *Iron Cages: Race and Culture in 19th-Century America.* New York: Alfred A. Knopf, 1979.

Toll, Robert C. *Blacking Up: The Minstrel Show in Nineteenth-Century America.* New York: Oxford University Press, 1974.

Tuttle, William M., Jr. *Race Riot: Chicago in the Red Summer of 1919.* New York: Atheneum, 1970.

Wayne, Michael. *The Reshaping of Plantation Society: The Natchez District, 1860–1880.* Baton Rouge: Louisiana State University Press, 1983.

Weaver, John D. *The Brownsville Raid.* New York: W.W. Norton, 1970.

Westin, Richard B. "Blacks, Educational Reform, and Politics in North Carolina, 1897–1898." In *The Southern Enigma: Essays on Race, Class, and Folk Culture.* Edited by Walter J. Fraser, Jr., and Winfred B. Moore, Jr. Westport: Greenwood Press, 1983.

Wheeler, Joanne. "Together in Egypt: A Pattern of Race Relations in Cairo, Illinois, 1865–1915." In *Toward a New South? Studies in Post-Civil War Southern Communities.* Edited by Orville Vernon Burton and Robert C. McMath, Jr. Westport: Greenwood Press, 1982.

Wilson, Charles Reagan. *Baptized in Blood: The Religion of the Lost Cause, 1865–1920.* Athens: University of Georgia Press, 1980.

Wright, George C. *Life Behind a Veil: Blacks in Louisville, Kentucky, 1865–1930.* Baton Rouge: Louisiana State University Press, 1985.

———. *Racial Violence in Kentucky, 1865–1940: Lynchings, Mob Rule, and "Legal Lynchings."* Baton Rouge: Louisiana State University Press, 1990.

[1]These citations develop themes suggested in the "General Introduction" and are designed to supplement the works cited in the Endnotes. In no sense comprehensive, the references are drawn heavily from the historical literature published since 1980, and reflect the ongoing reassessment of white racism in late nineteenth-century America.

INTRODUCTION

Volumes III and IV focus on the persistence of proslavery ideology long after slavery's legal termination. Without question, emancipation as an idea posed a serious threat to racial conservatives, north and south. After Appomattox many whites proved unable or unwilling to accept the notion of blacks as freedmen and women. In a multiplicity of forums, and for decades after the Civil War, they continued to praise slavery as the golden age of race relations in American history. The peculiar institution, whites said, educated, protected, civilized, and Christianized African Americans. Postwar proslavery theorists predicted that without the guardianship of whites, the ex-slaves would die off, revert to savagery, or, at the very least, fail miserably in competition with whites.

In *White Supremacy and Negro Subordination*, for example, which appears in Volume III, Dr. John H. Van Evrie drew heavily on contemporary racist anthropology and pluralist ethnology. Van Evrie based his analysis on the assumption that "the white citizen is superior, the negro inferior; and, therefore, whenever . . . they happen to be in juxtaposition, the human law should accord, as it does . . . in the South, . . . [that the inferior status of the black is] fixed forever by the hand of God." For years Van Evrie had argued that slavery, far from being an unusual status, was the natural condition for the African. He thus reversed the entire notion of slavery and freedom, espousing the view that blacks experienced freedom only when enslaved. "The negro," explained the New York editor in 1868, "forced from his normal condition, and into unnatural relation to the white man, must relapse into his African habits, . . . and . . . unless we take possession and restore the natural order . . . civilization itself will utterly perish, and the great heart of the continent be surrendered to African savagism!"[1]

Other examples in Volume IV, the pamphlets authored by the Reverend Amory Dwight Mayo and Dr. Paul B. Barringer, illustrate less crude but equally virulent strains of the ongoing proslavery argument. Though a Massachusetts native and renowned educational reformer, Mayo nonetheless employed positive images of slavery in his campaign to uplift southern blacks through education. According to historian Paul M. Gaston, Mayo typified "the new breed of Northern reformers who muted or abandoned whatever abolitionists [sic] and radical sympathies they might once have had and allied themselves with the spokesmen of the New South." Writing in *The Negro American Citizen in the New American Life*, Mayo utilized the slavery-as-school analogy, a familiar weapon in the arsenal of the old proslavery ideologues. Under the "schooling" of slavery, explained Mayo, the African American "learned the three great elements of civilization more speedily than they were ever learned before. He learned to work. He acquired the language and adopted the religion of the most progressive of peoples." Mayo even praised slavery because the institution allegedly "protected the Negro from his lower self . . . against vagrancy, laziness, drunkenness, and several temptations of a semi-tropical climate which are too much for thousands of his betters."²

Barringer, respected both in medical and academic circles, was descended from North Carolina slaveholders and credited slavery with providing contemporary blacks with whatever "civilization" they possessed. He argued that without the discipline of slavery, blacks not only were "steadily degenerating both morally and physically," but "reverting to barbarism with the inordinate criminality and degradation of that state." Racism was so pervasive that many otherwise enlightened southern Progressives shared these opinions. Indeed, to their mind, racial control through disfranchisement and other segregationist laws represented "progress," a move away from political "corruption" and a step toward "pure" government. According to southern Progressives, once the South could be "cleansed" of the Negro as a political factor, then real reforms could be instituted that could allegedly advance all residents of the region, including black southerners. By 1915 Barringer apparently had abandoned hope of attaining a satisfactory solution to the Negro question. He went so far as to propose to President Woodrow Wilson that the United States sponsor black colonization to Haiti as the only "real solution" to the race problem. "The present drift towards 'segregation,'" explained Barringer, "is but an indication that the races in the South have nearly reached the parting of the ways." Barringer, like other paternalistic southern Progressives, longed for the racial control of the Old South as they fashioned the New South.³

Endnotes

¹Fredrickson, *The Black Image in the White Mind: The Debate on Afro-American Character and Destiny, 1817–1914* (New York: Harper and Row, 1971), 92; Smith, *An Old Creed for the New South: Proslavery Ideology and Historiography, 1865–1918* (1985; Athens: University of Georgia Press, 1991), 46–47; Van Evrie, *White Supremacy and Negro Subordination* (New York: Van Evrie, Horton and Company, 1868), 17, 30.

²Gaston, *The New South Creed: A Study in Southern Mythmaking* (New York: Alfred A. Knopf, 1970), 101; Mayo, *The Negro American Citizen in the New American Life* (n.p., 1889), 3, 7.

[3]John David Smith, "An Old Creed for the New South: Southern Historians and the Revival of the Proslavery Argument, 1890–1920," *Southern Studies: An Interdisciplinary Journal of the South*, 18 (Spring, 1979): 80; Barringer, *"The Sacrifice of a Race"* (Raleigh: Edwards & Broughton, 1900), 28; Donald Spivey, *Schooling for the New Slavery: Black Industrial Education, 1868–1915* (Westport: Greenwood Press, 1978), 76; Barringer to Wilson, August 28, 1915, Paul B. Barringer Papers, University of Virginia Library.

THE

PUBLIC SCHOOL

IN

ITS RELATIONS TO THE NEGRO.

BY CIVIS.

———————

REPUBLISHED BY REQUEST, FROM THE SOUTHERN
PLANTER AND FARMER.

———————

RICHMOND:
CLEMMITT & JONES, STEAM PRINTERS.
1877.

[From the Southern Planter and Farmer, December, 1875.]

THE PUBLIC SCHOOL IN ITS RELATIONS TO THE NEGRO.

No. I.

In a series of articles over the signature of "Civis," which appeared in the *Religious Herald* last spring and summer, I demonstrated that the political principles which are invoked in the support of the public school are foreign to free institutions and fatal to liberty; that the theory upon which the system is based is well calculated to emasculate the energies of a people, and to debauch public and private morality; that the education of children is not the business of government, but the sacred and imperative duty of parents; that the assumption by the State, as the system requires, of the duties, privileges and prerogatives that belong only to the parental relation, is a wicked and dangerous denial of the reciprocal relations and obligations of parent and child, as proclaimed by nature and taught with solemn emphasis over and over by God, by Christ and his Apostles; that the cost of instruction at the public school is, as to those whose money supports it, greater than that of better instruction at the private school, and that the enforced charity is really an injury to the party receiving it and to the party robbed and wronged by unjust taxation; that granting, for the sake of argument, the system to be in itself desirable, Virginia is forbidden by simple honesty to patronize it, for she can only do it, as she is doing to-day, with money which is not her own, money withheld from its rightful owners, the creditors of the Commonwealth.

These positions and others of a kindred character, elaborated in the articles referred to, and fortified and illustrated by the facts of past and current history, have been assailed in various quarters, in some instances with marked ability, but in all with conspicuous and signal lack of success. Having shown that the public school is utterly indefensible, both as a matter of right and of policy, even if our population were homogeneous, I purpose in this article and in others, which may follow, to discuss the system in its relations to the negro that we may discover what policy is demanded alike by his interests and our own.

Ideas,—born of a spurious and pernicious philanthropy indigenous to other latitudes, which sees the mote in a brother's eye not the beam in its own, which substitutes its unsupported dicta for the doctrines of Revelation, for the teachings of science and for the lessons of history and of experience,—are gaining foothold in our

3

midst, are becoming crystalized in our laws, and unless arrested or eradicated, will speedily fructify in a bitter harvest of woe.

And in this paper I shall say, as I have heretofore done, just exactly what I think. At a time when expediency seems to be the test of morals; when, as in the corrupt days of the Roman Commonwealth, men have one thing shut up in the heart, another ready on the tongue, I know of no medicine so likely to work good results as the full and truthful utterance of one's honest opinions, without reference to the coward dictates of a pliant expediency.

Further, I must premise that I am the friend of the negro, but a friend to him in his proper place of subordination; a far better friend than those who inflate him with ideas of his importance, which will only lead him to his ruin. Born and bred on a plantation of negroes, the owner of slaves until robbed of my property under the forms of law, I have always entertained the most kindly feelings towards them, which I still cherish whenever in their speech and conduct they acknowledge their true position, a thing— so strong in them is the instinct of inferiority—they never fail to do, except in the very few cases in which their brains have been addled by the miserable teachings of a fanatical philanthropy. Having observed all my life I well understand the peculiar qualities of the race, and they are exactly such as fit them for menial offices and subordinate positions, and of necessity disqualify them for the higher walks of life, and particularly for the great functions of citizenship.

1. The negro is distinguished by extreme docility, a most desirable quality in a menial; a most dangerous, a fatal one in a sovereign. Who in this Southern land has not witnessed day by day the most lovely exhibitions of this quality in the negro, humble, trustful and obedient? And yet they are banded by the same quality, as voters and sovereigns, into an unthinking mass ready to execute, without questioning, any behests of their leaders. The same quality that fits them for subordinate positions unfits them to be voters, and voters they ought not to be.

2. Notice their improvidence for the future. They seldom project their thoughts into the future and will not deny themselves to make provision for sickness, or old age, or for their children. Remonstrating a few years ago with a negro woman who had formerly belonged to me, and she too the mother of several children, for the reckless waste of her wages, I was met with the astounding answer that she was afraid she might die and leave money behind her unspent. I have ceased my efforts since to assist them in making a provision for the future, convinced that poverty is necessary to drive them to those menial offices which underlie civilized society and which alone they are competent to discharge. How different with the white man, who gives his youth to labor that his age may be crowned with ease, and projecting his thoughts beyond the limits of his life, practices a daily self-denial that his children may have a higher career and a nobler sphere than were possible to him.

Those who will not acquire property, who live from hand to mouth, are always desirous of change, and have been so in every age of the world; any change may improve their condition, none can injure it; and hence they constitute ·the inflammable. material of mobs, riots and revolutions. How dangerous to put political power into the hands of such, and such negroes are, always have been, and always will be.

But this improvidence of the future, which so strongly marks the negro, and makes him so dangerous.as a political element, actually increases his value as a mere menial and dependent. Untroubled by the cares of the morrow, he reposes with calm confidence on the firmer nerves and clearer brains of his superiors to supply his wants, and is happy and content in his humble sphere of allotted usefulness.

.3. By virtue of the black pigment beneath his skin, placed there by Infinite Wisdom, though modern philanthropy tells us it is a great outrage, the negro is eminently a sweating animal. This is a fact of vast importance and should not be overlooked in the treatment of this subject. This coloring matter absorbs heat freely, carries it into the system, and there it drives the water to the surface, which in evaporation takes off a large amount of heat in the latent form. Evaporation is a cooling process. Thus as solar heat freely strikes in, tending to raise the temperature of the body beyond the normal point, perspiration and evaporation are induced and proceed at equal pace, by which processes this tendency is accurately counteracted, and the temperature of the body is kept constant. A horse ploughing in hot weather can kill in succession a dozen oxen urged at the same rate, chiefly because the horse sweats freely, the ox does not. The remarkable sweating capacity of the negro renders him objectionable in the cars, in the jury box, in the halls of legislation, in the crowds that assemble on the courtgreen, but wonderfully fits him for his proper functions as a laborer in tobacco and rice fields and on the great cotton and sugar plantations of low latitudes. In such work, which suits him as it suits no other race, and in doing which he is incomparably superior to any other race, he is useful and has been happy, and would be again if he were not constantly goaded by a fatal political policy and mischievous intermeddlers into visionary dreams and vague ambitions which stagger his feeble intellect, and, in many cases, render him restive and morose in the only sphere of life which he is competent to fill. Since this people landed on this continent, they have been gravitating from higher to lower latitudes, not by human but by Divine enactment, that they might find the physical conditions best suited to the law of their being, and, under the direction of a superior sagacity, follow those modes of life and perform that kind of labor best calculated to promote their own happiness and the general interests of mankind.

If it be said, as I know it will be said, that the qualities which I have attributed to the negro are in part the heritage of slavery, and that we are in duty bound to educate the race in compensation of 250 years of labor, my ready and triumphant reply is:

1. That Domestic Slavery brought absolute savages into contact with civilization and taught them to be skillful laborers in agriculture, in household duties, and, to some extent, in the mechanic arts; that it was to them a School of Association that raised the race to a higher plane of life than it has ever reached in any other age or in any other quarter of the globe; that in the opinion of those even who have most fiercely denounced the institution, it has rendered them competent to the highest functions of life, the duties of political sovereignty.

2. That compensation for service rendered has been thrice made by the generous supply of their wants as well in the helpless periods of infancy and decrepitude as in vigorous and useful life; and by the tuition which they have received in this School of Association, resulting so conspicuously in their moral and intellectual improvement.

The history of this race may be explored in vain for a case in which these people have risen by inherent energy to a condition of independent civilized existence; in vain for a single instance even in which after having been as highly civilized as is possible for them, and then left to themselves with the arts and appliances of civilization in their hands, they have succeeded in making progress or even in holding their own.

The Liberian colony founded under the most favorable auspices after vast expenditures of treasure, and anxious and protracted thought by many of our best and wisest men, constantly guarded by influences and propped up by material support from this country and England, is yet in a tottering condition and seems unable to defend itself against the assaults of savage brothers.

In some of the West India Islands—Hayti, for instance—where by British philanthropy negroes have been made almost the exclusive owners of the soil, coffee and other intertropical products, once largely exported, have almost ceased to be articles of export; and plantations, before magnificent and wonderfully productive, are rapidly relapsing, under the ownership of the blacks, into original wilderness. Raising, almost without labor, in their fervid and fertile soil only a few yams, they rely almost entirely upon the spontaneous productions of the earth to support their lazy and unprofitable lives. The moulding and controling influence of the white man being cancelled, they blend the teachings of the Bible with the baldest superstitions, and are fast reviving the feticism which their ancestors brought from the Guinea coast.

Were it not too painful to pursue the subject in that direction, I might find illustrations nearer home and show how corruption runs riot; and the car of progress turns back, and civilization, late in its noblest and loftiest type, wilts withers and dies before the hot breath of these black barbarians.

All the facts of negro history, his moral, intellectual and physical peculiarities, particularly his facial and cranial configuration, point to the same conclusion, to wit: that he belongs to an inferior type of the human family, to a lower grade of organization. No man, familiar with the facts involved and competent to form a sound opinion, can believe that the negro is the equal of the Caucasian. The truth is, the negro is incapable of independent civilized existence. His God-given instincts, stronger than the logic and a surer and safer guide than the teachings of philanthropy, impel him to rely for support and guidance upon a clearer and a stronger wit than he can claim. He is, by necessity of intellectual weakness, a parasite. This explains his extreme docility, which renders him so agreeable and happy, and valuable as a menial, so dangerous a tool in the contests of politics.

These people so impulsive and docile, so reckless of the future and so oblivious of care, so patient of heat and of labor, incapable of logical and consecutive thought, unambitious, unenterprising, unprogressive, we have among us. How shall we treat them? A problem in sociology so important has never before demanded a solution. The development of our material resources, the perpetuity of our form of government, the conservation of our social system, and the interests and happiness alike of both races, are involved in the solution. If calmly and dispassionately we consider the facts of the case, if we study the history of the negro, his idiosyncracies and capabilities, it will not be difficult to discover the line at once of duty and of interest. On the other hand, if we ignore the differentia of the races, the peculiarities which God has impressed upon the negro, and proceed to reconstruct him after the approved pattern of a silly fanaticism, we shall commit one of those terrible blunders which are worse than crimes.

There is one plan by which, without cost to the State, the highest happiness and utmost usefulness of which the negro is capable, may be accomplished; there is another which will effectually destroy both his usefulness and his happiness, and render him liable, at any capricious moment, like a blind giant, to seize and tear down the pillars of our political edifice, involving at the same time an enormous expenditure of money, which we cannot suffer without the sacrifice of the good name, the sacred honor of the Commonwealth.

In the next number of the *Planter and Farmer* I hope to make application of the foregoing to the subject in hand.

CIVIS.

[NOTE BY THE EDITOR.—We have two correspondents writing under the *nom de plume* of "CIVIS," both of whom are prominently identified with the educational and agricultural interests of the South. The author of this article is favorably known to the public by the contribution to the *Religious Herald* last spring and summer of a series of articles on the "public school" referred to in this communication.]

[From the Southern Planter and Farmer, Jan'y, 1876.]

THE PUBLIC SCHOOL IN ITS RELATIONS TO THE NEGRO.

No. II.

So different anatomically and physiologically are the two races from each other, that we are told on the highest medical authority that the treatment which is demanded for the recovery of a white man in fever and other forms of disease will be fatal to the negro; that the most successful practitioners educated at the North or in Europe, when they first come in contact with the negro and proceed to treat him in sickness on general principles, uniformly fail, and frequently with disastrous results, until by observation and trial they learn that special treatment is demanded by congenital peculiarities, both in organization and functions. We have already seen that the negro both in his intellectual and moral attributes is conspicuously inferior to the white man, so that there is a perfect correlation between his physical peculiarities and his immaterial nature. Inferiority is stamped plainly and indelibly on the negro alike in his intellectual, moral and physical being.

This line of demarcation between the races is not accidental or the result of outward surroundings; it has been fixed by the finger of God. Since the negro has been known to history, he has always been as we see him now. In our dealings with him, shall we ignore or attempt to obliterate this line of separation? It is greatly to be deplored, says modern philanthropy, that these differences exist. They constitute a great barrier to the success of its pet schemes of equality and fraternity. There have always been men, as there are to-day, wiser than God, and ready at a moment's notice to reconstruct the work of the matchless Architect. A distinguished scientist of our day has told us that the eye is a bungling piece of optical mechanism; and that, under his direction, the construction of that organ would have been vastly better. Not long ago, carpers and critics were fond of attacking the divine cosmogony, because three-fourths of the earth's surface is covered with water, an arrangement which restricts, they complained, our race to a small part of the planet. They, wiser than he who "spake and it was done, who commanded and it stood fast," would at farthest have covered only one-fourth of the earth with water, an arrangement which, we now perfectly know, would have rendered the land an absolute desert for lack of sufficient evaporating surface. I do not belong to the fanatical crew that dares to assail the Infinite Wisdom; that would

"Snatch from his hand the balance and the rod,
Rejudge his justice, be the god of God."

As far as I can understand the forms and forces of matter, I see the most wonderful harmonies, manifold adaptations of material things to our wants and happiness, and even in many phenomena, which bring sorrow and suffering, a vindication of the ways of God to man. When and where I cannot understand, I am equally content to wonder and adore; believing, knowing that when the unknown becomes the known, as at last it may, it will equally attest the infinite wisdom and boundless beneficence of the Great Contriver.

It does not, however, appear to me difficult to explain why the negro, not by accident but by the act of God, is made inferior to the Caucasian. It is in perfect harmony with the whole economy of the world. The law of nature, which is always the law of God, is inequality, not equality; diversity, not uniformity; and the happiness of the whole animal kingdom is best subserved by this arrangement. "One star differeth from another star in glory;" no two trees in the forest, no two leaves even, are exactly alike; and every man is different from all other men, that live, or have lived, on the surface of the earth. Civilization requires an infinite variety of work, which in turn requires for its performance infinite gradations of intellect. The man who, accepting his destiny as indicated by his humble capacity, performs the lowest kind of menial labor, does work just as necessary in the economy of civilization as the profound astronomer who measures and weighs suspended worlds, and marks out their circling paths. The truth is that the number of those required to do the loftiest work of which the human intellect is capable, is very small; while larger and still larger numbers are required for lower and still lower work, so that those occupations are most thronged which least require intellectual strength and activity. It always has been so; and, dream and speculate as we will, it always will be so. When Christ said: "The poor ye have always with you," he stated a general truth, applicable not only to the age and country of which he spoke, but to all ages and to all countries. Of necessity it must be so, it is right that it should be so. Bootblacks and scavengers, cooks and chamber-maids, farm hands, and operatives in manufacturing establishments, must continue until chaos comes again. These and kindred occupations, constituting the very foundation of civilized society, require for the utmost efficiency of the work, little or no scholastic training on the part of the mere laborers. Nor can it be said that such work would be better done if the laborers were educated. So far from this being so, the difficulty of having it done at all would be greatly increased; and when done, it would be done by no means so well. For several reasons, this must be so. The fact that a laborer is educated, or thinks he is educated, beyond his calling, unfits him for that calling. If a man is engaged in work below his education, he feels degraded by it, and that sense of degradation compels him to do inferior work. No laborer can do good work unless he is proud of his work. I know of no spectacle more pitiable than that of a man compelled by necessity to engage in menial labor for a support, whose education, either in fact or in his conception, fits him for a higher plane of life. He is far less happy, and does less work, and that less efficiently, than the simple laborer by his side, whose thoughts never rise higher than his calling, and whose guile- less heart is made happy by a word of praise from his employer.

Again, the more simple a piece of machinery is, the more man- ageable it is, and the better it does the work for which it was designed. When we complicate it so as to render it capable of doing several things, it will not do any one of these things so well as the simple machine constructed solely with reference to that thing. A mower and reaper combined is less efficient as a mower than a simple mower; is less efficient as a reaper than a simple reaper. And so that intelligence and culture, and only that, which is required for one's calling, best fits him for the duties of that calling. The bootblack is not a better bootblack, but a worse one, the ditcher is not a better ditcher, but a worse one, if he can also calculate a solar eclipse or read with a critic's ken the choral odes of the Greek dramatists.

A higher than human authority hath taught us that we cannot serve two masters. Faithfully and well to discharge the duties of one sphere of life positively disqualifies us for those of a lower or of a higher sphere. Contentment in our allotted place—and a place is allotted to us all—is at once the plain dictate of reason and the positive injunction of inspiration. A laborer will never do full and efficient work unless he finds not only his support but his happi- ness in his labor, content to leave to those more gifted than he, the problems of science and the perplexities of finance. And such a course is always the laborer's choice; unless the vile spirit of un- rest and discontent has been stirred within him by the constant teachings of a blasphemous philosophy.

The practice of men in the employment of menial labor is in entire harmony with our doctrine, and at once attests and demon- strates its truth. The farmer always prefers as laborers in his field those accustomed and competent only to such work; nor will he employ, except from necessity or as a matter of charity, applicants whose thoughts have taken a wider and a loftier range. To succeed in work that is below one's capacity and attainments is just as im- possible as to succeed in work that is above one's capacity and attain- ments; and this the practical man, who, in all matters relating to his business and interests, has more sense than all the philanthro- pists and reformers in the world put together, well knows, and acts accordingly. Not long ago, I had a conversation with a prominent gentleman, a farmer and preacher, who combatted this view; and yet in the conversation it cropped out that he had just refused em- ployment, though greatly needing labor on his farm, to two strong young men, fresh from the Normal School at Hampton, on the ground, as acknowledged, that persons engaged as they had been would not suit his work, nor it them. What this man did, everybody else, under similar circumstances, does. The simple fact that men uniformly so act, proves that such action is based on the strongest and most conclusive reasons. The cook, that must read the daily paper, will spoil your beef and your bread; the sable pickaninny, that has to do his grammar and arithmetic, will leave your boots unblacked and your horse uncurried.

Some—and a great many too—are and must be mudsills. Some are and must be "hewers of wood and drawers of water." Such is the decree, and the language quoted is that of the Almighty. This doctrine, so unpalatable to our fanatical optimists, has been most fiercely attacked; but these assaults, hot with wrath, have made no impression on the thick bosses of Jehovah's buckler.

Society, left to the operation of natural causes, will take its proper order of stratification. Each member, according to his inherent energy and capacity, will find his proper place in just gradation. To protect the individual in his rights, not to form society, is the function of government. As individuals have or lack capacity, they will rise or sink; and they will rise who ought to rise, and they will sink who ought to sink. To check, or attempt to check, one from sinking who ought to sink, is as great a cruelty to him and as disastrous to society as to prevent or attempt to prevent one from rising who ought to rise. That father would be cruel in the extreme and inflict a great damage on the community who should hold, or attempt to hold, in lowly life, a son competent to the grandest achievements; but not more cruel nor more injurious to society than that other father who places his son in a position above his capacity, and, say, holds him there, a position which requires of him duties that he cannot discharge, and devolves upon him responsibilities, that he cannot meet, rendering worthless, and, from a sense of worthlessness, wretched, one who, in his proper place, would have been both useful and happy. That every man should promptly find his proper level is demanded alike by the happiness of the individual and the general interests of the community. An attempt on the part of the State to place all on a common level, is beyond the range of its just powers, and is as silly as it is vain. The great Father of Waters, as he moves to the sea, bears on his turbid bosom many thousand tons of solid matter, which is accurately assorted and distributed along his course and at his mouths by the operation of physical laws too powerful for human agency to contravene; and so the laws of God's moral government, not less constant nor less powerful than those that control the physical universe, determine the stratification of human society. We may endeavor by legislation, as weak as it is wicked, to prevent this stratification or to make it homogeneous and uniform; but so sure as God is stronger than man, the attempt will end in failure, inflicting, however, untold misery on individuals and crippling, it may be, the industries of the globe.

We have drifted far from the simplicity of our fathers. They held that government is instituted for the protection of individual rights; now the individual is the prey of government, which crushes him with tyrannous exactions, while the highest aim of statesmanship consists in the discovery of new subjects of taxation. And now, when the President of the Republic, (can we call it a Republic?) "whereof," he sapiently tells us, "one man is as good as another," recommends in his last annual message to Congress, compulsory education by the Federal Government; and, with a logic, of which I will only say that it is worthy of its source, proposes to tax the church to support the school, backed in this latter matter, I regret to add, by the feeble support of the Governor of Virginia, it is high time that thoughtful men should bestir themselves, demand a new reckoning, and make the supreme effort, lest the ship of state drift into worse than Prussian absolutism. The fact that the President makes such a proposition, and that, too, in the most solemn and formal way, ought to arouse us from our lethargy and make us open our eyes to the alarming drift and tendency of the times. It is nothing less than that the Federal Government should stretch out its Briarean arms from the St. Lawrence to the Gulf, and from the Atlantic to the Pacific, and lay its cold and heavy hand upon all the children of "the nation," compelling them to schools supported by universal taxation, prescribing what they shall learn, and what they shall not learn, forbidding the reading of the Bible and the bare mention of the name of Christ, forming their minds and their morals, taking charge of their health and their habits, constituting itself a sort of wet nurse to the little urchins, and leaving to parents, upon whom alone is devolved, as well by instinct and affection as by the repeated and most solemn injunctions of Inspiration, the education of their children, little more than the function of reproduction. Under such a system, the path to despotism is short and plain; and we may expect to see, as we most abundantly do see, wherever the scheme has been long intrenched and so has had time to fructify, an utter relaxation of parental and filial obligation and manifold forms of atheism and irreligion. But the Federal Government has as much right to intervene in this matter as the State Government; it belongs to neither. The education of children belongs to parents and to them only; nor can they delegate or surrender it to the civil authority, State or Federal, without guilt.

But, it is maintained, that a necessity is laid upon Virginia to support the public school because of the presence of negroes as citizens in our midst, whose equality is asserted by the law and maintained by the power of the Federal Government.

Let us look into this. When an inferior and a superior race come into contact with each other, one of these three things will take place. 1st. The inferior race will disappear; or 2d. The races will amalgamate; or 3d. The inferior race must submit, under forms more or less despotic, to the domination of the superior race.

1. When Europeans landed on this continent, their instincts demanded that so vast and fertile a domain, pregnant with such mighty and brilliant possibilities, should not be left to the proprietorship of

wild savages, incompetent to cultivate the soil or explore the mine. They were but cumberers of the ground, and must give way to those who could utilize the gifts of nature to the general benefit of mankind. On the other hand, the proud spirit of the haughty Indian, after many a bloody protest, it is true, sullenly recognized the inevitable logic of this demand, and so he has constantly retired before the advancing wave of civilization. Taught by instinct, he felt that he was unable to compete, for the means of living, with a race whose superior sagacity moulded the forms and bent the forces of nature to their will. Thus, the mighty tribes that once lorded it over this continent, following the course of the sun, and vanishing, as they retired, like April snows, are represented now in our western wilds by only a few degraded and broken spirited remnants, the miserable victims of the cruel charity of the Government—for governmental charity is always cruel, and corrupting too—famishing on fibrous beef, and poisoned with putrid pork. As the tide of life moves further westward, the Indian, as heretofore, must abandon his reservation, and soon his only place will be in history. This is one method of solution, which we have witnessed with our own eyes, and, so sure as the laws of nature are constant, we shall witness it again, unless we change the hideous policy to which we are committed.

2. Under favoring circumstances and conditions, the races will amalgamate. Nature implants in the superior race antagonisms and antipathies to the inferior, which except under abnormal circumstances, effectually protects the purity of its strain. The greater the disparity, the stronger these antipathies, and therefore the less the liability to amalgamation. But howsoever great the disparity, amalgamation is inevitable under certain conditions, as where the inferior race vastly outnumbers the superior, or when the two races are kept together by external force. The amalgamation of the blacks and whites—a crime against blood and lineage, against man and God, against which I raise my hands in horror and disgust, and exonerate my conscience, if I can do no more, by a solemn and indignant protest—is encouraged and invited by the law, which recognizes the political equality of the negro, and ties the races together in the bonds of political partnership.

If the negro, as the law assumes, is equal to the great functions of citizenship, is a copartner with us in a common government, to discharge the same duties, meet the same responsibilities, and share the same destiny, then the races ought to assimilate as thoroughly as possible, and every bar to their perfect blending ought to be removed. Mixed schools, which we barely escaped—if, indeed, we have escaped —only because race instinct, though weakened and blinded by the hot passions born of strife and blood, was stronger than the logic of the law, in which the same training and instructions should be given and antagonisms worn off by constant contact and association, is the necessary, the logical demand of the doctrine of equality. Nor let us deceive ourselves by saying that political equality is one thing and social equality another. An adjective will not save us. Equality is equality. If the negro is fit, as the law in question declares he is, to make laws for the control of our conduct and property; to give orders as a colonel or general, which we must implicitly obey; to sit in senatorial robes; to wear the spotless ermine; to occupy the chair of Washington, he is certainly fit to eat with us at our tables, to sleep in our beds, to be invited into our parlors, and to do all acts and things which a white man may do.

The intent and animus of the law, the pressure of the whole machinery of the Federal Government, and of the State Government too, in so far as it recognizes the equality of the negro in its insane attempts to qualify him by education for the rights and duties of citizenship, tend to a common point, viz., to wear off race antagonisms by contact and association, to pave the way consequently to assimilation and amalgamation, and thus degrade into mulattoes and molungeons, the noblest type of the noblest race that ever floated on the tide of time. No thanks to the law if this result does not promptly and fully ensue. It is as criminal as if miscegenation were the order of the day; for it plies all its logic and displays all its seductions to effect that object, from which we are saved, in so far as we are saved, only by those antagonisms and antipathies of race, stronger than human legislation, implanted in us by our Maker to protect purity of blood and accomplish the "survival of the fittest."

If it be said in reply that this very principle of race antagonism is an effectual bar to hybridization, I answer:

1. That if such be the tendency of the law, it must produce its effect; that it is as impossible to annihilate a force in morals as it is to annihilate a force in physics; that the law makes its fiercest assaults upon the very principle which is relied upon to combat or modify its tendencies, and that this principle is liable to be so weakened and emasculated by the varied appliances operating against it, as to be unable at last to antagonize the baleful tendencies of the law. The law, however weak in comparison with the antagonizing principle, must produce its effects, which will become more manifest and more disastrous as the law becomes stronger and the opposing principle weaker. And this is exactly the tendency of things. As we submit to this legislation, and applaud and adopt it, its power over us becomes greater and our repugnance less to it and to its results, so that a time may come when, both from the increasing strength of the law and the growing weakness of human virtue, our race may be hopelessly ruined.

2. Beware how you subject human nature to temptation. For us, as weak as we are sinful, the only safe philosophy is found in the prayer of our Savior, "Lead us not into temptation." How dare we support and sanction a law which daily displays before society and our children a constant temptation to corruption of blood? It is a crime against decency and morals, against race and blood, against God and nature.

If we are not utterly debauched by the temptation, the law is not the less criminal; for we are saved, so far as we are saved, by a principle outside of the law, antagonistic to it, the eradication of which is the supreme object of the law, and of those who conceived and framed it.

But we have no option, we are told, except submission. I reply that we can submit without guilt to anything that we cannot prevent; but that when we adopt, and applaud and defend this law, and, with superserviceable weakness, extend its application, we are as guilty, we are more guilty than its original framers. And this thing, and nothing else, we are doing, when we go to the exhausted Exchequer of the Commonwealth, and take from it money—money that does not belong to the State, but to its creditors—and apply it to the support of the public school that the asserted doctrine of negro equality may be made good. In this we cannot offer the plea of compulsion; no federal law requires it; we do it of our own volition; and in doing it, we grant that the negro is competent to political sovereignty and endeavor to prepare him for it; and thus we commit ourselves to the dogma of negro equality and become responsible for all its hideous consequences. This law, born of blood, is destined to die, as the passions engendered by war subside, unless we adopt it and approve it, and so infuse new life into it, and proceed with supreme guilt and folly to incorporate it into our State legislation. Shall we do it? God forbid.

3. A third course has been indicated, the discussion of which is reserved for another article. CIVIS.

———

[From the Southern Planter and Farmer, February, 1876.]

THE PUBLIC SCHOOL IN ITS RELATIONS TO THE NEGRO.

No. III.

If we do not wish the negro to vanish like the Indian from existence, nor to amalgamate with the whites, and thus to originate a population as worthless as the mongrels of Mexico, all that is left us is simply to let him alone, and leave him to occupy his natural position of subordination. This is the position which the negro instinctively seeks, nor is he happy or comfortable in any other. Everything has been done that diabolical wit could suggest to make the negro assert his equality, and yet he will not; incendiary philanthropists have passed through the length and breadth of our land, and endeavored to scatter firebrands among his race, and still he is quiescent; the Federal Government has expended millions of treasure and mobilized mighty armies to infuse into him sufficient courage for the maintenance of the mendacious dogma, and yet no sooner has the tread of armed legions faded from his ears than he turns to seek his only safety in obscurity. Coming from the hot crowd, where he has been galvanized by inflammatory rhetoric into a spasmodic feeling of importance, so soon as he touches the cool air and comes in contact with a white man, all his injected courage oozes out, and by his language, his attitude and bearing, he proclaims his inferiority. In all the annals of history I know of nothing so striking and so conclusive as the humility, the general quiet behavior, of the negro, though every effort is made and every possible suggestion offered to vex and goad him into a contrary course. They are sometimes, it is true, lashed into local and temporary disturbances; the wonder of wonders is, that these disturbances are not general and constant. The negro, true to nature and true to truth, stoutly denies the heresy of equality. And why should we endeavor to make him belie the instincts of his nature, and seek to force him into a position in which he knows he is unable to sustain himself? There are no people in the world so kindly and so indulgent to the negro as the white people of the South—none so bitterly and implacably hostile to him. When he comes, as he generally does, humble, docile and obedient—in a word, as an inferior—he receives the most kindly and generous consideration; but when, as is sometimes the case, he assumes impudent airs and utters impudent words, or in any way deports himself as an equal, then he stirs the blood and fires the pride of race, and he must take the consequences or wilt at once into submission. The unvarnished truth must be told, and the sooner we recognize it in our conduct the better for us all. *The whites and the negroes cannot live together as equals.* Why cannot this be done? our modern reformers ask. I answer: because God, for wise reasons not difficult to be understood, has made it impossible. It is forbidden by a law of nature, which applies not only to the human race, but to the entire animal kingdom. If a game cock and a dunghill rooster be placed in the same barnyard, the latter must submit, or he must die. Numberless illustrations of this principle will occur to the readers of this journal, accustomed as they are to observe the habits of animals. This race antagonism becomes stronger as we ascend the scale of animal life, and is most pronounced in man, for the plain reason that its object—the preservation of purity of strain—is more important than in the case of the inferior animals! Inferior and superior races, whether of man or of the lower orders of animals, cannot live together except as inferiors and superiors. If we put them on a plane of equality and hold them there, the weaker dies. The law of the Federal Government declares the equality of the negro; but the declaration of the law does not make the dogma true. It were as easy to make the James river the equal of the Mississippi, or the Alleghany mountains as lofty as the Andes, by a presidential pronunciamento.

The public school system recognizes the doctrine of negro equal-

16

ity, and professes to prepare him for the highest functions of life, the duties of political sovereignty. If he is, by congenital inferiority, not competent to such functions, the attempt to prepare him for them is a manifest absurdity. If he is competent to such functions, then inferiority does not belong to his race. Having shown, in former articles before referred to, that the public school, even without reference to the question of races, is utterly indefensible, both as a matter of morals and of policy, I oppose it in its application to the negro race:—

1. Because it is an assertion, in the most dangerous form, of the hideous doctrine of negro equality. How this blasphemous heresy seeks the amalgamation of the races as its culmination, was clearly shown in our last article. I cannot dwell on this topic; it is too revolting, it is too disgusting for contemplation.

2. I oppose it because its policy is cruelty in the extreme to the negro himself. It instills into his mind that he is competent to shine in the higher walks of life, prompts him to despise those menial pursuits to which his race has been doomed, and invites him to enter into competition with the white man for those tempting prizes that can be won only by a quicker and profounder sagacity, by a greater energy and self-denial, and a higher order of administrative talent than the negro has ever displayed. In such a competition the negro inevitably goes down. To invite the negro from those pursuits which require firm muscles and little intelligence to those callings which demand less muscle and higher intelligence, is to invite him to his sure extermination. To require the ponderous Percheron to equal the fleet Arabian courser, as he sweeps the plain, or the latter to draw the heavy loads which scarcely tax the muscles or warm the shoulders of the former, would be the last degree of cruelty to the animals, and render them at the same time worse than worthless. More cruel are we, and a vastly greater damage do we inflict upon society, when, prompted by a silly fanaticism, we seduce the negro from those occupations in which alone he can be useful and content, and tempt him to a competition which he cannot accept without his ruin. It is as pleasing as it is instructive to witness how labor is allotted here in the South. We find negroes universally preferred and almost exclusively employed as cooks and chambermaids, as barbers and bootblacks, as laborers on the farm and in tobacco factories. As I write, my head is dull and my eyes are heavy from loss of sleep caused by the sickness of an infant child; and yet the nurse, a negro girl of seventeen years, upon whom the heavy work has chiefly fallen, and whose sleep has been interrupted several times every night—during some nights many times—is as fresh to-day as when the doctor was summoned two weeks ago. I have known her to be aroused five or six times a night, and yet not to lose from these several interruptions combined a half hour's sleep, for in thirty seconds after relieved of active duty she is soundly asleep again. This result, I am sure, is due to a low type of cerebral organization, to her mental inactivity, which really fits her for the duties of her

2

place, but would be a supreme disqualification for the higher avocations of life. She is withal tenderly affectionate to her charge, cheerfully responds to all the calls made upon her, and I prefer her in her place to any white girl in the commonwealth. Would it be kind to her, would it be just to society, which must always demand just such duties as she performs, to tempt her to aspire to a higher position denied her by Him who made her as she is?

In such pursuits as I have indicated, the negro is preferred from a thorough conviction, born of observation and self-interest, the safest guides, that he is more docile and manageable, more efficient and happy, than whites are when engaged in the same sort of work. But the negro has no administrative faculty; he cannot forecast and plan, he cannot arrange and combine. How stupid to teach, or attempt to teach, a being so organized, that a time will come when he will be able to determine the parallax of a fixed star, or solving the problems of political economy, will at last realize the conception of the poet and "read his history in a nation's eyes!" Let him imbibe the fatal lesson and proceed to grapple with the Caucasian as a competitor for a livelihood, on a plane too lofty for his intellect, and his doom is sealed. Let him confine himself to menial pursuits, to certain kinds of mechanical labor, and he will have a wide berth; he will encounter no opposition, and if he does, can conquer it, for in such labor he excels. Moreover, in such callings he has the kindly encouragement, the protecting sympathy, of the superior race, and thus his comfort, his happiness and his usefulness are best accomplished. But let him attempt to move out of his orbit and seek a higher circle, to wrest from more skilful hands the work for which he has no aptitude, then he will find every inch of ground fiercely and stoutly contested; then he will arouse into opposition the pride of race, which will vindicate its native dignity, and with unpitying triumph bear him hopelessly down. His strength, his only strength, is his weakness. Now, the theory of the public school denies all this, and, in endeavoring to qualify the negro as a co-partner with the whites in the administration of the government, asserts in the strongest way his unqualified equality. It were strange, indeed, if a doctrine so flattering to the vanity of a weak and credulous race did not find, though opposed to their instincts, some adherents among them. Hence, we find that in our cities and villages, where they have been most plied and corrupted by this doctrine, they are asserting, to an extent greater or less, their importance with a result that is mournfully told by mortuary statistics. Awaiting my family physician in his office a few days ago, and picking up a copy of the *Virginia Medical Monthly,* I noticed that in all the cities reported (Richmond, Norfolk, Lynchburg, Petersburg, Selma, Mobile,) the death rate is notably greater among the blacks than among the whites. Why this persistent uniformity? The negroes to-day all over this country are dying more rapidly than the whites. Once it was not so. They increased with marvellous rapidity, the supreme proof of physical comfort. Let the negro imbibe more and still more of this false and poisonous philosophy, and, led by its malign inspirations, leave those lowly walks in which alone he can make a living and be happy, then will the swift extermination of the race put an eternal quietus upon all our speculations as to his status in politics and in society.*

3. I oppose the public school, because it brings paralysis to our industrial pursuits. We are poor to the point of derision; yet exhaustless wealth lies hidden in our soil. Broad acres of deep alluvium, which would yield to honest toil some sixty and some an hundred fold, lie untilled, and only serve to poison the atmosphere with mephitic exhalations. The utilization of our natural resources is our only pathway to prosperity. The great need of this Commonwealth is labor—labor that can be relied on and controlled. Work, work, work is our salvation. And yet, instead of encouraging labor, our legislation puts it as much as possible under ban. The framers of the patchwork constitution under which we live have displayed a fertile ingenuity in creating the largest number possible of public offices, that idlers and incompetents might occupy them as bomb-proofs from labor. Constables and sheriffs, assessors and tax gatherers, publicans of one sort or another, swarm through the Commonwealth and devour our living and eat out our substance. To tax, tax, tax, is to our Virginia statesman the full conception of his duty, while the revenues thus wrung from a reluctant people are applied not to satisfy the supreme demand of honor, but to support burglars and thieves in comfort and idleness, and foster the mischievous experiments of quixotic philanthropy. Session after session the Legislature is approached by immigration agencies for appropriations to enable them to bring laborers from abroad, and yet we turn and expend annually with suicidal folly, vastly larger sums of money to render worthless, and worse than worthless, a vastly better class of laborers in our midst. Can the force of folly

---

*I have calculated the ratio of white and black mortality for the cities of Richmond, Norfolk and Lynchburg, Va.; representing a total white population of 51,952, and a total colored population of 41,713—total population, white and colored, 93,665. The mortuary reports for these cities, in my possession, cover a period of twenty one months (March 1874 to November 1875, inclusive). During these twenty one months, there was a total white mortality of 1,900, a total colored mortality of 2,599. In other words, there was one white death to every twenty seven of the white population, and one colored death to every sixteen of the colored population. The reports from Petersburg, Virginia, cover a period of only three months (September, October, November, 1875). The white population is 8,744; the colored population 10,185. During the three months, there were fifty-three deaths among the whites, and one hundred and four among the colored, or one white death to every one hundred and sixty five of the white population, one colored death to every ninety-eight of the colored population.

It may be of further interest to note that regarding the first three named Virginia cities, during the twenty one months stated, there were four hundred and eighty still-births; of these the race is not given in thirty-three cases, but one hundred and forty-six white still-births are tabulated, and three hundred and one colored—making the total of four hundred and eighty. Omitting any reference to the thirty-three still-births, the races of which are not given, the ratio of white still births is one to every three hundred and fifty-six white population, and the ratio of colored still-births, one to every one hundred and thirty eight of the colored population.

further go? Up to 1860 the exports of the South in the shape of
tobacco, cotton, sugar, &c., were several times greater than the exports from equal areas in any other part of the Union, and kept the
balance of trade in our favor—(there lies the secret of our financial
troubles). I have seen the statistics, though I cannot lay my hands
on them now, which demonstrate that our Southern agriculture,
during the period alluded to, gathered from our fertile soil more
wealth than was ever acquired by similar means since the dawn of
authentic history. These grand results were chiefly due to the labor of negro slaves, who almost fed and clothed the world. The
crude products of their labor were fashioned by superior skill, all
over the civilized globe, into infinite forms of comfort, of elegance,
and of luxury. And in such congenial employment the negro was
comfortable and happy to an extent never realized before by any
other laboring class since time began. His eyes stood out with fat-
ness, and joy exultant burst from his tuneful throat. With happy
confidence he relied upon a clearer head to direct his steps, and
loved the generous hand that supplied his wants. This race, perfectly adapted, as we have seen, by their moral, intellectual and
physical attributes, to field labor in low latitudes; better for such
work, incomparably better, than Irish or Scandinavians, than
Scotch or English, than Dutch or Swiss—better even than the olive
pigtails of the Flowery Kingdom—we teach, or attempt to teach, to
despise those lowly walks in which alone they can be useful and
happy, and disregarding the laws of nature, which can never be
violated with impunity, to aspire to the shop and the counter, the
office, the pulpit, the bar, the bench, the hustings, the warrior's
wreath, the statesman's civic crown. Are we in our dotage? Debased and corrupt, have we at last become the victims of that supreme infatuation, which forebodes destruction from the gods? The
negro, tutored under the old regime, inoculated therefore with just
conceptions of himself and others, and so protected against the
malignant virus of modern philanthropy, is still the best field laborer
in the world. The negroes who are growing up, or have grown up
in the last decade, are sadly unreliable. But if they are idle and
thriftless, the fault is ours, not theirs. That they should behave as
well and work as well as they generally do, is a great marvel. The
thrusting of the negro into politics, against every dictate of prudence and common sense, without a precedent in all the annals of
time to sanction it, is what ruins him as a laborer. Is he not a factor of the government? Dim visions of ease and idleness flit before
his beclouded mind, and stagger his feeble intellections. The President of "the nation" invokes his assistance and leans upon him for
support. Flattered by and feeling his importance as a political element, bearing the weight of empire on his shoulders, he is no longer
content to crush the clods, nor proud to guide the shining plough
and turn the stubborn glebe. The lofty duties of citizenship call
him from the swamp and the ditch, from the farmyard and the
field. With simple wants, which—so feeble is his moral sense—he

can supply without labor, and almost without danger, is it strange that it is unsafe to rely upon him for faithful and steady labor? And shall we, at the expense of the bleeding honor of the common-wealth, endeavor to raise the negro to a class of duties which he will never comprehend, nor with safety can even attempt to dis-charge, and in the process utterly unfit him for that kind of labor which is the great demand of the day, and in the performance of which he excels every other people on the earth.

4. If all I have written be destitute of force, still there remains an objection to the system, which is *absolutely conclusive*, unless indeed the sense of honor is dead within us beyond the possibility of resus-citation. Simple honesty forbids that we should support a mam-moth charity, however worthy, with money which does not belong to the State, money wrongfully withheld from its rightful owners, the creditors of the Commonwealth. To support the system, even granting it to be desirable *per se*, is, under existing circumstances, a high crime; a crime of the deepest dye and most malignant type, which no argument, no necessity can justify.

We owe a debt of more than thirty millions. It was contracted by our own people through legislatures fairly chosen and represent-ing the will of the people. If it had been created by the new element forcibly injected into our economy, as is the case with the debts of some of the States south of us, repudiation might perhaps be enter-tained. But *we* created it. Nor was it created for objects which have been swept away by the convulsions of war. We are to-day in the enjoyment of the benefits purchased by this debt. We are not required to pay for a dead horse. A magnificent monument, by which we propose to perpetuate to coming ages the form and the features of the Father of his Country, stands on our Capitol Square, but it is still unpaid for. How dare the State insult the memory of Washington by an act of grand larceny! If his spirit could infuse that inanimate bronze, his indignant soul would shiver the effigy into atoms! What Virginian does not burn with indignation and blush with shame, when he sees the Commonwealth, late the synonym of chivalry and honor, chaffer and higgle with her creditors for abate-ment and compromise! If an honest man be pressed with debt, he makes all the money he can, reduces expenses to the minimum, and turns over to his creditors the excess of income over barely neces-sary expenses. But if a man, burdened with debt, support a style of living more costly and luxurious than he indulged in his prosperity, and plead his poverty as a justification of non-payment, he simply adds mendacity to theft. Let States be judged by the same rule. From them is due, in a higher sense, a pure allegiance, an unquali-fied obedience to justice. What shall we say to the plea of poverty put up in behalf of Virginia, when we know that with an area one-third less and a population a fourth less than in 1860, the expenses of the Government are more than two and a half times greater than when the State was in the plenitude of its wealth. The Governor in his last message, through many paragraphs of pompous rhetoric,

recommends a ruthless retrenchment in all the departments of the
Government, and to the same end, a remodeling of the Constitution;
but when he sees the inevitable application of his ideas, adds with
bated breath: " This recommendation means no interference with
the public school system." " O, most lame and impotent conclusion!" This system which abstracts $500,000 per annum· from
State funds, and embracing local taxation, costs considerably more
than a million, we are required to support, while the honor of the
State is bleeding at every pore, and its creditors are coolly told to
stand aside until we have concluded a costly experiment in governmental philanthropy. Shall we have the brazen effrontery to plead
our poverty in justification of our conduct, when we expend annually $1,584,000 to meet the expenses of our State Government, not
including interest on the public debt; while from 1850 to 1860, the
annual average cost of a vastly better Government, embracing a
larger area and a greater population, was only $588,000. How can
we look our creditors in the face and talk about our poverty, and
propose postponement or reduction of interest, when rioting, it would
seem, in excessive wealth, we appropriate from State funds alone to
the costly luxury of public schools an amount, which, fifteen years
ago was sufficient to defray all the expenses of the Government?
If the expenses of our State Government were one-third what they
are or less, we should have a Government incalculably better; for all
money raised by taxation beyond what is simply necessary is only a
fund for corruption. Our people groan beneath excessive taxation,
not because they are unwilling to bear the just burdens of government; but because they know that their hard earnings are used, not
to save the plighted faith of the Commonwealth, but to support the
lazy incumbents of unnecessary offices; to provide fuel and lodg-
ings, food and raiment, for rogues and scoundrels, three-fourths of
whom would be more suitably punished at the whipping-post; to
meet the heavy demands of a bald experiment in universal education, based on false theories of government, false doctrines in morals,
repugnant to the traditions and to the genius of our people. If we
would apply to the State debt the sums annually appropriated to
the support of the public schools, we would be able to pay full interest and create a sinking fund besides. Thus easy it is to pay our
debt; to throttle the vampire that is sucking our blood; to get relief from that incubus that paralyzes our industries and keeps capital from our borders. Doing this, Virginia will be welcomed, thrice
welcomed, and received with happy plaudits, into the family of
honest commonwealths. Doing this, joy will suffuse her face, and
honor, quickening her pulses into healthful and happy play, will
send the life current in tingling ecstacy through her veins. Doing
this, the dark cloud of repudiation will vanish into thin air, and
Virginia, radiant with her ancient glories, will stand forth, " re-
deemed, regenerated, and disenthralled." Can we hesitate?
      A State that will not pay its honest debts, has lived too long. The
very existence of a State, so dishonored, is a crime, and the prolific

parent of crime. The State is to its citizens the rule of right, the very embodiment of inviolable justice. To enforce among its subjects a just regard for mutual rights, the State imposes fines and forfeitures, uses chains and manacles, builds jails and penitentiaries, constructs the gallows and the guillotine. But when the State becomes itself an evil-doer, commits those acts which it punishes in its subjects, tramples under foot the eternal justice which it professes to enforce and to dispense, then it debauches the morals of its subjects, who have been taught to look to it for inspiration and for guidance.

There is among us in this latter half of the 19th century, a laxity about debts, public and private, which would have disgraced the ethics of pagan Rome. They called a debt *aes alienum*, another's money; with us, when a man gets another's money, by borrowing or otherwise, it is, in many cases, most effectually his own. Stay laws and bankrupt acts, at once the evidence and the means of corruption, enable him in many ways to bar payment. Nor does he lose caste by his ill-gotten wealth. Luxurious parlors open to receive him, and are honored by his presence; his wife and daughters flaunt in silks and flutter in brocade; his splendid equipage flings mud from its whirring wheels on the obscure pedestrian with whose money, perchance, it was bought. When, even in the corrupt days of the Roman commonwealth, Cicero was approached with a proposition for new tablets—obliteration of debts—the indignant Consul answered he would give new tablets, but under the auctioneer's hammer. Nor is it difficult to find the cause of this woful putridity of morals. The two Governments under which we live, have, for fifteen years, shown an utter disregard, have affected on the grand scale, an utter annihilation, of the property rights of the citizen; have themselves committed, over and over, those crimes which just governments always punish in their subjects. Is it strange that the individual should forget the distinction between mine and thine, should have his sensibilities utterly obtunded, when the State, to which he has been taught to look as the impersonation of justice, as his exemplar in morals and in conduct, abuses the confidence reposed in its honor, and denies the obligations of its plighted faith? If the State, upon which rests supremely the obligation of immutable justice, can plunder and rob on the grand scale, why not he in feeble imitation on the small?

And so, descending step by step, we have learned to entertain the idea of repudiation. Calmly we walk to the edge of that awful chasm and look down into its dismal depths. Shall Virginia take that fatal plunge? No sacrifice would be too great to prevent it. But none is required. It is only necessary to be content to live as we lived in our purer and happier days. If we do this guilty thing, it will be the blackest picture in the book of time. The act will have no extenuation. For one, I say it deliberately, I prefer the annihilation of her sovereignty, the obliteration of her name from history, and from the memory of men.

If Virginia is to commit this crowning infamy, I trust it will appear that they, who can justly claim the proud heritage of her glory, were guiltless of the sin; that Virginia, brave in war and wise in peace, renowned in history and in romance, the lofty idol of gallant and knightly sons, preserved, so long as she was free, her honor unsullied; that the noble mother, convulsed with mortal agony—herself no longer—stooped to this last disgrace only after she had been bound and manacled, and a baser blood had been injected, at a tyrant's bidding, into her indignant veins.

CIVIS.

[From the Southern Planter and Farmer, May, 1876.]

THE PUBLIC SCHOOL IN ITS RELATIONS TO THE NEGRO.

No. IV.

The negro, we are told, is a voter, and our own safety and protection demand that we should educate him and so prepare him for the intelligent discharge of the duties of citizenship. To this I answer:

1. That fully believing that such a result will never be reached, I am utterly unwilling to expend vast sums of money, wrung from an impoverished and tax-burdened people, in a silly attempt to accomplish an impossibility.

2. If the negro, or rather his special friends for him, assert his equality, then let *him* make good the assertion. That they, who with hot indignation deny the revolting doctrine, should yet be heavily taxed to prove it true, is an extreme experiment on human patience. And yet, if with meek pusillanimity we submit to heavy taxation in the furtherance of negro education, we thereby put into the problem an element that renders its solution impossible. Under such a system, any success or seeming success, which the negro may accomplish in what our modern reformers term education, would leave still unsettled the question at issue. Negro children go to school, it is true; but they go because the feast is free and the school-house is a shelter from labor. That yearning for knowledge, which is the only test that it will be effectually acquired or usefully employed, is not the motive that takes the negro urchin to school. Should such a motive possibly exist, the system leaves no room for its display or development. By money extorted from capital and labor, negro children are coaxed and petted into the acquisition of the rudiments of learning, into a certain facility in the mere imitative processes of education. From such data the conclusion is reached that the negro is capable of education in the true sense of

the word, and is competent to the loftiest functions of life—the duties of political sovereignty. Not more absurd would the conclusion be that oranges may be profitably grown in Virginia as a staple crop because the seed will germinate in our soil, and the plant, if protected from the rigor of our winters and forced by artificial heat, may be made to bear a scanty crop of imperfect fruit.

3. There is one way, and only one, in which it is possible for the demonstration to be made. Let the negro, in his own way, without help or hindrance from any quarter, make good his claim that he may be safely invested with the rights of citizenship, then, and not till then, will the demonstration be satisfactory and complete. The negro has his destiny in his own hands; he is in a civilized society, with all the arts and appliances of civilization at his command. If he is competent to rise from his present position, and capable of becoming a useful citizen, an integral part of the body politic, no help, no stimulation, is necessary to bring about the result. Indeed, he would rise and make good the demonstration of his capacity and consequently of his rights, not only without assistance, but in the face of hostile legislation. Never had a semi-civilized race so splendid an opportunity of demonstrating their capabilities. So far from not learning, they cannot help learning, if only they have the ability and the desire to learn. To tax our people, already pinched with extreme poverty, to provide for the blacks the means of free education, is simply an attempt to bribe and coax them into learning, and is, in itself, a complete confession of defeat. The soil is so barren that it must be stimulated into temporary and spasmodic productiveness by copious applications of guano obtained from a foreign locality. Withhold the artificial stimulus, and the soil lapses at once into its original infertility.

Now, we tax ourselves to the point of actual suffering, we stretch the power of taxation to the very verge of confiscation, and attaint the sacred name of the Commonwealth, to settle a question in sociology, the solution of which is rendered impossible by the new element—unnecessary and deceptive—with which we complicate the problem. That individual negroes may be stimulated by the system into a mechanical familiarity with the elements of education, so-called, no more settles the question of the capacity of the race than the fructification of a tropical plant in a hot-house proves that it can stand the rigors of our climate and may be made to entrench itself permanently and profitably in our soil. But if the negro, moved by his own instincts, stimulated by his own aspirations, make good, in his own way, by his own strength, and at his own expense, his fitness for citizenship, then the question is put beyond cavil, and the doctrine of negro equality is settled affirmatively and forever. If, under the circumstances indicated, he should fail, however, to make good his claim, then it would as clearly appear that he is congenitally an inferior, and that his proper position is menial and subordinate. We are guilty, then, of the supreme folly, of the outrageous wickedness of expending annually vast sums of money,

8

extorted by unjust taxation from a disheartened and poverty-stricken people, upon the pretended education of negroes, with the view of settling the question of their fitness for citizenship, while this very expenditure in their behalf renders a correct solution of the problem an utter impossibility. On the other hand, without the expenditure of a single dollar, the question would settle itself naturally, and so settled, would lead us to the only safe and wise conclusions.

Let not the reader imagine that I am arguing for the exclusion of the negro from the public schools. Having shown in several articles, before alluded to, that appeared in the *Religious Herald*, that the system is utterly indefensible, even without reference to the question of mixed races; that it is in irreconcilable conflict with the American theory of government and with the Bible doctrine of parental duty and responsibility; that it debauches public and private morality; that unless arrested, it will be the death of liberty, if, indeed, it has not already inflicted the fatal blow, I favor the abandonment of the scheme altogether.

Are the "children of the State" then, says an objector, to be allowed to grow up in ignorance, and by their ignorance imperil the morals, the property and the institutions of the country? To this I answer:

1. That if the education of children be left where God and nature has placed it, in the hands of parents, some will be educated and others will not be. As a general statement, those will be educated who ought to be educated, and those will fail to be educated, or rather will remain untaught in letters, whose education would neither increase their own happiness nor advance the general interests of society. Those, or their parents for them, who have an innate yearning for a loftier and nobler sphere; for the pleasure and the power of real mental development; for the good it will enable them to accomplish, and the influence it will enable them to exert, will not be baulked in the accomplishment of their ambition. They will reach their goal through years, it may be, of toil, of hardship, of self-denial; and this very discipline of trial and difficulty will be the most important element of their education; will make them stronger, purer, better. In the education of such, society is profoundly interested; and they will be educated as certainly and far more effectually without the pestiferous and dangerous intervention of government.

But they who have no such longings will, in the main, be left out: and it is better for them and for society that it should be so. Their instincts do not seek, their modes of life will not require, scholastic arts. Their attainments in letters accordingly will range from zero upwards, but never high. Such people must spend their lives in physical labor. Is it hard that it should be so? Very hard, in the estimation of our fanatical optimists, but not so in truth. Such people would be extremely unhappy, and useless as well, if placed upon a plane above their instincts and beyond their capacity. Speculate as we will, a large part, perhaps the larger part, of the human family is doomed to manual labor. We cannot extricate them from that condition. In it they are happy and content unless disquieted by the false teachings of a mischievous fanaticism. The prime necessities of life, as food and fuel, raiment and shelter, have always demanded, and always will demand, the mechanical labor of half the world. Let it not be imagined that steam or electricity will at length so perform the work of human muscles as to leave all men abundant time for intellectual cultivation. Science suggests no such dreamy vista. The locomotive has but increased the demand for transportation, the spinning jenny for textile fabrics, the sewing machine for excessive embroidery and ornamentation. As the facilities of work are increased, the demands for work will grow proportionately. The wants of society, artificial or necessary, will always multiply as fast as the means of supplying them.

Now, they who do this work cannot be scholars. A man who has followed the plough all day long cannot study when he comes home at night. All his time of rest is demanded to repair the muscular and nervous exhaustion of a day's labor. If, in his early youth, he has made some proficiency in literary arts, they fall into disuse, as a fact, and from necessity, in his toiling manhood. The laboring class will also be a reading class when, and only when, Plato's Utopia is realized. The attempt to lift our whole population, white and black, into a literary atmosphere would be supremely silly, even if we possessed the fabled gift of Midas, whose touch turned every object into gold. The fantastic enterprise, under existing circumstances, when we are unable, or profess to be unable, to pay the interest on our public debt, and to solve the daily recurring problem of food and clothing for our families, is an outrage upon simple honesty and common sense.

Nor can it be successfully maintained that the education is promoted of those even for whose special benefit the public school is intended. Those whose instincts lead them to seek education will be better educated, as already shown, without the costly patronage of the State. But the others, without such instincts, may attend schools; compulsory laws, as in the Northern States, Prussia, and elsewhere, may enforce their attendance; the desire to study, the thirst for knowledge, however, is lacking, and cannot be supplied by legislation. Without this essential condition of success, the whole ʰusiness is a farce. The feast is spread, but the urchins do not relish it; you may force it into their stomachs, but then it is physic, not food; it cannot be assimilated; it does not strengthen, it weakens, the intellectual organism. The "Pierian Spring," a little turbid, perhaps, bubbles before their eyes; but they are not thirsty, and will not drink. You may force them to swallow draught after draught; but then it is only a disgusting drench, not the living water of intellectual life.

2. To grow up ignorant of letters is not necessarily to grow up in ignorance. I have been all along using the term education with a sort of silent protest. A man is educated, who can observe intelligently, compare and reason, and reach just conclusions, with or

without book learning. A knowledge of letters is not education, but only a means, and frequently a very imperfect means, of education. That man is educated for his sphere of life, and is happy and useful in that sphere, who well understands and discharges its duties. I daily meet uneducated men, whose knowledge of newspaper and what is called popular literature, is flippant and voluminous. I daily meet educated men, good citizens, and good neighbors, some of whom cannot even read, while others abandon in mature and busy life the scholastic arts acquired in their boyhood.

My next neighbor is a quiet, kindly man, a valuable citizen, an industrious and successful tiller of the soil. If you go to his farm in the busy season, you realize at once, from the steady progress and thorough character of the work, from the absence of all hurry, bluster and confusion, that he is indeed a master workman. I have seen him directing the work of thirty laborers. Some are hauling up wheat, some are threshing, some are fanning, some are ricking the straw, some are putting away the chaff, some are measuring the grain, some are hauling it to market; and all these operations are so ordered that they go on at equal pace; there is no jar, no loss of time. Can such a man, averaging from 25 to 30 bushels of wheat per acre on a large farm, competent to direct this work in such a systematic and judicious way, be justly called an uneducated man? And yet this man never reads, and, I am told, is unable to read. If, indeed, he is uneducated, then I wish we had more of the same sort.

During the late war, Stonewall Jackson came at nightfall to a swollen stream. A supreme necessity required that he should cross it before day. He called his engineers to him and explained the situation. He also sent for a man, who sustained an anomalous relation to the army, and whose sterling worth and strong common sense had frequently attracted the General's notice. "What can you do for me?" said Jackson. "Let me pick a hundred men, and I think I can put you over," said our hero. The detail was granted; and before day he returned to old Stonewall: "Ginral, the bridge ar built; your army can pass over. Your drawin' men will show you their picters in the morning." And yet by the modern test this man, who built the bridge before professional engineers had completed their plans and specifications, was an ignorant man. If, indeed, he was, then the familiar line is true in a sense which the poet never intended:

"When ignorance is bliss, 'tis folly to be wise."

Consider the ancient Athenians. Such was their critical acumen that with ease they followed Socrates in his subtlest disquisitions; such their polished taste that the use of a false quantity by a speaker forced him from the bema; such their quick intelligence that their appreciative plaudits were the highest meed of their orators and the sure passport to fame. And yet these people, innocent, in the main, of letters, and therefore, according to the modern standard, uneducated, have fairly illumined the track of history with the brightest record of public spirit and of patriotism; have left for the constant study and imitation of succeeding ages the loftiest achievments in poetry and in eloquence, in philosophy and in art; and have infused their spirit as an eternal inspiration, solace and guide, into the language and literature of every civilized people that have since figured in the annals of time.

We are indeed a progressive people! Education, which concerns that incorporeal essence, the mind or soul, we have learned in our day to determine with an accuracy fully equal to that with which a merchant measures his calico or a butcher weighs his beef. Our modern reformers turn to the Federal census, and because they find that the percentage of persons unable to read and write is greater in Virginia than in Connecticut, reach the conclusion by the application of their simple rule, that Connecticut is exactly four and a half times better educated than Virginia. The fact that Virginia has given to the country and to history the purest and ablest patriots and statesmen, the most brilliant and gifted orators, the ablest generals, the noblest displays of generosity and self-abnegation, while the contribution of Connecticut has been little more than painted hams and wooden nutmegs, has no relation at all to the matter of education!

But whether children are to grow up ignorant or not is not a proper question for government. The fact that it is assumed that government may take the whole matter of the education of "the children of the State" into its parental hands most painfully shows how far we have been corrupted from the simplicity of our fathers. Such an idea never entered the minds of such babes in statesmanship as Mason, Monroe, Marshall, Pendleton, Randolph, and so on, but was reserved to illustrate, in our day, the luminous patriotism of Judge Underwood and Doctor Bayne.

According to the American theory, government is not personal or parental, but is a mere agency which we may alter or abolish at pleasure when it fails to accomplish the purposes for which it was instituted. Government is the creature of society, not society the creature of government. The government belongs to the people, not the people to the government. It is the proper function of government to protect the rights of individuals, not to form society.

Now, our government, State or Federal, cannot undertake the education of the people without violating its foundation maxims. If our government can prescribe when our children shall go to school, where, and to whom, what they shall learn and what they shall not learn, it is plain that it can mould to its pleasures the feelings and sentiments of the rising generation. It forms society. A party in power can easily perpetuate its existence. In some of the States, the whole public school machinery has been run avowedly in the interests of the Radical party. Under such a system the voters of the country are fabricated and fashioned by government. The government is not the reflex of public sentiment, but public sentiment the reflex of government. The opinions of individuals do not form the government, but government the opinions of individuals. This is done confessedly in bepraised Prussia and in other absolute governments. Under such a system, the people may be called voters; but they are tools, pliant tools, ready at a moment's notice to do a tyrant's bidding. No room has been left for the development of individual opinion, as necessary to free government as air is to life; but a generation has been welded by uniform processes into an unthinking mass, not competent to direct, but prompt to obey, the government, which has infused it with its ideas and moulded it to its will.

To support the public school is to abandon the American theory of government. Nor is it calculated to abate our fears when we observe how responsive the States are to the suggestions of the central government, which, not satisfied with pliant servility, is evidently preparing to clutch the whole system and wield its incalculable power in the furtherance of its projects.

Another view will demonstrate that the public school system and the American theory of government cannot exist together. We maintain the perfect separation of Church and State. Absolute religious freedom, we proudly claim, is the gift of American thought to humanity. Here, we assert, Catholics and Protestants, Jews and Mahommedans, Infidels, Pagans and Atheists, stand politically on the same footing. All are free to believe or disbelieve what they please, and incur by their belief no disqualification of any sort whatever. A man is responsible only to his Maker for his religious belief, and government cannot tax for the support of any form of religion. Such is our boast, such our creed. But this creed is attacked so soon as the State undertakes to educate. The vexed question of Church and State obtrudes itself, and will not down. Shall religious instruction be given in the public school? If so, then that instruction will offend some, who will maintain, and, according to our political compact, will justly maintain, that they are taxed to propagate religious error. Shall religious instruction be excluded from the public school? If so, then the public school, in the clear opinion of the great bulk of Protestants, is an institution in the interests of Atheism and Infidelity. To exclude the precepts and the doctrines of the Gospel, and its motives and inspirations, from the hungry, plastic minds of children, is, they tell us, to put contempt upon religion and to compel their children to receive hostile, perhaps fatal, impressions. They are taxed that their children may learn to trample under foot the lessons of religion and the blood of the atonement. Whether, therefore, religious instruction be given or excluded, the great American doctrine of absolute religious freedom is violated.

Shall the Bible be read in the public school? If so, what version? If the Catholic version, then Protestants are taxed to support the doctrine of penance. If King James' version, then the Catholic is taxed to propagate heresy, and the Jew to maintain the pretensions of an imposter. The State cannot prescribe a religious creed; it has covenanted to respect the religious faith of all its citizens alike, and not to inquire into the truth or error of their tenets.

Let the Bible be a sealed book in the public school, demands the Atheist or the Infidel, Let its doctrines and teachings never be announced to furnish motives of conduct to the pupils. Be it so. Then religionists of every class will complain, and justly, that they are taxed to destroy religion and to foster infidelity. The minds of their children are hungry; if truth be excluded, they must feed on error. Those minds are plastic, and must receive impressions. If Religion be forbidden to write its lessons on the soft tablets of their hearts, Vice will brand them with his mark and seal them as his own.

Nor is it possible to divorce religion from secular instruction. There is religion in the copy-book and in the primer, in history, in science, in literature. Every teacher makes impressions for or against religion.

Under such a system, what chance is there of sound, moral culture when a chapter of the Bible can be read only by sufferance; when the only infallible source of ethics must be positively excluded or timidly employed. The mere cultivation of the intellectual powers, without the proper cultivation of the moral faculties, furnishes no safeguard against vice and crime. It enlarges the desires, it is true; but this enlargement is not accompanied by corresponding moral restraints to prevent their unlawful gratification. It only puts into the heart a stronger temptation, and into the hand a keener instrument for crime.

Such has always been the fruit which this tree has borne. It first took root and flourished among the ancient Spartans, and soon their creed was perfidy, and their virtue, theft. In an article in the *Religious Herald*, I proved by the inexorable logic of the census tables that crime and communism are most rife and rampant exactly in those communities where the system has been longest entrenched. The State, in order to prepare our children for the safe and intelligent discharge of the duties of citizenship, must inform their minds and mould their morals! This work, by the voice of Nature and the law of God, belongs to parents, and to them only; and government has never in a single instance usurped the parental function without emasculating, debasing and corrupting the character of its subjects. If this be our reliance for the intelligence and morality necessary to the perpetuity of free institutions, then we are leaning upon a broken reed, we are treading upon treacherous ashes, we are building upon the unstable sand.

But the system, we are told, is upon us by the conqueror's act, and submission is at once our necessity and our policy. To this I answer:

1. That there is no evidence to show that the Federal Government required the incorporation of the free school system into our State Constitution as a condition of reconstruction; and if it did not, the argument is plainly false.

2. But, it is replied, that while the Federal Government did not expressly make this avowal, it was known that such was its pleasure and its purpose, and that the State would not have been re-admitted into the Union unless our Constitution had contained a provision for the support of free schools. This may be true; it may not be true. It is a matter of conjecture. But granting it to be true, I have this to say: Virginia is now a State of this Union. She is as truly a State as Massachusetts, and as sovereign within the limits of State action. Provided she does not violate the Federal Constitution, she is as free as any other State to regulate her internal affairs in her own way. All that the Federal Government had a right to expect, all, in fact, that it did expect, was so to start us in our new career as to make it morally certain that we would move in the path of its appointment. Fastening upon us negro suffrage and the public school, it knew that the difficulty of making a change would be exceedingly great. But if from inherent energy and virtue we surmount the difficulty, the Federal Government will only be baulked in its own game—a game it had no right to play, and certainly will have no right to complain. If good faith to the Federal Government indeed demands the eternal integrity of the present Constitution of Virginia, by what authority, then, is our present Legislature engaged in an attempt to affect important alterations? If Virginia is indeed a State, with all the rights of any other State, then the payment of her debt supremely touches her honor. But, if, as is secretly assumed but not roundly asserted, she is not a real State, but an outlying province; if, by foreign force, a form of organic law is fixed and fastened upon her that prevents the development of her resources and renders compliance with her plighted faith impossible, then it were well that the fact should so appear, and cancel her obligations. If such, indeed, be her condition, then let the Federal Government tear from her shield the sham sovereignty we should in very shame refuse to flaunt. Let the full truth be openly avowed. Sorrow, humiliation and shame have been the fruit, the bitter fruit, of falsehood, pretense and self-deception. If such indeed be the condition of Virginia, then she is dead; dead from the blow, which, with superhuman courage, she vainly essayed to parry. But proclaim her death, and the circumstances of her death, and so save her honor. Yes, it were better to annihilate right out her pretended sovereignty, and so free her fame from the foul stain of violated faith, than that she should live on, but in a moribund state, while dishonor feeds and fattens on her decaying vitals. So dying, her pale ghost, as it descends to the shades, pale from sorrow and from torture, but still pure, will be welcomed to the tender embrace of the bravest of her sons: of him, whose effigy, the gift of kindred blood, was lately inaugurated amidst the loud roar of artil-

lery and the mournful dirge of martial music; who left, as his last legacy to the Commonwealth he could not save, the immortal words, " Death is preferable to dishonor."

No, no; I cannot admit the conclusion of those who say that the conqueror has left us the form but nothing of the reality of freedom; that he has imposed upon us the responsibilities of sovereignty but denied us the liberty of meeting its demands; that he even consents to the destruction of the government he fought to defend in order to wreak the more fully his malignant vengeance on us. No, no; we can change the Constitution of our State, if we please ; we can do this and be guilty of no breach of faith—express, tacit or implied.

3. When the present Constitution of Virginia was adopted, it was simply impossible to do the wise and proper thing. The conqueror, after a hard and doubtful contest, was flushed with victory, hot with wrath, and thirsting for vengeance. Thus inflamed, he did things injurious to both sides, which a returning sense of justice and the mellowing influence of time, lead him to cancel or modify.

On the other hand, Virginia was absolutely paralyzed with despair. She had made the supreme effort and had failed. Bleeding and prostrate, she lay at the conqueror's feet. If at such a time she accepted ruinous and degrading conditions; if, in the hour of her mortal weakness, she went farther (as I think she did) in the way of submission than was required, and, to appease her powerful and vindictive conqueror, assumed burdens which even he in his hot exasperation did not seek to impose, is she now, when she is somewhat recovering from her deadly stupor, and the blood, though slow and languid, is beginning to creep and tingle through her veins, still to suffer, and to suffer forever, the crucifixion of those cruel fetters? Virginia was not even present in the Convention that formed this Constitution. A few, indeed, impotent to restrain, stood by in silent agony and saw their mother mutilated and mangled by aliens and enemies, when there was neither strength in her arm nor mercy in her woe. And yet we are told that a Constitution thus formed, and imposed upon us, is an eternal contract, and that it is wrong even to attempt to free the Commonwealth from its hard and ruinous conditions.

We are trying to inaugurate the "era of good feeling," to "shake hands across the bloody chasm," and be friends again. God speed the happy day! But that day will never come so long as unjust and injurious terms, the heritage of defeat, are submitted to on the one hand, or enforced on the other. We can never feel kindly towards the North so long as we chafe under these cruel exactions; the North can never respect us or extend to us a sincere and honorable friendship so long as with lying lips we profess to love the chains that gall us. The only condition of solid peace, of honest friendship, is that the perfect equality of the States should be felt, asserted and acknowledged. In order to the restoration of fraternal relations, we must make a full, frank and manly assertion of our sentiments. To conceal or qualify them is but to confirm the oppression which the advocates of such a policy profess to fear. As time mellows the temper of the North, and the hot passions, born of blood, subside, the generous instincts of the victor, stimulated and strengthened by an ever-growing conviction of identity of interests, and by the sad spectacle of a brave people writhing under dishonorable terms accepted in the weakness of despair or imposed in the cruel wantonness of power, will seek to erase the traces of fratricidal conflict and to blend the late hostile sections into friendly and honorable union again. But this consummation will never be reached so long as we profess to be satisfied with—even to support and defend—the degrading terms of which the conqueror himself is getting to be ashamed. By manly conduct and bearing, by language open, frank, ingenuous, let us maintain our self-respect, and so we will secure respect and consideration from our enemies—enemies no more, at last friends. I offend a powerful friend. My condition is such that an adjustment is necessary. He has me in his power, and imposes conditions which wound my pride and self-respect, but I accept them from necessity. We resume our relations; we maintain the forms of friendship and courtesy; but it is a hollow and a treacherous peace. If I should tell him I was easy and content under the galling terms, he would hold me, and justly, in contempt. I can never feel kindly towards him; he can never restore to me his confidence and respect; we can never be friends again, until by concurrent action the degrading terms are cancelled. The application is easy.

That there is nothing in our relations to the Federal Government to prevent our abandonment of free schools, the friends of the scheme in Virginia have again and again proclaimed. When the Civil Rights Bill, requiring mixed schools—the logical demand, by the way, of the system—was under debate in Congress, they constantly declared that that feature, if retained, would effectually kill the public schools in this and in all the Southern States. There is a way, then, to get rid of this system, even according to its supporters, for the Constitution of Virginia is now exactly what it was then.

But, says an objector, the theory of public instruction so generally prevails, and is still making such rapid headway, that it is idle to resist the current, and that it becomes us to submit as gracefully as possible to the inevitable. I answer as follows:

1. If the system is utterly wrong both in morals and in policy, as I have shown it to be, it is the duty of good men to oppose it, and that without reference to the question of the success or failure of their opposition. In the language of Burke: "When there is abuse there ought to be clamor; for it is better to have our slumber broken by the fire-bell than to perish in bed amidst the flames." It is better for us, it makes us purer and stronger, to encounter defeat in a brave contest for the right than to triumph in the wrong. In fact, a constant contest with evil is the unending duty of humanity. To submit to it, and hence to be corrupted and debauched by it, is

the soft persuasion of the lax morality of our day. I daily meet men who say: "I fully accept your views, but the thing is upon us, and we have only to submit." Of course, the system will prevail; if those who are opposed to will not oppose it. The devil himself is upon us; must we, therefore, cease resistance, and passively submit to his pleasure?

Others say, in terms of confidential cowardice, that, while they utterly disapprove the scheme, yet so many who have votes or patronage are in favor of it, their interests forbid them even to divulge their opinions. But they, upon whom the burdens of government chiefly fall, whose opinions, therefore, are most entitled to consideration, who have never been candidates for office, and never expect to be, with but few exceptions, oppose the scheme. It is fastened upon us by the brute tyranny of numbers, supported by the votes of those who give it no money, and by the money of those who give it no votes.

2. But I am not at all certain that the system is necessarily upon us forever. It is not gaining, but it is evidently losing strength, even in the North. The tree is beginning to bear fruit, and it is not luscious fruit. The great State of New York is in a ferment about the matter. So with some of the Northwestern States. Even in Masachusetts, the machinery has to be continually tinkered and altered. Everywhere it excites discontent and opposition, and causes bad blood. Most men cannot reason except from facts; they must learn only in the school of experience. The facts have not been favorable to the system; the experience has been bitter. The insuperable difficulties that belong to the system, as, for instance, compulsory attendance and religious instruction, display themselves under the test of actual experiment, and threaten it with overthrow. The school fund has in many cases become a fund for corruption, and has been used notoriously in the furtherance of political schemes. The educational system, a part of government, and therefore subject to all the fluctuations and corruptions of government, has in some instances been so saturated with the putrid waters of party politics that parents, unable to reason from principles, instructed at last by facts, stand aghast at the contamination to which their children are subjected. The system is not becoming stronger; it is getting weaker. A reconsideration of the whole matter is the growing demand and tendency of the times.

3. But so far from accepting the opinion so flippantly proclaimed, I know that the system, sooner or later, is doomed to utter overthrow. Founded on false principles of government, false doctrines in morals, its cornerstone injustice, like all other false systems, it will at last tumble down. It is a violation of those eternal principles of God's moral government, as steady and as constant in their action as the laws that control the physical universe. The results of the violation of those principles are as inevitable, though, perhaps, not so patent or so prompt, as those which follow a disregard of physical laws. "The mills of the gods grind slowly," but they grind;

and their perfect work will at length be accomplished. We may obstruct the operation of these principles, as we may obstruct the action of physical laws, but never in either case safely or permanently. They will display at last their invincible power by sweeping away all obstructing causes, and the consequent devastation will be greater in proportion to the strength of the obstructions.

We may arrest for a time the flow of a river to the sea. As the waters come, and fret and foam against the embankment, we may make it higher, broader, stronger; but no obstruction which human power can build will be able finally to withstand the resistless momentum of that ever-swelling flood. And the longer we stay its course, the greater will be the desolating force of that angry tide when at last it has forced its way.

False moral systems, once more popular and more prevalent than the one we have subjected to examination, have in like manner been swept away, and their wrecks bestrew the path of history. "Truth is great, and it will prevail."

But shall we weakly wait until this system has borne its full harvest of evil fruit; until, leaving us no fragment of our distinctive civilization, it has accomplished our social subjugation, without making the supreme effort for its extirpation? If we cannot destroy it, we can certainly so modify it as to strip it of some of its most objectional features. The scheme intended for the benefit of individuals, not for the protection of property, should, if we can do no more, be thrown upon the poll tax solely for support. The most intelligent and worthy friends of the system themselves favor this plan; and with proper effort, the necessary change of the constitution could be easily effected. But there is a remedy, an effectual remedy, if only we have the courage to use it; there is a way out of the wilderness, which will lead us to relief not only from this system, but from other evils also, daily becoming more and more intolerable, the brood of the same hideous parentage.

Universal suffrage, the sum of all political evils, without which the free-school system could not be sustained in Virginia, must give way to qualified suffrage; and the best qualification is a property-qualification. Start not, and say the remedy is impossible; be patient, let us see.

If indeed it be impossible, then we may fold our hands in despair; we are a ruined people, utterly ruined. A government that does not protect property rights, fails to discharge the most obvious and important function of government, and is a monstrous oppression. Universal suffrage puts property under the control of those who own none, and to be able to control property by legislation is in effect to own it. It is the unvarying testimony of all history, and the impregnable conclusion of sound philosophy, that the ratio of increase of non-property-holders is greater than that of property-holders, and this becomes more conspicuous as population becomes more crowded. A time comes in the history of every State when non-property-holders constitute the majority, the large majority as population becomes dense. Under universal suffrage, the majority, owning no property, control the property in the hands of the minority. They will tax it so as to make it tributary to their interests, increasing the tax more and more for their own benefit, until property yields more revenue to the public than to its nominal owners, and this is practical confiscation. Or, they may demand and enforce actual partition and inaugurate downright communism. The effect, in either case, is the same. When confiscation by either route is reached, revolution, bloodshed and chaos are the results, succeeded by the dead calm of absolute despotism. Universal suffrage is, *ipso facto,* a confiscation of private property. The tendencies of our legislation to such an issue are so painfully patent that I need not stop to point them out.

This result, sooner or later, would be reached; but now, more quickly and with circumstances of aggravated horror by virtue of the alien and baser blood forcibly injected into our political system. We must not criminally shut our eyes to the bitter harvest of woe we are preparing for ourselves and for our children. The discovery of "manhood suffrage" is the fatal achievement of those communities which boast their free schools and superior enlightenment; and whose educational policy, discredited everywhere by its results, is commended to our support. The fundamental error that pervades the northern mind, adopted and defended by Dr. Wayland in his "Elements of Moral Science," and so to some extent prevailing in the southern States (the book having once been largely used as a text in our colleges), is the doctrine that rights are unaffected by condition. In this doctrine "manhood suffrage" had its origin and finds still its support. But the doctrine is as false as it is mischievous. Our rights grow out of our condition. Condition defines and determines our rights. A minor has rights, but other and different rights when he gets to be a man. Savages have rights, but other and different rights when they become civilized. The poor man has rights, sacred rights; but other and different rights when he has acquired property, He has the right to protection for his life, for his business, and in all lawful means of bettering his condition and advancing his happiness. But he has no right to control property that does not belong to him; in other words, he has no right to suffrage.

A property-qualification for suffrage is recommended by the following considerations:

1. It is just. Nothing is plainer than that they who own the property of a country, and must bear well nigh the whole burden of taxation, should control legislation.

2. It is the only politic and safe plan. To acquire property is a much better educational test even than the ability to read and write. Any fool may learn to read and write, but to make a thousand dollars requires much more intelligence, and is a far better test of worth. To own property identifies one with the State, and his intelligence is quickened and stimulated by his interests.

But, says the demagogue, must a man be required to fight for a country in which he cannot vote? Must he be required to shoulder the musket and not be allowed to cast a ballot? I answer: fighting and voting are very different things. The fact that a man makes a good soldier does not at all touch the question of his fitness as a voter. Fitness to fight and fitness to vote, are not convertible terms.

Why does he fight, and what does he fight for, if he cannot vote? I answer: he fights for the country that protects his life, that protects his business, that protects his hopes and his prospects, and will protect his property when he acquires it. If suffrage be so dear, I answer further, that he fights for the country that will give him suffrage in due time when he will be prepared to exercise the right, now valuable, for the general good, and for the undisturbed possession and enjoyment of the fruits of his honest toil. We have had restricted suffrage in Virginia, and nobody was oppressed or aggrieved, but all were more content and better protected, because the government was in safer and better hands.

We, are told, however, that, universal suffrage having been inaugurated, it is now impossible to recall it. But the privilege has become so worthless and has been attended with such ruinous consequences of the certainty of a still more abundant harvest of sorrow in the future, that thousands are ready to disfranchise themselves if, by so doing, they could restrict suffrage and put it on a safer basis. Let us not be discouraged by the remark, so common, that political powers, when once extended, can never be peaceably revoked. Our condition is utterly exceptional, and history throws no light upon the problem left to us for solution. The conditions are new and abnormal, and we may reach an issue as novel in history as the case itself.

If it were proposed to amend our State Constitution by engrafting upon it a property qualification for suffrage, applicable alike to both races, who would support the amendment? I answer:

1. All, with the rarest exceptions, possessing the required qualification, the class who are most interested in good government, and upon whom its burdens chiefly fall.

2. Thousands upon thousands, who have little or no property, but who have energy, intelligence, the hope and the capacity of acquiring property. They would gladly abandon a polluted and worthless privilege to acquire in due time a valuable right which they would exercise in the protection of their property. With proper effort, the support of almost every voter belonging to this class could be secured for the suggested amendment.

3. But not these two classes only, who own the property, and represent the intelligence, the morality, the energy and enterprise, of the commonwealth. Their influence is necessarily and justly great, and this influence they would properly exert in securing the support or cancelling the opposition of others more or less indifferent.

Opposition to the amendment would come, as a general statement, almost wholly from that class who are so low that they do not even hope to rise. Its defeat, if defeat must come, would demonstrate that the political power of the State is lodged exactly in those hands least competent to use it. Into this wretched condition has the grand old Commonwealth already come? I do not believe it. But she is approaching that condition with each revolving year. Her rescue is easier now than it will ever be again. The attempt is worthy of our noblest effort, demands our utmost energy. Let the real people boldly demand this change, and bravely attempt to put it through, and success is certain. Let them turn away from the cautious counsels of timid editors, with whom the subscription list outweighs good government and the triumph of truth. Let petty politicians, tempted perhaps, for selfish ends, to head the ignoble opposition, in whose eyes a vote is more important than a principle, be made to understand that in this hour of supreme peril, they must stand aside. Not only life, and property and good government, but our honor and our social status and the very sanctities of the fireside are imperilled. Let us endeavor, if we despair for ourselves, to open a future for our children, and leave to them at least the heritage of hope.

Oh! my countrymen, my countrymen, will you go on in unthinking apathy, and weakly close your eyes to the thickening horrors of the future? If we falter now, when every thing is at stake that makes life dear, then it will appear that we have experienced not only political but social subjugation; that we have neither "freedom in our love, nor in our souls are free."

CIVIS.

THE

SOUTHERN NEGRO AS HE IS.

BY

G. R. S.,

BOSTON.

"For many are deceived by their own vain opinion; and an evil suspicion hath overthrown their judgment." — *Apocrypha.*

BOSTON:

PRESS OF GEORGE H. ELLIS.

1877.

41

42

THE SOUTHERN NEGRO AS HE IS.

THE radical change in the policy of the Republican party towards the South, under the present administration, increases and intensifies the interest of every thoughtful man in the great social problem of the Negro. He is curious about his past, inquisitive as to his present condition, and anxious for his future.

His curiosity and inquisitiveness are easily satisfied, but in them he finds little solace for his anxiety; and the more diligent his research, the more do his solicitude and perplexity increase. In short, the future of the Negro is enigmatic and obscure, and certain facts being known (which only those can know who have associated with him in childhood, and guided him in maturer years), it then can only be indistinctly suggested.

It is a great and prevailing mistake to suppose that the Negro is easily understood, or as readily classified as an ordinary specimen in an anatomical museum. Exact knowledge of him is not acquired by the ordinary traveller in a flying trip to the South, nor, indeed, in a six months' or six years' residence there; on the contrary, nothing but an experience gained by constant intercourse in the field, workshop, and household, can furnish the proper data for a correct opinion of his present status.

A gentleman of culture, who has devoted much study and thought to the subject of the Negro character, says: "Even we who have lived our whole lives among them, are *strangers* to their inner life. Yet those whose opportunities bear no comparison to ours, have more confidence in their opinion

than we have, knowing, as we do by experience, the wide difference which interferes with our mutual understanding."
"In regard to our views of the Negro, they are at least very friendly to him. I think he has behaved *remarkably well*, and I wish the race the highest success it can attain in the future."

Unfortunately for ourselves and the Negro, we "small philosophers of Massachusetts" have formed our estimate of him as a social element from certain preconceived and indistinct notions, rather than from experience and well-established facts; in many instances yielding up reason to our sympathies. It is our object, so far as it is possible within moderate limits, to present in a cursory way some leading *facts* as to the present condition of the Southern Negro, morally, socially, and politically. An able correspondent of one of our liberal papers in Boston says:—

"By the proclamation of President Lincoln, in 1863, upwards of four million of slaves were suddenly made free, and shortly after, nearly one million were clothed with the rights, privileges, and responsibilities of American citizenship. These acts, so meritorious in themselves, added at once to the already diluted and degraded suffr..ge of the country an ignorant mass of voters, numbering about one-seventh of the then voting population of the States. A more ignorant and degraded class of people could hardly have been found. Held in bondage for considerably more than a century, after being drawn from a barbarous condition in Africa, they were allowed, and even encouraged, to grow up without education, without morality, and with scarcely more than animal instincts. Naturally they are a kindly people, and their quickness at imitating and copying what comes in their way helps them to acquire, in many instances, gentle ways and habits. Some of them have doubtless been helped by kind masters and mistresses, and by association with white people, and not infrequently by their aptness for simple kinds of music, and for a comforting but superstitious religion. It has been their misfortune, a cruel wrong inflicted upon the race, and not any fault of their own, that they have learned so little. Pages and volumes may be written to recount the wrongs they have suffered. We are not blaming them; we are not apologizing for them; we simply try to look at the actual facts as they exist.

"What sort of a person *is* the average colored voter in the South? We have nothing to do with the creations of fiction, with the prose of Harriet Beecher Stowe, or the poetry of Whittier. Nor in our judgment of the whole race must we be misled by such men as Frederick Douglass, or Joshua B. Smith, or James Wormley, or Revels, or Lynch.

"Of the million of colored voters, more or less, by far the larger portion were known as 'field hands,' ignorant, degraded, licentious, and improvident. In the cities there were exceptions among the mulattoes and quadroons. Some body servants and house servants were exceptionally bright, and exceptionally fortunate in opportunities for improving themselves. But the great mass of colored people in the South are as unfitted to care for themselves, much less to intelligently exercise the suffrage, as can possibly be imagined. Their condition is well-nigh hopeless. They are simply animals. Let us not deceive ourselves, lest by any chance we do them a great and irreparable wrong. I have myself seen colored *statesmen* in the South who could hardly turn their hands or their feeble minds to any labor, even the unexacting one of polishing their own boots. I can testify from observation that the intelligent colored waiters one sees at Saratoga, or Newport, or Sharon Springs, and the quick-witted copper-colored followers of the art tonsorial in our Northern cities, are as far advanced in intelligence and manliness over the most of their Southern brethren as day is brighter than the night. In America every man who stands erect on two legs is a citizen, and however humble he may be, has his rights, which are sacred. Secure to the Negro all his rights by impregnable bulwarks; but for his sake, as well as the larger interests of the country, let us not forget that in most cases he is a child in knowledge, and an animal in instincts and habits.

"When we dismiss from our minds all sentiment and fancy, and all the overdrawn pictures of eloquent oratory and tender poetry, and look at the Southern Negro voter as he is, and apply to his case the principles of statesmanship rather than the vaporings of heated imagination, we shall find him a perplexing study, that will puzzle the largest-hearted and the wisest."

Some time since, we prepared a series of questions under the three heads previously mentioned, which several prominent gentlemen of abundant experience and culture have kindly answered; and we give the answers *verbatim* with an occasional explanatory comment or addition of our own, suggested by inquiry and observation, as presenting, in the most concise, forcible, and practical way, the Negro as he appears in the light of ripe experience, constant observation, and accurate knowledge, to those who are always in contact with him, and are most deeply and personally interested in his present condition and future development.

THE NEGRO MORALLY.

1st. *In what degree do the emotions distinctive of vice and virtue exist as principles of action?*

"The Negro is naturally emotional; he is naturally religious, but his religion is almost entirely sentimental and emotional; he has very little active sense of virtue and vice *as such*, or as principles of action. The *love* of virtue and hatred of vice have little hold on him. When tempted, he generally considers the *immediate consequences* of his action, rather than the question of *right* or *wrong*, and is decided by the seeming probabilities of the case."

2d. *In what degree do the emotions of love and hate exist?* (Involving conjugal, parental, and filial love, resentment and revenge.)

"The conjugal tie is exceedingly weak, and conjugal fidelity generally disregarded. The parental and filial emotions are also very feeble. To his *own* children he is disposed to be overbearing and cruel; to those of the *whites* kind and attentive."

Sir John Lubbock, on marriage and relationships among the lower races of men, says : —

"Marriage and the relationships of a child to its father and mother, seem to us so natural and obvious, that we are apt to look on them as aboriginal and general to the human race. This, however, is very far from being the case. The lowest races have no institution of marriage; true love is almost unknown among them, and marriage in its lowest phases is by no means a matter of affection and companionship." *

Resentment and revenge are not *characteristics* of the Negro;

* "Origin of Civilization and Primitive Condition of Man."

he harbors no malice, but his resentment is frequently aroused, and if not at once gratified, soon passes away.

3d. *Has he an accurate conception of his negative duties to others?* (Relating to the taking of life, property, and virtue.)

"When he takes life, it is usually under the *sudden impulse* of passion stimulated by drink, and seldom from revenge, or as a deliberate and planned act. As to property, he has very little perception of *meum et tuum;* it is hard to induce him to believe that stealing, particularly of small things, is a *sin.* Sensuality is the besetting sin of the Negro in both sexes. He has little idea of the restraints of the marriage tie, divorcing himself without the aid of courts, and taking another wife in some distant place, defying identification."

4th. *Has he an accurate conception of the positive duties arising from friendship, and from benefits received?* (Involving gratitude, justice, and mercy.)

"His sense of friendship, gratitude, justice, and mercy is small,— large professions, small performance. There are, however, instances of the very strongest devotion to his benefactors."

5th. *Has he an accurate conception of the positive duties arising from contracts and citizenship?* (Involving the relation of personal service, and patriotic and civic duties.)

"A contract binds him only so long as he thinks it for his advantage. He does not scruple to evade or violate it, because he attaches no sanctity to his promise.

"It is scarcely to be expected that he could, in so short a time since his emancipation, understand much, if anything, of the nature and obligations of citizenship. The future may produce a change, with the change in his political status."

6th. *Has he an accurate conception of his duty to the Deity?* (Involving the character of their worship, and their lives as members of the visible Church.)

"He is *intensely* emotional and superstitious. Religion in some form seems almost a *necessity* to him, and many of the sentimentally religious do seem to have some conception of their relations to the Deity; but there is a vast amount of the *feticism* of their ancestors in Africa, and of modern paganism about them. As to a clear and correct conception of the nature, attributes, and offices of the Holy Trinity, it is rare among the Negro people. In the duties of practical religion they are very deficient."

Sir John Lubbock, in his chapter on the "Character of Religion among the Lower Races of Men," says: "In fact, the so-called religion of the lower races bears somewhat the same relation to religion in its higher forms that astrology does to astronomy, or alchemy to chemistry. Astronomy is derived from astrology, yet their spirit is in entire opposition; and we shall find the same difference between the religions of backward and of advanced races."

We will add that the average Negro is a firm believer in sorcery, enchantments, charms, and the ordinary practices of witchcraft; his worship consists of vehement, impassioned, ecstatic prayer and exhortation; profuse psalm singing (frequently absurdly improvised), the whole often culminating in the "*holy dance*" or "*walk in Egypt*," a relic of African barbarism, in which the contortions of the body furnish a safety-valve to the intense mental excitement. The dawn of day, and absolute nervous and physical exhaustion, call them back to labor and refreshment, frequently prefaced by a walk of several miles to their miserable and cheerless cabins.

In the cities, among the "fashionable" negroes, who closely imitate the whites, the "*holy dance*" is dying out, and is rather looked down upon; but on the plantations it is still kept up.

The ceremonial of baptism is peculiar, and consists of preliminary services in the church; a procession is then formed, headed by the pastor, who is followed by the converts, all in emblematic white robes and white cotton gloves, the congregation bringing up the rear, singing psalms and hymns and spiritual songs, through the streets of the town to the bank of the river. There, after prayer, exhortation, and more singing, they are dipped in the muddy water, and struggle out

2

through the yellow, slimy mud, shouting, in religious frenzy, "Glory to God!" In the afternoon all again repair to the church, the converts dressed in *ball costume* and bridal array, to hear more preaching, and join in congratulations and singing. This is kept up until evening, with gradually increasing fervor, until the climax of the holy dance.

Petty thieving in the ordinary Negro mind does not conflict with his good and regular standing in the church; in fact, small thefts are not considered sins; or, as an old Negro woman expressed it when reproved for robbing the turkey-roost and then presenting herself at the communion-table, *"Do you suppose I would allow a miserable turkey gobbler to stand between me and my blessed Saviour?"*

We were much surprised to find the *black* church membership in Georgia so much smaller than the *white*, but do not know if the proportion is the same in the other cotton States. We, however, give below the membership in Georgia:

The Baptists have 193,600 members; one to every six persons, of whom 81,000 are negroes. The Methodist Episcopal (colored), 13,752; the Methodist Episcopal (North) 12,000 colored, 3000 whites. The African Methodist, 40,000. The colored Presbyterian, 1000. Total *black* membership, 147,700. Total *white* membership, 262,800. Showing of the white population of the State, one church-member to 2.43, and of the blacks, one church-member to 4.02.

THE NEGRO SOCIALLY.

1st. *Has he a liking for labor as labor?*

"There is no fire in his bones impelling him to labor. There is no impulse in his climate or surroundings, no sufficient need, no inherited habits, no illustrations before his eves. The 'Country Parson' says that even the *whites* could not stand this test; hence, any real love of labor, as such, is either by inheritance or habits founded on the consideration of its fruits. He never seems to feel restless because idle, or to seek work just to be doing something. If his physical wants are supplied, he is perfectly satisfied to do absolutely nothing."

In some of the sea-board counties of Georgia, where fish and game abound, many of the plantations have been abandoned on account of the difficulty in obtaining *continuous labor* in cultivation; the negroes preferring the irregular and indolent habits of the aborigines, and going to labor only when the necessity for clothing compels them to do so.

2d. *Has he a liking for labor as the means to an end?*

"If the reward or inducement be sufficient, he labors very cheerfully; but his satisfaction lies in the result attained, not at all in the fact that it was attained by *his labor.* He would prefer it a *free gift.*"

3d. *What is his character as a laborer?*

"His physical capacity is good. His ability to stand exposure to the sun, miasma, and fever, and to work without exhaustion, are unusual, and instance the survival of the fittest. The wear and tear of his nervous system is small, for he is not eager in his work. If his employment *suits* him, he is very capable and most cheerful. A great deal has been said about the Negro's inferiority to the white man as a laborer, and in many pursuits it is doubtless true, especially so in job-work about towns, where so much depends upon method and economy of time; and also in employments requiring skill and intelligence rather than capacity for physical endurance. But for regular plantation work with the plough, hoe, and axe, the Negro will accomplish as much in a day as any laborer, and will laugh and sing over it; at the close of the day, he has plenty of life left for a coon-hunt or a dance until midnight. He is, however, a routinist, rarely endeavoring to change or improve upon what he has hitherto done, and slow to learn improvements in method from others. Merely muscular labor is his forte. As a laborer, under proper control, he is the best that can be had at present."

4th. *Is he provident?* (Involving the support of his family.)

"He is improvident. Many of them know this. Even if rations are supplied in abundance they will not hold out; much less do they foresee wants and provide for them. He is not provident for his *personal* wants, much less for his family. Apprehension of them is no check to the increase of race."

"Whether this is a natural defect, or the result of slavery, in which state his *owner* was his Providence, and he knew that his family would be provided for, we know not; but, whatever the cause, his improvidence is remarkable. There are, of course, exceptions; but in a majority of instances, when a Negro comes into possession of money, he puts it to immediate use in gratifying any whim for trifling or useless things, and very rarely puts by any for future needs or necessities. His family have always managed to live in the *past*, so his faith wavers not as to the *future*."

5th. *As a laborer, does he require surveillance?*

"He needs watching; he does not like it, but needs it like a child. He will make constant mistakes in details unless observed, and be very negligent, slighting his work. His judgment is not to be relied on to meet unexpected emergencies."

In this particular it is doubtful if there is much difference between him and the common laborer of the North.

6th. *Is he easily controlled?*

"As a laborer he is very easily controlled, seeming to have an instinctive sense of subordination."

7th. *Is he self-sustaining?* (Away from the encouragement and influence of whites.)

" He is self-sustaining only by the smallness of his wants. He lacks perseverance and energy to work continuously, and cannot resist the temptation to take numerous holidays."

8th. *Has he any desire for education?*

" He is not deficient in the *desire* for education. It is, however, indefinite, and based on love of display and novelty, and an ambition to read and write like 'white folks,' rather than on a love of knowledge. The average of intelligence among them is very low, and is likely to remain so."

9th. *What progress does he make, and what is its limit?*

" In some cases the young Negro is precocious, and will learn the preliminary branches as quickly as the white boy; many have made remarkable progress in branches requiring memory alone; but, as a rule, the desire and capacity both seem to exhaust themselves about the age of (15) fifteen. As a rule, he has better memory than reasoning faculties, yet he improves under cultivation. Sir Samuel Baker compares his first rapid progress to that of one of the inferior animals."

All idea of social or mental equality with the whites is apparently abandoned. Schools are abundantly provided and liberally maintained by the whites; and in the State of Georgia alone 55,000 negro children attended the free schools in 1875. Generally there is no social disorder, and the two races live together in relations of mutual assistance and dependence.

10th. *Has he any social ambition?*

"In towns and cities, from contact with, and in imitation of, the whites, he shows social ambition to some extent. On the plantation there is scarcely a trace of it. The *aristocratic* city Negro copies the white in dress, manners, conversation, and religious worship, and has a great desire to shine. Vanity, not *pride*, is a leading characteristic."

11th. *Is he inclined to, and easily instructed in, mechanical employments?*

"He is decidedly inclined to, and easily instructed in, the coarse and common trades, such as shoemaking, tailoring, blacksmithing, carpentering, joining, rough painting, bricklaying, etc.; and, were he thrifty and forecasting, he could make a living and save money. He rarely becomes a first-class mechanic, and a 'white boss' is generally a necessity."

The Mulatto and Negro differ very decidedly in capacity, mental and physical; the former having the larger mental, and the latter the larger physical development. The greater the proportion of white blood, the greater the mental capacity; and, consequently, the colored men who acquire political prominence, or unusual skill in the trades or the arts, are generally found to be largely indebted to the admixture of white blood. The intermarriage of mulattoes is seldom productive; when it is, the offspring is feeble and sickly, and reared rarely and with great difficulty.

12th. *What is the character of the rising generation?*

"It is thought they are deteriorating in every way; physically, from want of care and proper parental management; mentally and morally, because not controlled as in slavery times. The parents are usually either inert or violent. The comparative worthlessness as laborers of the rising generation is one of the gravest difficulties."

Our opportunities for observing the moral condition of the free plantation laborers have been limited in number, and we hesitate in making any positive statements as to their condition as a whole. But under slavery, the slave, as well as the

master, had many advantages. The latter was bound by his
personal interests to keep the slave well housed, well clothed,
well fed, physically cared for, and decently moral. To the
former, these were all blessings which in a state of freedom
he is generally denied. In the place of a cleanly whitewashed cabin, which he was forced to keep in order, he has
a miserable hovel; his clothing is an apology; his food is
inferior in quality, and irregular in quantity, or he is without
it altogether; his health and sanitary condition he does not
understand, and has no care for; his morals are, what might
be expected as the natural result of these conditions, generally debased. The planter now naturally considers himself
absolved from all consideration or supervision of the mental,
moral, or physical condition of his laborer; and, as a conse-
quence, the Negro left to himself and away from all restraining influences, without education or established principles,
inherent or acquired, is in a deplorable situation. On some
plantations we have visited, adultery, bigamy, and all manner
of lewdness exist to a frightful extent without remonstrance
from the proprietor. We were present at one time on a
plantation where a Negro had committed rape on the person
of a young Negro girl, and afterwards compromised with the
father by *the promise of a payment of ten dollars!* In the
State of South Carolina where the Negro has had control,
and notably in the city of Charleston, the older negroes are
respectful; but the younger and rising generation, from
neglect, bad advice, and the want of proper education, are
sullen, wilful, impudent, and excitable, ready and willing at
any moment to join in a mob or riot on the slightest provo-
cation. The blacks and whites both commonly carry arms
and concealed weapons; and throughout the Southern country, outside the cities and larger towns, the pistol is as much
a "*vade mecum*" as a plug of tobacco. Resistance to
white domination and control has been openly taught in the
church, in the school, and in the political arena, which may
account for much that is bad in the present state of the
young. There is abundant evidence to show that under
slavery, and during the war (as hateful and disorganizing as

slavery and war are), the Negro was a better member of society than he is to-day, in his transition state, or, perhaps, ever will be. A reverend gentleman well known in South Carolina, and who now is over a large colored congregation in Charleston, says: "I had during the war the charge of a large parish of over five hundred communicants, on one of the sea islands, where the majority of the population is of the worst class of semi-civilized negroes; and during all that time I never saw or heard of an instance of insulting or impudent conduct on the part of the blacks toward the whites."

But in South Carolina the conditions have been exceptional, and the result is exceptionally injurious to the blacks and whites as well. Totally unfitted by instinct or education for the right of suffrage, or the holding of office, its unreasonable and improvident exercise has been attended by the worst consequences to the State. And the effect of this sudden and conscious inheritance of political power upon the black population, and particularly the rising generation, is as already described.

In Georgia, where latterly the Negro has not been driven to the polls, but allowed to exercise his right or not as he chose, his specific gravity as a political element is somewhat indicated. Under ordinary circumstances he has little interest in, or knowledge of, national or local politics, and he voluntarily denies himself the right to vote; and however paradoxical, unreasonable, or unphilosophical it may appear, the Negro in Georgia, where he has *no* control, is a very much better citizen in every way than he is *now*, or *has* been in South Carolina, where he has had a large share in the government. Education and larger experience may change and improve his present moral and political condition.

13th. *Are the females withdrawing from field labor, and in any sense becoming a burden on the males?*

"The females are very generally withdrawing from field-labor, claiming that their husbands must support them 'like white folks do.' The planters, however, generally demand their labor in any unusual pressure, particularly in cotton picking, as some return for free quarters and fuel during the year. When so employed they are paid wages."

The drift of female labor is towards large centres of population on account of the increased opportunities they afford for social intercourse in the way of religious and society meetings, for satisfying a natural fondness for sights and shows, and for engaging in *"aristocratic"* labor, such as "taking in washing," etc.

14th. *Is insanity frequent?*

"Insanity is now more frequent than formerly in servitude, when it was almost unknown, unless hereditary. In December, 1875, the State lunatic asylum of Georgia had a total of five hundred and eighty-seven patients, of whom ninety were blacks; and the proportion of the latter is thought to be increasing gradually." The rate of mortality, especially in children, has very much increased.

15th. *To what degree does he possess reasoning faculties?*

"As a rule, the Negro reasons imperfectly; his intellectual faculties are weak. His memory, however, is more retentive than his judgment is clear; or, in other words, of the two powers, memory and judgment, the former is the more capable of performing its functions."

3

THE NEGRO POLITICALLY.

1st. *As an element in politics has he any distinctive character?*

"The *color line* has controlled, and is likely to control. Of the general interests of society he has little conception, and he thinks only in a rude way of his own color. When fully wrought upon by his preacher, or others having influence, and brought into line on a pure *class* and *color* question, he is difficult to move. He is afraid of the vengeance of his own race, and of social ostracism by his fellows.

"Singularly, in all such cases, the women are specially bitter against deserters, being often known to abandon their husbands for voting contrary to their wishes. But unless solidified upon some *class* question, their votes are most easily controlled."

The fear of the loss of their freedom so recently gained, is the great political *lever* by which false and designing men have swayed the colored vote in one coherent, solidified mass for their own base purposes and selfish ends. The United States local officers were supposed to hold the keys to the temple of freedom, and to be able to shut them out, at will.

In blind, childlike confidence did they look up to them, as representing a beneficent government, and as friends upon whom depended the perpetuity of their freedom; to them, they yielded an obedience, simple, absolute, servile.

Has this confidence been betrayed?

Let the depleted and bankrupt treasuries,

The recent anarchical condition of South Carolina,

The depreciation of property and labor,

The abandonment of plantations,

The general stagnation in business,

The insecurity of property,

The increase of taxation,

In short, all the evils disastrous to labor which follow corrupt government, answer.

If the office-holders and others who have brought about this state of things alone suffered, it would be a sufficient compensation; but the Negro voter, remembering the broken promises, his disappointed hopes of Elysian fields, and happy Rasselian valleys where the call to labor never sounds, has lost faith, and is beginning to feel that he has been wronged by his new-found friends, and is again returning slowly, but surely and confidingly, to his former advisers.

2d. *Has he any rank as an element of progress and higher development?*

"None whatever, as a class."

His imitative power is great; but the faculty of origination is wanting. Where the white race leads, he will follow, but always at a distance, in the ratio of their respective capacities.

3d. *What are his qualifications as a voter?*

"At present, except under circumstances described above, the old phrase, 'floating vote,' expresses him as a voter, with a tendency to side against property, intelligence, and virtue; not from opposition to them *as such*, but because of his indistinct conceptions and want of understanding."

From want of opportunity for education, he is of course ignorant, and his negative qualifications may be summed up as follows: —

He neither reads nor writes. He is immoral. He reasons imperfectly. What he is told he remembers confusedly. He has no power of analysis. He is gregarious with his own race. He is easily influenced, but cannot be depended upon, even if he *accepts* a bribe. He has little of what is called "common-sense."

In all these particulars he differs little from the ignorant white voter of the North; but with us at the North the igno-

rant whites are very greatly in the minority, and the danger
and inconvenience in the administration of the government
of the smaller towns, arising from their presence, is very
slightly felt; while under similar conditions at the South, the
Negro is greatly in the *majority*, and the difficulty of managing such a mass of irresponsible voters in the interest of good
government is very great, and serious, if by any exciting
cause he is brought to the polls. In fact, the *possible* condition of all the Southern cities and towns, with perhaps a few
exceptions, is what the *actual* condition of New York is to-day.

4th. *As a factor, in the increase of population, what is his
probable future?*

" He is probably a diminishing factor. Under slavery the
Southern negroes increased rapidly. Children brought no
additional cares. The mother enjoyed certain privileges, im-
munities, and exemptions, all of which are now wanting; and
there was no lack of medical attention or supplies. This
state of affairs was guaranteed, not less by humanity than by
worldly thrift. Now, another child brings additional expenses,
and they prefer *not* to have them. The root of the cotton-
plant is known to all Negro women as a powerful emmena-
gogue, and, being everywhere obtainable, it is extensively
used. This is having a decided influence in diminishing natural increase; and the census of 1880 is looked forward to
with extreme interest. To this is to be added the further
effects of poverty, entailing lack of medical service and med-
icines, of proper food, clothing, and shelter, and in general the
absence of the care taken by their former owners; and the
greater prevalence of epidemic diseases caused by their herd-
ing together in crowded and filthy quarters in towns and
cities. Free from control, dissipation is more frequent and
disastrous."

We have not attempted any elaboration of the ideas stated
and suggested in the above replies; and have not entered,
nor do we propose to enter into any discussion of, or sugges-

tions as to, what *should have been* done with the Negro when he first received his freedom, or to offer any criticism or censure upon what *was* done, or any speculations as to his future. Our object is simply, to the best of our ability, to state the facts of his present condition, obtained from the best sources, and from personal observation.

The correspondent before referred to, sketching his present condition, says : —

"How to help him in his sore need, is rather the province of the philanthropist. To him in the end must we leave the Negro after all. Just now we are regarding him simply as a political factor in the body politic. We have tried him as a legislator, a supreme judge, a major-general, and a policeman. Generally he has been a failure. As a laborer under kind instruction he has often proved a success. And yet, as one sees the hundreds of idle blacks that swarm over the Capitol, lounge in the sun on Pennsylvania Avenue, or crowd the railway-stations and small towns of the South, ill-clad, lazy, worthless, but grinning through their thick lips as if life were all frolic and fun, one cannot help asking the question, whether the intellectual faculties in this race will ever sufficiently predominate over the purely animal instincts to enable them to profit by *any* amount of instruction and advice. Even the severe school of adversity seems to teach them but little. I speak now of the pure Negro, not of the mulatto or quadroon. I envy even the hopefulness of those who believe in any happy future for these poor, ignorant, and despised ones. In God's providence, they doubtless have their purpose. I do not think that their highest function is office-holding or voting. We had no right to suppose they would succeed in this. We have made them the laughing-stock of a whole people. We have brought them to a condition in which they must now stand alone, or fall. To sustain them longer by bayonets is unsafe and impossible. Let us not despair, however. Their removal from politics will at once quiet all opposition to them, and they will go to work to make money and set their little homes in order. This will be a positive gain, both to our politics and business interests.

They begin already to again trust their former masters. Again they seek their advice, and vote with them upon local interests and often upon national ones. The more intelligent of them can already see that when they divide into both parties, they will be sought and flattered by politicians, instead of being 'bulldozed' and murdered. God speed the day when they shall have the courage to vote *any* ticket or *all* tickets, so that it shall become the interest of all parties to consult their interests! Then only will the race taste political freedom. Time and education will slowly help them to rise in the scale of civilization. But the future is sad for them at best. Their young die in large numbers for want of proper nurture, and it must be at best through great tribulation that they finally work out their earthly salvation, and are able to stand alone."

From what has already been stated and suggested, some conclusions as to the capacity of the race for the higher forms of self-government, in its present stage of development may be drawn.

With no correct notions of morals or religion, no accurate conception of the positive duties arising from citizenship, improvident, ignorant, and not self-sustaining, the race is at present entirely unprepared 'or the responsible duties of freemen; and naturally when the Southern Negro has been called upon to govern he has signally failed.

He is not to blame for this, and is not blamed; his misfortune is understood, and by those who knew him best his failure was foreseen. But notwithstanding this knowledge of his incapacity, the whites, North and South, have, from political or other motives, in many instances recklessly imperilled their own interests, and those of the Negro, by forcing him into positions for which, either by habits or education, he was entirely unfitted.

Many illustrative facts could be given, but one or two will suffice. Hamburg, in the State of South Carolina, is on the Savannah River, and directly opposite to Augusta, Ga. This place was last year the scene of a riot, the particulars of which will be remembered, and in which, in our opinion, the blacks as well as the whites were to blame.

Hamburg was formerly an active, thriving place, with a bank, warehouses, etc., and a good many fortunes were there made, we are told. Before the war, it was the rival of Augusta in cotton-shipping. At its close, it fell into the hands of the black majority, and was fully officered by them. The bank and warehouses are now closed or destroyed, the streets grass-grown and deserted, and its business entirely lost. The city of Charleston, S. C., was also in the hands of the black majority. General stagnation in business followed; money was appropriated, but never spent for the objects for which it was appropriated; the streets were neglected; the sidewalks broken and disordered; the buildings, public and private, in a state of rapid decay and general neglect; and the devastation of war and fire was unrepaired. Improved property was *given away* for ten years, on an obligation to pay the taxes.

If we now turn to Liberia, concerning whose present condition and future prospects, or destiny, scarcely any two observers can agree, we find a government conducted *by* the blacks *for* the blacks, and under which the white man is disfranchised and unrecognized.

Without attempting to settle any disputes, we will try to find a few facts upon which we can all stand.

Looking first at the increase in population. We find that the American Colonization Society in 1820 sent out their first company of eighty-six colonists.

In 1847, when the republic was organized, the Americo-African population was 5,000; aborigines, occupying their territory, 100,000.

In 1856, Americo-African population, 8,000; aborigines, 250,000.

In 1859, the American Colonization Society had sent out to that date 10,000 emigrants at an expense of $1,800,000, of whom only *one-half* were then residents!

In 1873, the Americo-African population was 20,000; aborigines, 700,000, including the two large, powerful, and hostile tribes of Mandingos and Grebos; the former all Mohammedans, and both recently (1876) in a state of insurrection against the Liberian government. It is a remarkable fact that a very large proportion of those emigrants who have been sent out, as well as those who have gone out at their own expense, have returned, and a larger number would have returned if they could. "The colored people are satisfied with their homes here, and resent any measures to remove them."* The earlier colonists have shown a heroism in defence against the savages, as well as in disease and in famine, worthy of any race; and we fear the same heroism will be again demanded in the present generation.

The financial credit of a government or people is a sure indicator of its permanent or temporary condition; and the statement is rather disparaging to Liberia that " a few years ago $500,000 were borrowed in London for 'internal improvements,' which, after deducting two years' interest, paid in advance, agents' commissions, etc., netted to Liberia $200,000 *in gold and useless goods*, which soon disappeared *without an internal* improvement."†

Her inability to pay either principal or interest is now apparent, and unfortunately "she lies at the mercy of her bondholders."‡

In agriculture very little progress has been made. Horses, mules, and asses cannot ei dure the climate, and soon die: the very luxuriance of vegetation increasing the difficulty and labor in the growth of crops. But very few manufactures have been established.

In 1857, thirty-seven years after the arrival of the first colonists, with a population of 8,000 Americo-Africans, her schools and churches were supported by American Christians, and to-day there is very little, if any, interest in higher education, or the support of common schools! The experience of Liberia is that of the South, as before stated. The desire and capacity of the Negro for education seem to ex-

* Paper read at the Sixtieth Annual Meeting of American Colonization Society by E. P. Humphrey, D.D., LL.D.

† Commodore Shufeldt's Address before American Colonization Society, Jan. 18, 1876.

‡ Commodore Shufeldt.

haust themselves at an early age. "I regret to say that a college has been lately established in Liberia. . . . I regret it, because it will involve an outlay that might be better used in common schools. . . . The present state of society in Liberia has no demand for such a thing."*

The climate and surroundings, the abundance of natural products of the soil to be obtained without labor, the absence of the necessity for clothing or habitations, except of the rudest sort, render the Americo-African, as well as the aborigines, indolent, indifferent, improvident; and any natural impulse for higher development is entirely wanting. If the impulse is implanted, and left to itself to increase and multiply, without constant encouragement and assistance from a superior race, it will soon exhaust itself. Archbishop Whately says: "We have no reason to believe that any community ever did, or ever can, emerge, unassisted by external helps, from a state of utter barbarism into anything that can be called civilization."†

"It is evident that physical geography has blighted Africa with the curse of barbarism,"‡ and if she is ever to be Christianized and civilized, as we hope in the providence of God she may, it will only be accomplished by the blacks, as humble instruments in the hands of a superior race. All travellers agree that Mohammedanism is spreading over Africa with marvellous strides, and the work of evangelization accomplished will of course be in proportion to the means used. But progress must of necessity be slow, "and with regard to education and civilization we must be satisfied to work gradually, and not to attempt to force our European manners and customs upon a people who are at present unfitted for them."§ Referring to the results of colonization in Africa, Chaplain Thomas remarks: "We would not be understood as attributing any unworthy motive to the zealous friends of the Americo-African in Liberia; they are noble

* Rev. C. W. Thomas, M.A., "West Coast of Africa."
† "Political Economy," p. 68.   ‡ Bowen's "Central Africa."
§ Com. Cameron, "Across Africa."

4

and liberal men. But we wish to intimate, that, in looking at and describing the condition of their long-cherished scheme, their desires too often color their statements."*

It must be admitted that the picture we have drawn of the Negro, as a *race*, is not a flattering one; and we wish that in some particulars it was not a true one. But we have for him no word of reproach; there is room for nothing but pity. When he received his freedom he was a child in intellect, in education, in dependence, in simplicity; and he has become what children with coarse animal instincts usually become without proper training. The Negro character, however, has its lights as well as shadows.

There *are* pious and godly men and women; good husbands and devoted wives; fond and loving and careful parents; devoted and sacrificing friends; honest and upright citizens. As a laborer, he is willing, cheerful, and of great physical capacity; insensible to exposure, miasma, and fever; easily controlled, and is altogether the best that can be had.

In the States where they have not of late years been forced into the political arena, the blacks are quiet and unobtrusive, attending, in large centres, to all the duties of life to the limit of their capacity, in the same manner as the whites in the same condition of life. In the State of Georgia they are credited as owning $8,000,000 in property. The schools for colored people are well patronized, and the number attending school very large and rapidly increasing. A gentleman in Augusta, Ga., tells us he has sold over two hundred house-lots to colored people, who have paid for them in small instalments since the war. The more thrifty in towns own a mule and cultivate their little lots about their houses, and engage in all sorts of employment adapted to their capacities, dress like "white folks," and go to meeting on Sundays.

In the country, they own, or lease and cultivate, small farms of one hundred acres or more, paying the rent in the product. A Southern gentleman, formerly a large slave-owner, tells us of one who has been his tenant for several

* Rev. C. W. Thomas, M.A., "West Coast of Africa."

years, and describes him as being, in all his dealings with him, prompt, courteous, careful, and, by instinct, a perfect gentleman.

As a rule, however, we fear that they are not successful as proprietors. The country Negro does not pay the attention to dress which his city brother does; but always goes to "meeting," if one is held within walking distance.

The wages paid on large plantations are very small compared with our Northern rate. The able-bodied men get $8.00 per month and found in rations of one-half pound of bacon and two pounds of meal daily, for each full hand, besides rent of cabin. The women get $4.00, $5.00, and $6.00, according to working ability, with rations. The daily rations are valued at ten cents, and are served only to the *laborer*, and not to his or her family.

Tobacco is used by men and women alike. By the courtesy of a large Southern planter who allowed us the use of his books of account, we were able to make some curious memoranda as to the domestic habits of the Negro. And among them in the use of tobacco, we found that the foreman of the mill, a superior hand, who was paid $10.00 per month, spent $3.30 in the weed. Some who were paid $8.00 per month spent, respectively, $2.15, $1.65, .80, $1.20, $1.00, and $2.00 in a month. An engineer who received $15.00, spent $4.35 in tobacco. A woman who was paid $4.00 wages, spent $1.65. In fancy goods for the women, such as highly-colored hats, dresses, parasols, and fancy high-heeled shoes, etc., and for the men, fine hats, fancy stockings (which, with the shoes, they take off and carry in their hands to the vicinity of the meeting-house), candies, canned lobsters and peaches, cigars, etc., etc., some of the hands spent, respectively, $1.90, .62, $1.00, .55, $2.00, .84, $1.75, .70 during the month. The average amount spent monthly for tobacco, by men and women, was $2.00 each: for luxuries, etc., $1.17 each. Total, $3.17, or 35 per cent. of the average wages. The average wages for men and women are $9.10 per month; deducting the amount spent as above, we have a balance of $5.93 left to each hand monthly, for the support of his young children, and, frequently, the wife, in food, clothing, and the usual necessaries of existence. For an average family of five non-working members, it would afford to each one the pittance of twenty cents daily. It is not much to be wondered at that he is frequently driven to rob a hen-roost, or shoot a stray pig, to satisfy the cravings of a hungry family.

The question is often asked, "Is there any antagonism of races in the South?" Under the usual normal conditions, there is not. In South Carolina, where, as we have before stated, antagonism has been encouraged in the negroes, and in Mississippi, Arkansas, and Louisiana, where they have been unduly excited in a variety of ways, and openly taught that the object and purpose of the whites was to *re-enslave* them — which result would follow immediately upon the success of the Democratic party, — there has, undoubtedly, been bad feeling; and excesses and crimes have been committed by whites and blacks, and probably a greater number by the whites than by the blacks,—as when the former are attacked or seek revenge, their means and opportunities are greater and more numerous. But for this great change in the disposition of a race once proverbially docile, obedient, and law-abiding, and now intractable, impudent, and dangerous, there must of necessity be an adequate exciting cause. The Southern people understand the Negro well, and they know that this unnatural lawlessness is *foreign* to the race; that it is not innate in them, and does not proceed, generally, from any injury or oppression undergone or experienced; but is the offspring of an over-heated imagination and very excitable temperament, wrought upon by outside agencies for the accomplishment of political results. Consequently, as far as our observation extends, we have yet to find any evidence of the existence of indignity or bitterness on the part of the whites towards the blacks, excepting, of course, those cases in which the life and property of inoffensive persons have by the latter been wilfully destroyed; but, on the contrary, we have found pity for the colored people, and contempt and disgust for their unprincipled leaders, everywhere expressed. This sympathy for the Negro is, in many cases, active and practical. We know of many Southern gentlemen who now support whole families of their old slaves and descendants, numbering ten or twelve each, not having the heart to turn them out upon the world; and yet, strange to say, these same negroes, submitting to other control, will vote against what their old masters suppose to be their interest in the support of honest government, and still return to the paternal roof-tree to be supported and protected as formerly.

We at the North understand very little, and it is, in fact, impossible for us to fully comprehend the love and affection which the Southern people have for their old nurses and house-servants; and there are many instances of the former having separate establishments and comfortable homes provided for their declining years as a reward for faithful service, in which they are cared for and supported with tenderness and solicitude. We personally know of heads of families who, since the war and the misfortune following, have deprived their own children of certain rather expensive necessaries and luxuries in order to bestow them on some faithful old servant. There are other instances in which the loss of fortune, and consequent poverty, are mutually and inseparably borne by master, mistress, and servant alike, — literally "bearing one another's burdens." To the credit of the colored people, be it said, that this extreme kindness and affection are frequently reciprocated; and during the war when distress, misfortune, and want were everywhere felt, the faithful blacks were able in many ways, impossible to their masters or mistresses, to relieve distress, furnish comfort in misfortune, and supply physical wants.

W. Lawrence, in his "Natural History of Man," speaking of the whole race, says: "Many of them, although little civilized, display an openness of heart, a friendly and generous disposition, the greatest hospitality, and an observance of the point of honor, according to their own notions, from which nations more advanced in knowledge might often take a lesson with advantage."

When their freedom was first declared, it was followed by a general desertion and changing of masters, sometimes very abruptly and unpleasantly; but it was usually borne by the whites with composure, understanding, as they did, that it was the only method known to the blacks by which they could *test* their freedom, and ascertain its actual existence. But the older servants gradually returned to their old homes, and to their former occupations. These separations of master and servant were frequently more painful to the former than the latter. We have seen the eyes of an old mistress fill with tears as she told us of the going away of a favorite servant, in a manner which appeared to her unfeeling.

The repugnance to colored people universal at the North, among all classes and shades of political opinion, however we may attempt its concealment, from party or other motives, has no existence at the South. Suckled and fondled in infancy, petted and indulged in childhood, and revered by them in later years, the Southern people still feel for them a kindliness and sympathy by us unfelt and unrecognized.

We will not attempt to discuss the problem of the Southern Negro's future in this country; but there are a few thoughts naturally suggested by what has gone before, which we will briefly state.

It is evident that from climatic and other influences, and consequent low mental capacity, no *comparison* can properly lie between the black and white races. It is said that " no European people has been in a condition comparable to that of the present dark-colored races, within the reach of any history or tradition."[*] It is evident that the black is, and will continue to be, a *dependent race.* It is evident that, owing to natural repugnance, there is no hope for them in amalgamation with the white race. It is one of the possibilities, but not one of the probabilities, of the future.

It is evident that the dissolution of our philanthropic societies at the close of the war was a *very grave error.* That, although the prominent object of the anti-slavery

---

[*] W. Lawrence, "Natural History of Man."

societiès was accomplished by devastation and war, the opportunity for the exercise of true philanthropy and an enlarged Christian charity was then, as never before, presented. That, owing to this neglect, the colored population of the South have lost moral ground which will never be recovered. It may be said, and is said, that the South must take care of its own population. Undoubtedly they have the disposition, and generally do what they can, to aid them, by furnishing means for education, etc.; but they have not the means to do much, and in the hurry and anxiety incident to getting a living, and in replacing the old, or building up a new fortune, the social and moral condition of the black man is neglected or overlooked. Christian men and women, North and South, may well ask why the solicitude and Christian charity so universal for the colored man before his freedom, without any particular thought of the obligation of his master, should now be partially withdrawn, or cease altogether, when charity has a free course, and the negro stands before us armed with freedom, and clothed with all the rights of a freeman, but, as we have seen, totally unprepared for his duties as such, and sorely in need of the helping hand and outstretched arm of the philanthropic Christian, for guidance and support in his hour of trial.

It is evident that we can best help him by recognizing his actual condition and capacities; that we cannot expect great progress or high culture, and that his interests and our own, as common citizens, will be best promoted by abandoning the forcing process, either in education or politics.

It is evident that the halo of false sentiment and poetic fiction which naturally surrounds an object distant and obscure, is a serious injury to the Negro, in causing demands to be made upon him, and upon those among whom his lot is cast, which neither he nor they are able to meet, and thus contributing to the misunderstanding, which, owing to mistakes as to facts, too much prevails.

It is evident that colonization has a feeble hold upon the Southern Negro. He prefers the support, assistance, and sympathy of the white race. In fact, he is our *ward in honor*, and we are bound by humanity, by the credit of a superior civilization and race, by the oppression and injustice he has already suffered at our hands, to raise him, by education, to a higher plane than he now occupies, and to fit him for the exercise of his civil rights.

It is evident that his rights, political and social, are in no jeopardy at the South, so long as he does not lend himself to foreign politicians to be used as a tool in carrying out their designs, subversive of good government and good morals and against common property.

In conclusion, we commend the thoughtful consideration of this subject and the facts presented, to those who, under the new administration of Southern affairs, honestly desire a better, a more accurate and just knowledge of the present condition, value, and capabilities of that race, now endowed with the highest honors and privileges of American citizenship.

THE

RELATIONS OF THE CHURCH

TO THE

COLORED RACE.

—o—

SPEECH OF THE REV. J. L. TUCKER, D. D.,

OF JACKSON, MISSISSIPPI,

BEFORE THE CHURCH CONGRESS, HELD IN RICHMOND, VA., ON THE 24–27 OCT , 1882.

—o—

This speech is here somewhat enlarged, but adheres to the line of argument adopted at the Congress. As originally delivered the speech was cut short at the end of twenty minutes, by the Secretary's bell.

——— :o: ———

JACKSON, MISS.:

CHARLES WINKLEY, STEAM BOOK AND JOB PRINT,

CAPITOL STREET.

1882.

The Great Speech,

REV. DR. J. L. TUCKER,

OF MISSISSIPPI,

On the "Relations of the Church to the Colored Race," delivered
before the Church Congress, held in Richmond, Va., Oct. 1882,
is now ready for distribution.

PRICE, by mail, postage prepaid, 25 cents each.

by Express, $20 per 100 copies.

ADDRESS, CHARLES WINKLEY,

Jackson, Mississippi.

SPEECH OF THE REV. DR. TUCKER, OF JACKSON, MISSISSIPPI,

BEFORE THE CHURCH CONGRESS, HELD IN

RICHMOND, VA., OCT. 24–27, 1882.

——o——

The selection of this as a topic for discussion is an indication
of a growing feeling that the relations of the Church to the colored race are, or ought to be, somewhat different from the relations of the Church to the white race. This is true, and the
reason for it lies in the vast mental and moral differences between
the races.

The Church must know the facts before she can make wise or
successful plans; and I pray God to help me tell some of these
facts to-night, that those who do not know the race experiment-
ally may be able to perceive something of the difficulties which
lie in the way, and which have caused the apparent apathy of
Southern Christians concerning the moral and religious condition
of the negro race.

To speak as I propose to speak to-night has been in my mind
for at least ten years, but I have been restrained, as many others
have been, by three considerations: One, the fact that Northern
people, having a sentimental idea of the negro, probably would
not believe the facts; second, that the politicians of both races
who cater for the negro vote, would make any man who told the

75

substance: and further, that they have no comprehension of what that substance ought to be. There are exceptions, but not many. When we speak of them as a race, this statement is true.

I am well aware that there are many listening to me who do not know the colored people, and who will be unable to understand how this statement can be true; not being able to conceive how the substance of Christianity can be separated from its form. Let me therefore briefly glance at the past, and show how it came to be so. And those of us who know the faults of the negro race and who often lose both patience and charity because of them, will find it well to consider philosophically how the negroes came to have those faults, since we are not guiltless in the matter.

THE NEGROES IN AFRICA.

Doubtless most persons present have read books of African travel, but probably have read them without gaining any true comprehension of the social state of the African tribes. We are so accustomed to the family as the basis of all civilization, that when we read of an African household or family, or husband and wife, we attach our meanings to the words and not the African meanings. The travelers use these words because they have none other; they are obliged to use the terminology of civilization; but the resulting confusion of thought is as great as if a chemist were obliged to describe chemical action in the terms of botany, or a geologist to describe the formation of rocks in the phraseology of a prayer meeting. In actual truth the African at home has "wives" as he has sheep, oxen and other stock, buys and sells them freely, makes presents of them occasionally, pays tribute with them sometimes, and values them chiefly at so much per head. Human life has no sacredness, and men, women and children are slain as beasts are, and even more carelessly as less valuable. Human suffering excites no pity, and blood flows like water. Their wars are wars of extermination or slavery, and some of the tribes, as the Fan tribe, feast upon the slain. Among some of them also, the aged and the infirm are killed as the easiest way to dispose of them. Du Chaillu and other travelers could find no traces among the tribes of the West Coast, from whom the slavers procured their cargoes, of any belief in or idea of a future state; and describes their religion as a mixture of witchcraft, bloodshed, fiendish orgies and terror-driven superstition. All travelers agree that in the languages of most of the native tribes there are no words to express the ideas of gratitude, of generosity, of industry, of truthfulness, honesty, modesty, gentleness and virtue. Where there are no words there are no ideas. That is to say, narrowing it somewhat, that what we call morality, whether in the relations of the sexes, or in the sense of truthfulness, or in the sense of honesty, has no lodgment whatever in the native African breast. It is necessary to understand these facts and to understand them clearly, in order to properly estimate the progress the race has made in this country, and to understand the roots and causes out of which have grown their present ideas and practices as regards morality.

When I have stated these facts at other times, I have been accused of putting them forward as my "views." I desire it to be understood, therefore, that I did not create these facts, and that I am not responsible for them. I assert, however, that they are absolutely true. The concensus of all authorities establish them beyond the power of any man to overthrow them. We of the South should remember these facts, for the recollection of the state out of which the negroes came, only a few generations ago, would often modify our harsh judgment of the colored people and dispose us towards patience and charity.

THE TRAINING OF SLAVERY.

When the negroes were brought over to this country their condition was what I have briefly described. They were absolute barbarians Slavery did something for them; they were under outward restraint. There were many masters who endeavored to teach them at least the elements of civilization, and on many plantations the points of marriage, truthfulness and honesty were enforced by precept and by punishment. It must also be said that on many plantations the house servants only were instructed, and the field hands had no preceptor but the driver's whip; and the field hands were the great majority in number. They

77

were not willing scholars. I know of no race who would be under such circumstances. They soon learned to feel the injustice of slavery, and it seemed to them that those who so wronged them in so great a matter could not be sincere guides in any minor matters. Their owners must want them to be virtuous, truthful and honest, not from any good motives, but simply to make them more valuable as property. Being punished for transgression in these things, they quickly learned to conceal the transgression. Being told that these things were right, they learned to protest that they believed in and practiced them. Being banded together in suffering, and having their own society among themselves, their own ideas, their own superstitions and beliefs, having the secret practice of their religious rites to hold them together, and the tradition of former lives in freedom as guides to them as to what was right for negroes to do and believe—they opposed a passive wall of resistance against the intrusion of new ideas. Yet there was the power of the lash behind the new ideas What could they do? They did what was natural under the circumstances, what any race would do—they accepted the outward form but refused the inward substance of the new ideas. They seemed to believe and obey, but really disbelieved and disobeyed. To please their masters they would proclaim the beauty of virtue and truthfulness and honesty, while not clearly understanding the meaning of the words. Thus they soon learned to use the phraseology of righteousness as a cover for wrong doing, and in time grew to think that the two belonged naturally together. I beg you to make note of the force of this point, as it explains much that would otherwise be inexplicable in their present condition.

I suppose that any race, unintelligent and slow to comprehend as the negroes then were, if suddenly confronted with new ideas in violent contrast with all hitherto cherished customs, and if driven by fear of punishment into an adoption of the new ideas, would learn the required phraseology while rebelling against the substance. It must be remembered too that the language was new and difficult, much more rich in words than the negroes were in ideas. It was not suited to their modes of thought. But if they could not comprehend meanings they could comprehend the lash; and when they learned the words and phrases which they could use as shields against punishment or as instruments wherewith to gain the good opinion of their masters, they adopted them as a cover under which they could live and act as they pleased The fear of punishment taught them what to say, their passions and traditions taught them what to do, and they were not able to perceive any incongruity between the two.

I desire to make this matter plain to you, for it is the key to much that puzzles one in the negroes to-day. There was in the native African no idea of a moral difference between truth and falsehood; when brought here he learned that certain acts were followed by punishment unless he could use words in such a way as to cover himself. Often he did not quite comprehend the meanings of the words, but as they served his purpose he learned to trust to them for safety without any sense of guilt. This is in truth hypocrisy, an hypocrisy most difficult to overcome because it is unconscious. The great mass of the negroes did not know that they were hypocrites, and do not yet know it.

My friends, reflect a moment. We are ourselves more or less drawn or driven into hypocrisy or something very like it, under stress of fear, and we often feign to be something better than we are, half unconsciously. Children do this continually, and the mass of the negroes are very like children in mental development. When we are conscious of this we have a sense of guilt, but I appeal to you if children do not have to be taught the sense of guilt? What wonder that the negroes, "untutored barbarians," suddenly confronted with an alien civilization which they could not understand, which was thrust upon them by force, learned lying, stealing, and adultery, not simply as they knew those things in Africa but with a bitterness of rebellion against coercion which made the practice of these things seem almost like patriotism; and the effort to deceive their masters, like loyalty to their race and native land!

Please do not think that I am speaking contemptuously or even unkindly. I am simply trying to give to those who do not know

79

the negro race a somewhat adequate idea of their present condition, with the philosophical reasons for that condition.

It is the history of slavery in all countries that it teaches hypocrisy, we may even say, compels hypocrisy; for this is the slave's only weapon, his only defense, his only protection against wrong.

To my mind it was not without reason that when the Ten Commandments were given to a half barbarous people, just escaping from slavery, the sole commandment about truthfulness was simply—not to bear false witness against a neighbor. Any higher or deeper idea of truth must have been beyond their power of conception.

SUCCEEDING GENERATIONS.

With each succeeding generation after the native Africans there came, of course, a modification and improvement; but race movements are always slow, doubly slow when education is interdicted. The slaves could not read, were not taught and had little beyond their own traditions to guide them. Vague items of information of other lands and better circumstances occasionally reached them; but these were not fully comprehended. To them the world consisted of toiling field hands, indulged house servants and pampered whites; with a hope of something better to come after death, and a vague idea that there was a better land somewhere towards the North. Their only enjoyment lay in meeting together for religious indulgence, and the only excitement and zest in life was in the pursuit of the pleasures which the white people said were wrong. In India, under English rule, the caste system still prevails largely, the native religions still hold sway over the people, and all progress is exceedingly slow, although education is not interdicted. Yet the various races of India were on a far higher level when the English conquered them than the Africans were when brought over here. The negroes have made very great progress in many things, and if their progress has been slow in morals, that is not to be wondered at; and we must remember that it is but sixty or seventy years since the importation of native Africans on a large scale ceased.

STEALING.

It never seemed wrong to the slave to steal from his own master He was but property himself, and it was "all in the family." Besides, he worked for nothing and it seemed to him but justice that he should enjoy some of his master's good things for which his labor paid. Something of this feeling the owners also had, so that petty pilfering was looked upon by both races as a matter of course, a thing to be winked at. See the result of such a feeling and such a training. That result was simply to destroy the sense of wrong in this matter almost wholly. If one desired now to train up a child to steal no better course could be pursued; for of course the negro parents taught their children how to pilfer so as not to be suspected, at least so as not to draw down too heavy a punishment, and the parents profited by the child's dexterity. This was always in all countries one of the natural results of slavery.

Nor did the slaves feel it to be anything but venial to steal from each other. The field hands would steal from the house servants arguing that they ought to have some chance to get partly even; the house servants could easily recoup themselves, and the final loss fell where it ought to fall, upon the master. They would rarely steal money, even when they had opportunity. This one fact throws a flood of light upon their estimation of the morality of stealing. The habit of pilfering would lead eventually to the taking of money, but they had the sense of guilt in this which they did not have in any other stealing. Stealing from neighboring plantations was also venial in their eyes. In Africa they had led a predatory life and the habit and instinct of it continued. When in danger of detection and punishment the slave had no sense of sin in lying. To protect himself by lies seemed to him natural and just. It was his only defence against what he believed to be an unjust punishment. Of course the lying about one thing led to lying about another. I have heard them argue with each other as to the permissable extent to which lying might go, asserting that it was simply impossible for colored folks to get along with white people without lying to them at least "sometimes."

MARRIAGE.

The slaves could not understand why a man should have but one wife. The white people taught them that as a matter of religion; but instinct, natural desire, and the customs of their race taught them the very contrary. It was a part of the religion of their oppressors, and as such was *prima facie* oppressive in itself. Loyalty to their race, as well as custom and desire, moved them to reject this item.

That the white people were at heart no better than themselves, they were positive. Had they not proof? Whence came so many mulattoes? The intrigues which the white men supposed to be secret were well known in all their most minute details to the negroes, even to the young ones. They were boasted about, carried from plantation to plantation, gloated over as additional evidences that their own customs were more natural, more honest, more true. Furthermore, the negroes concerned in these intrigues at once took higher rank among the women, obtained privileges, better dress, less labor, and some influence to help the others in their hard lives. What wonder that such a thing became a coveted honor among them, coveted by their relatives, even by their parents as well as by themselves, to the utter destruction of the very sense of virtue!

Again: They had but little security for permanence when they did marry. It is a necessary concomitant of slavery that families should be separated, husbands and wives and children sold apart from each other. The gigantic wrong includes all lesser wrongs. I cannot speak at length upon this point, for it involves facts which will not bear publicity. To my mind their present moral condition in this matter of the relation of the sexes is but the natural outgrowth of the training of slavery upon the habits of the native Africans. We should not too severely blame them, but we should bestir ourselves to teach them better. Were the full facts known I believe that there would run a thrill of horror, yes, and of sympathy, through the whole North, resulting in a great movement to raise them up to a higher plane of life.

RELIGION.

There was one part of the religion of the whites which they accepted with avidity; namely, the person and errand of Jesus Christ. Something in the story of the Cross appealed to them with a force unknown to those who live easy and comfortable and self-indulgent lives. They believed in it with all their hearts and souls, for in it was a divine pity, a divine promise of succor. But this belief made no difference in their daily lives. They could grasp the vague ideas of pity and of hope, but could not grasp the sense of duty. Duty always came to them under the sternness of oppression, and they could not connect the idea of love with that of duty.

I beg you to note this point also. To them it was slavery that brought duties. They had never known of any constraint upon desire except the constraint of slavery. However kind and pleasant an owner might be, yet the lash lay behind disobedience. Feeling the monstrous wrong of slavery it seemed to them that all duties of all kinds, religious, moral, or physical, all labor, all constraints upon desire, were parts of the wrong thing slavery. When white teachers taught them that they should govern their desires, they thought the white man was but trying to enslave their souls as well as their bodies. When taught that certain acts would displease the Lord Jesus, they thought that the white people were trying to make them believe that the Lord Jesus was a slave driver too. They could not understand how any obligation to do or not to do, could be separated from a state of slavery. To their perception the white people, who were free, did just what they pleased in all things, whether in abstaining from labor or in gratifying desire—of the latter they had proof—. It seemed to them that whoever loved them would set them free, and freedom meant absence of all constraint, positive or negative. Satan can always vary his temptations to suit the circumstances of those whom he would destroy. And so the religion which they did accept from the white people grew to be a matter of emotion only, having no constraining force upon their conduct. Religion meant love, and love meant freedom, and freedom meant absence of duty, moral or physical. They were taught that they had to "get religion" by some process of conviction and conversion. He who "got religion" therefore, got a sense of God's love for him, and thenceforward was free so far as any moral law or moral guilt was concerned. Man's law might constrain his actions, but man's law was slavery; God's law was freedom. Faith was the one thing needful, and would cover a multitude of sins. He who became a Christian had no further fear of God's law, and felt an intensified antagonism against man's law. The only interpreter of man's law was the slave driver. He was to them the law-maker, book of statutes, prosecutor, judge, jury and executioner, all in one. When freedom brought them relief from the overseer, they thought there would be no more law of any kind to trouble them.

Furthermore, the removal of the constraint of slavery brought a relapse into many practices of African barbarism. Witchcraft had never lost its hold upon them, and with freedom, increased its power. The weaving of spells upon enemies, the carrying of charms and the trust in various incantations, were mingled in a most inextricable way with love for God and trust in Christ. I could give many instances of this, occurring from time to time within my knowldedge down to this present year. The town negroes were comparatively free from these superstitions, but their freedom must be spoken of as comparative only; on the other hand in the country districts often a whole neighborhood of negroes would be terrified at the advent of some "witch," would endeavor to move away, and where that was impossible, to propitiate such a person in trembling fear. It is my judgment, formed upon close observation and enforced by personal inconvenience and losses, that these superstitions, which are really remnants of African devil worship, have had since the war and up to within a few years, a stronger influence upon the race than any other force whatever, moral or physical. There was the worship of God by the lips, in prayers and hymns, but the practical worship in fear of consequences and acts of propitiation was of the devil.

To engraft the old customs upon the new religion was easier than to discard them, and accordingly this was done. We know

that something similar was done in ancient Rome, and even the
Bishop of Rome became "Pontifex Maximus" by direct inheritance from the high priest of Roman paganism. What wonder
that the ignorant negroes, unable to read the Bible for themselves
did this more completely?

Of late years the town negroes have emancipated themselves
more than ever before from these parts of the old race traditions;
but this cannot be said of the country negroes.

All these things of which I have spoken and of which I have yet
to speak, have combined to produce a strange obliquity of moral
vision, a strange perversion of judgment, a curiously conglomer-
ated religion—which it is exceedingly difficult for any white people to understand, and utterly impossible for those to understand
who have had no practical experience with the race.

My friends: What I have here briefly described is their religion to-day. It is an outward form of Christianity with an inner
substance of full license given to all desires and passions. There
are many exceptions, thank God for them. Every Southern man
knows exceptions; and to many of their preachers the moral condition of the race is a matter of great humiliation and concern.
But in spite of all exceptions, what I have said is true of the
great mass of them.

Again, I beg you to believe me when I say that I am not speaking in contempt or in anger or any such feeling. My heart goes
out to the colored people with a great and longing desire to do
them good. My ordination vow constrains me and the love of
Christ constrains me to labor for them; I would fain see the
church, yea and all christian people, awake to the great duty of
caring for their perishing souls. But every thinking man knows
that any effort towards any end must conform itself to the circumstances surrounding it. The effort will fail if aimed to overcome
obstacles that do not exist, while ignoring obstacles that do exist. I have heard of a recent gift of a million dollars for the
benefit of the negro; yet if my understanding of the disposition
of that gift be correct, it might almost as well have been thrown
into the sea. A hundred thousand, rightly invested, would do
far more good. And so I speak as I do to-night, praying God to

give force to my words, that those who desire to help the colored people may have some conception of the things wherein they need help.

THE INSTINCT OF CONCEALMENT.

One thing they learned in slavery which they had not known before, and that was to act together. They were drawn together by the sense of mutual suffering, a common fate, a common oppression. They were in feeling banded together against the white race, and it became a point of honor with them to stand by each other. Often they would suffer to extremity before they would betray each other, even in acts of sin. Parents taught their children that the one thing utterly despicable and vile and unforgivable was such a betrayal to the white people; and their punishment for this act, even when it was unpremeditated or unconscious on the part of the child, was terribly severe. This mutual defence of each other was their only safety. They felt that at any time their very lives might depend upon their fidelity to each other. You must understand that this fidelity could only consist in lying for each other, and supporting each other in denials and protestations. My friends, I do not blame them for this. It came not from bad hearts, but from the circumstances of slavery superimposed upon the circumstances of barbarism.

Under such training, it was from the first an instinct with them and quickly became second nature, to conceal all that concerned them from the whites. Instinct and second nature it is yet. They will make excuse for each other, deny for each other, steal for each other, lie for each other, not only in great matters, but in all manner of small matters. Lie gratuitously and uselessly from the first mere instinct of answer to a question. And mingled with the lying and stealing will be all manner of pious protestations and edifying talk, and calls upon God to witness—which will also be sincere. This is the amazing thing in it! It is this strange sincerity in hypocrisy which often angers those who know the race to the loss of all patience with them or belief in them. And it is this unconsciousness and sincerity in hypocrisy which often misleads those who do not know them into supposing them to

86

be—poor and ignorant, indeed—but honest-hearted, humble-minded, consistent Christian people, who are, from some unaccountable prejudice, greatly maligned and abused by Southern whites.

A few years after the war a party of gentlemen, mostly Clergymen, representing a great Northern church, came into Mississippi to visit and inspect the colored churches of their denomination and to devise methods of aiding them. The negroes gathered to welcome them and there were a series of great meetings. The Northern visitors preached and heard certain negroes preach, looked on at the eagerness and earnestness of the colored congregations, listened to the fervent prayers from both men and women, heard the pious talk, the ejaculations of thanksgiving, all the verbal evidences of true religion, and went home saying, "what earnest, what humble minded, what grand Christians these poor negroes are!" Had they sought information from their white brethren of the same church, South, they would have been told that while the earnestness and fervor were there and were correct enough, yet there was no real substance of religion beneath it; that the very opposite of Christian lives were led by almost every one who listened to them or to whom they listened. But their hearts were full of anger against the South then, they refused to listen to the Southern people who asked permission to speak to them, rejected evidence, and departed shaking the dust off their feet, thinking that no Southern man could be just to the negro. Yet the negro preacher in whose church they held their largest meetings, at that very time was living in open and undisguised adultery. This sufficiently illustrates his idea of morality and the duty of a Christian; his idea of theology was shown by another act. Shortly after the visitors left, this negro preacher offered a so-called "Paschal Lamb" in "sacrifice," in a way which violated every sacrificial idea, and was a mingling of African rites and Mosaic names. The lamb was selected, slain and roasted, and placed upon a table in front of the "altar." There was a great meeting, loud and continued praying and singing, which lasted all night long, during which there were many trances and convulsions. The lamb was cut into little pieces in church during the night, and the pieces were eagerly bought by the congregation; some of them were eaten on the spot, and some tied up in little bags to be worn around the neck as charms. There was a considerable pecuniary profit, though I do not think the preacher had the profit for his main object.

The Northern visitors knew nothing of this, but went away with the firm conviction that the negroes were the same sort of Christians that they were themselves. The result of their visit was that considerable sums of money were sent down to the colored people to encourage this sort of religion; and then, as it seemed to the visitors that the colored people were doing very well, all help ceased.

It was the instinct of concealment in the negroes which so covered over the facts of the case from the visitors that they never even suspected the truth. This instinct of concealment is powerful yet in the race, and most powerful where there is the least intelligence. When questioned they will answer or deny as they think will please you and make them stand well in your eyes. They are very shrewd. They will give you the information you want, provided it be not true. If true, and if it be such as would excite your disapprobation, you cannot get it. They are suspicious of all inquiries. It seems to them that your only object in desiring to know anything about them is in some way to do them harm. An ordinary negro simply will not tell you the true facts about his life, or the lives of his friends, or the habits of his race. An educated negro may answer truly, after a struggle with himself; but then he will tell you no more than he perceives you know already. The instinct of his race is strong in him, and will be strong in his children, probably for generations. There are a very few highly educated ones who will do more; but their own race call them "white folks' niggers," look upon them with suspicion, and conceal from them as carefully as from the whites. There are exceptions to this, too, for I know myself a few educated colored men who are not afraid to tell the truth about their race, and who yet possess the confidence of their people; but I am giving facts that are generally true.

THE EFFECT OF FREEDOM.

With freedom came a great subsidence into evil. The outward restraint was gone and they rejoiced and revelled in following out the bent of their passions. Hundreds and thousands of marriages were at once dissolved without formality, and new ones formed also without formality. For several years immediately succeeding the war, the great mass of the negroes were continually migrating from one district to another, with the intent that if slavery were restored no owner should be able to find his own slaves again. Many families moved together in this migration, but very many more broke up and separated into their component parts. Liberty meant license to most of them. Slavery had forced them to work, freedom should give them rest. What we call laziness and vagaboudage, they called freedom. Agriculture was carried on during those years under very great difficulties, and with each season there was a great change of laborers. Live stock disappeared through the whole South like magic—killed by the negroes for subsistence. A single year of freedom caused as much as or more loss to the South in this item, than all the gigantic loss and destruction of the four years of war. Amongst the white people there were terrors and alarms everywhere; there was a state of apprehension, of excitement, of fear, and of anger, that was but little short of anarchy. While amongst the negroes, amid all their joy and exultation there was, underneath the surface, a seething mass of new sins of a character indescribable—unnamable.

Simultaneously with this great outburst of evil negro churches sprang up everywhere, built largely by Northern money, in which there were shouting, praying, singing, all manner of excitement, hysterics, trances, loud calls upon God; but in which there was no religion, at least none of that kind which has its issue in an holy, humble and obedient walking before God.

The colored people did not believe that religion had anything to do with conduct and resented any attempt to convince them of it. The first effort I made among them was to open a night school on a plantation on which I was working some fifty hands just after the war, in 1866, before I became a Clergyman. To this school all the colored people on the place came and some from neighboring plantations, three times a week and on Sunday afternoons, to learn to read, and to hear the Bible read and explained. For a month or two all went well, until one Sunday afternoon, when I read and explained somewhat carefully the Ten Commandments. This broke up the school. The men were sullen and would not talk, but the women were outspoken and indignant: "Fo' de Lawd, dat air wor an impersition. Dat mought be white folks' Bible, but 't worn't no hones' Bible. Moses never spoke no sich trash. 'T worn't no sort a 'ligion fur black folks." For months afterwards through all that neighborhood, those ten commandments were used as awful warnings to the colored people to keep to their own teachers and their own religion and let the white folks alone.

PROGRESS SINCE THE WAR.

The seventeen years since the war have brought great changes to the colored race, great improvements in many things to some of them, but no change in morals. The decadence into evil of which I have just spoken, has not been followed by any upward growth in morals. Sins are more persistent than virtues. Their pecuniary condition is greatly improved, especially in the cities and towns. Those of them who are willing to work are in no danger of suffering, except in cases where an utter want of thrift, and utter folly in spending money, overbalances the earning power. They are slowly acquiring property, slowly learning how to take care of what they have. There is certainly in progress a modification in their ideas as to the meaning of freedom, and as to the necessity of labor; and there is a slowly growing feeling that their lack of greater material progress has its causes in themselves, out of which the white people can help them if they only will. But this improvement in condition is not shared by the plantation negroes. I have read accounts of improvement in the country districts in some parts of the South where the white people are largely in the majority; but such cases are but side eddies on the borders of a great stream. The vast majority of the race live away from towns and cities. We have counties in Mississippi where the black population is twenty or thirty thousand, and the white population only some few hundreds. There we have Africa over again, only partially restrained. In such districts there is almost no improvement in physical condition or in willingness to labor. But what more especially concerns the Church is their religious and moral condition, and in these there has been no perceptible improvement since the great descent into evil after the abolition of slavery. In the midst of a prayer I have known them to steal from each other, and on the way home from a prayer meeting they will rob any hen-roost that lies conveniently at hand; and this without any thought of sin against God, and even without any perception of an incongruity. The most pious negro I know is one confined in a penitentiary for an atrocious murder, who can see no especial sin against God in his crime, though he acknowledges an offense against man. He cannot be made to see that God must be angry with him, and thinks all intimations to that effect in prayer or exhortation, founded in personal dislike or prejudice, or because he is not well dressed and has a sore on his leg. Absolutely he cannot conceive of any other reason or motive for "taking part against him" and imputing sin against God to his crime.

I have known a negro preacher guilty of incest, another of habitual theft, a third with two wives being married to neither, a fourth who was a constant and most audacious liar—yet who were earnest and successful preachers. I could give names, dates and witnesses for these and twenty other similar cases, and it would be easy to find any required number more. Yet the four men of whom I speak were not conscious of hypocrisy, and their known sins did not diminish their influence with their race. It was impossible to hear them preach or pray and doubt their absolute sincerity.

I do not mean to say that all negro preachers are such men, for I personally know those who are not, some of whom I am glad to call my friends; but I desire you to notice the great force and significance of the fact that these sins do not degrade their ministers, nor materially lower their standing in the colored churches.

All over the South they are now living openly in these sins, and especially one of these sins; and neither preachers nor people regard them as sinful or as militating against ministerial duty or acceptance with God. In very many cases the lay leaders in their congregations are men and women of known and open bad character.

There are in all the cities and larger towns, numbers of families who are thoroughly respectable in every way, a credit to their race or to any race, to whom these things are painful and humiliating; but such exceptional instances there always were. Perhaps there are a greater number of such families now than there were twenty years ago. .I would not speak positively, but I doubt it. On the other hand, in all the country districts the removal of the restraints of slavery, such as they were, has resulted in an open abandonment of even the semblance of morality, and the loss of almost the idea of marriage. Why, in one county in Mississippi there were, during twelve months three hundred marriage licenses taken out in the county Clerk's office, for white people. According to the proportion of population, there should have been in the same time twelve hundred or more for negroes. There can be no legal marriage of any sort in Mississippi without a license. There were actually taken out by colored people just three! I ask you to ponder the significance of this fact. Soon after the war the legislature passed an act legalizing the union of all who were then living together, marrying them whether they wished or not; and for years afterwards the courts were crowded with applications for divorce from colored people which had to be granted mostly, since there was ample cause for divorce under either the divine or the statute law. I know of whole neighborhoods including hundreds of negro families, where there is not one single legally married couple, or couple not married who stay faithful to each other beyond a few months or a few years at most, often but a few weeks. And if out of every five hundred negro families one excepts a few dozen who are legally married, this statement will hold true for millions of the colored people; and these things that I tell you to-night are but hints. I dare not, I cannot tell the full truth before a mixed audience.

It is utterly useless to deny these facts, for they can be substantiated by overwhelming testimony from both white people and the better class of colored people, and especially by personal inspection if any one doubts testimony; and it is worse than useless to shut our eyes to the facts. The colored people are among us for all time. They touch us at all points. They affect our political life, our business life, our social life, our religious life; our very civilization in the years to come will be, must be, largely influenced by them. If they were decreasing in number, or improving in morality we might rest in quiet, and let time solve the question. But the weighty fact is that they are increasing in number, increasing much more rapidly than the white people, and are *not* improving in morality—the statistics of marriage licenses show this—and the heaviest per centage of increase is among the most ignorant class of them, those who live on plantations. We can not afford to leave them in their present condition; were there no other motive self-preservation alone would demand of us that we make a great effort towards bettering it. The public school system is inadequate. The people are widely scattered and only half of the population pay taxes, for the great mass of the negroes have no property to tax. To pay for schools for themselves and the colored people too, is a burden beyond the ability of the white race. It is a heartless thing to blame the Southern whites for not doing that which had they been twice as numerous and twice as rich, would still have been far beyond their means.

The great facts stare us in the face—that the race is increasing largely in numbers; that since the war but few of them have come up above the moral level of the race; that the average level in material prosperity is but little higher than it was before the war; that in morality there has been a great deterioration since the removal of the restraints of slavery; that there is now no upward movement whatever in morals, and if there is any change it is downward.

Brethren, consider these facts! See the awful meaning of them! We see almost a whole race going down into perdition before our eyes; for the Scripture saith that because of these things cometh the wrath of God upon the children of disobedience. Look back upon the history of twenty years, marked with war and pestilence, and tell me if there has not been a curse upon the South! There is a pressure from God upon us to carry a pure Gospel and a true religion to this people, and woe to us if we refuse.

PLAN OF WORK.

But when we essay to do this duty there are three great obstacles which meet us at once, viz: The reluctance of the white people to work among the negroes; their own profound distrust of white teachers and white teaching; and the fact that they already have a religion which suits them better.

These obstacles can be met and overcome in this way. First find a white parish that is already working among the colored people; not individuals simply, but a parish I can tell you of several such. Begin there, for there you have two of the three obstacles already overcome, and the third one at least partially overcome ; for the white people are already working among the negroes and the negroes are already receiving aid and instruction. It will take years to overcome the race prejudice so far as this in any fresh place. The negroes' preference for their own idea of religion must be overcome by carrying to them overbalancing benefits, and by patiently and perseveringly and lovingly trying to teach them better things. But cheap plans will do no good whatever ; neither will gifts of money like some recent ones, diffused everywhere. Concentrate your work and make strong centers from which good influences may radiate.

If you build a cheap Chapel for the white race, West or South, they will take it, use it and thank God for it. But the negroes already have cheap Chapels of their own, and do not want yours unless they can practice their own religion and morality in it independent of your control. Suppose you build a cheap Chapel and in it preach to them of Christ—you will quickly find that they know more about Him, or think they do, than you do, and will out-talk you with a fervor and unctiousness that will put you to shame. Tell them the story of the Cross—there is no white congregation that will be half so responsive. The air will be full of thanksgivings and exclamations of worship ; but they will not therefore forsake one sin or practice one virtue If you be very young and innocent, or if you be a stranger from the North, you will come to the conclusion that these people have been greatly maligned and abused, and that they are more devout and more religious than the whites. While in this frame of mind you will simply be an instrument of the devil to keep the negroes down; since ignorant work based upon false conclusions, is at least as bad as none at all. For heaven's sake let us have our eyes open and know what we are about in this matter. If in your cheap Chapel you strike at the root of the evil and insist that religion must govern the actions, if you insist upon virtuous, truthful and honest lives, and if you rebuke openly for sins in these matters; then the negroes will forsake your cheap Chapel, and go to their own cheap Chapels where they can be as fervid as they please and free from an inconvenient morality. No, cheap things are useless. Let me sketch out a plan.

Find a parish in some of the larger centers of population, where the native white people, who know all the conditions of the problem, are already at work among the negroes, and strengthen that parish for that work ; so will you encourage the white people where they greatly need encouragement, and will build up where it will do the most good, a feeling of protection and kindness towards the negroes. And so, also, will you obtain permanency for the work, for parishes do not die as individuals do. Give such a parish every facility for its own work as well as for this missionary work. Build a transept for the colored people if it be thought best for the two races to worship together, separate, yet upon one floor and under one roof and toward one Altar, as they are separate in race yet worship one God—which seems to me to be the true and catholic idea—or build a separate Church for the colored people, if that be thought best; only in this case have it close by, so that the white people can go there to hold classes and teach, and will be personally interested in keeping it morally clean and sweet.

To this end the white people must own the property, holding it as trustees. Make the Church attractive, warm in tint, decorated—so as to please the negroes' love of color and form. Give to it a good organ, not a melodeon, but a good church organ, and an organist who can teach the colored people to sing. Let the service be full and rich, with choral song and plenty of it. These things will be irresistibly attractive to them. Furthermore, give that Church a day school. Education and religion must go hand in hand if you would permanently elevate the negroes; while their facilities for obtaining education are so defective and their craving for it so great, that by this alone you would win their undying gratitude. But if you would chain the white people to the work and make them enthusiastic over it, you must give them such a school also; two schools, one for themselves as well as one for the negroes. They too need and crave education for their children, while all over the South the facilities for obtaining it are scanty and the cost is great. Surely you will not have less sympathy for the white people than the colored? Two schools will double the expense, but I tell you that this is the true way to succeed. You simply cannot evangelize the negroes on any large scale without the aid and sympathy of the Southern whites; and you will show but a cold Christianity if you are blind to the needs of your own brethren and alive only to those of the negroes. Give to your workers as well as to the work; so will you unite the two races by mutual benefits as they must be united to attain any permanent success. The white people will know that you help them because *they* help the negroes, and this will bring you love and gratitude and faithfulness from both races. I urge this point with great earnestness for it is my firm conviction that in it lies the key to success, certainly to any great success. Devise liberal things if you would have liberal returns.

Besides the schools, give to this parish an hospital. There can be one ward for poor white patients, but the hospital should be used mainly for the negroes, who need it most. Hundreds of them die for lack of medical attendance and medicine, and because of careless nursing and insufficient nourishment. Give also a building for an Orphanage. These, the schools, the hospital and the orphanage, would need endowment, for neither the negroes nor the white people could support them. It is enough to require of the white parish that it shall furnish the workers to give *life* to your gifts to the negroes.

Further, supply facilities for a labor intelligence office, for reading rooms, for a library, for a night school for the benefit of those who can not come in the day time, yet want to learn ; also for a sewing school to teach this most necessary part of a woman's work, and by and by to train seamstresses ; also for mothers' meetings. In almost every town of any size there are a number of ladies ready to band themselves together to work for the Lord Jesus in any way that the Church may point out to them as their duty. They only ask for food, clothing and a certainty of care in sickness and old age. I can find twenty such, ready for this or any other work, asking no wages, but only a home. Give to this parish, now, a Sisterhood Home. You may call them Deaconesses, Sisters, or what you will, only give them a house to live in and a modest income to live on, and they will do your work thoroughly and well with hearts and hands. Were they to work exclusively among the white people they could support themselves ; but *you* will want them to work among the negroes also, for you, to be your teachers and nurses, your agents for Christ's work ; and the negroes cannot pay even the little they would ask. Build them a home, therefore, close to the hospital and school and orphanage, and provide them with an income sufficient for their modest wants, and they will carry on these institutions for you. I have had recently applications from colored women of the better class, asking to be sent as servants to such a sisterhood. Some of them had heard of my desires for their race and seemed to think that the accomplishment was near at hand. They would gladly cook, wash, nurse the sick in the hospital or care for the children in the Orphanage under the direction of the white sisters, without wages, if they could only be sure of a home.

One thing more ; there ought to be industrial schools added to such an institution, that the colored youth might be taught trades. These are costly, but their value is simply beyond estimate. The Hampton Institute in Virginia is doing a noble work in this respect as in others. Would that we had a Hampton in Mississip-

4

pi. Had we such, it ought to be stronger, more positive, more radical in its teachings concerning religion. The mass of the negroes have a false religion. I emphasize this. It is a false religion ; and the right teaching should go down to the very roots of the matter.

When you have such a parish thus equipped, you will have the negroes looking on and saying: "Is that the white folks' religion? To educate our children, to nurse the sick, to care for our orphans, to help us get work? The Lord Jesus must be there : we will go and learn of him."

Do you see my points? First, that the negroes are not yet well enough educated, not yet on a high enough level to make good use of any help you may extend to them, if left to themselves. Second, that the Southern white people who know all about the race and how to deal with them, are the only ones who can work judiciously to lay sure foundations. Third, that you must engage the interest of the Southern whites by helping and strengthening them also; for by this means you will most surely stir them into action, both by awakening their consciences and by showing them a feasible plan of work.

APPEAL.

Brethren of the North, we do not need any man to tell us our duty. We know well enough what it is; but we are appalled at the gigantic difficulties in the way. We do not wholly agree as to methods of work, but that is because we see no way of doing anything without the expenditure of more money than could be raised in all the South. It seems a hopeless problem for this reason. One thing we are agreed in and that is that work should be concentrated. A little here and a little there are simply wastes of money and time. What we need is a plan beyond which we can see success, and money enough to support that plan. I tell you that the Southern people are heart-sick at seeing failures, until at last they have become contemptuous. Various Northern Missionary bodies have poured money into the South since the war, by the hundred thousand; and every dollar of it, so far as I know and believe, which was not given into white control, was wasted. The Methodists, for instance, would not consult or trust their own white brethren South, and are punished for it by having done harm with every dollar; building up strongholds, meant for God, but which the devil occupied in disguise, and taught the colored people to worship God with their lips but himself in their daily lives. And so when Northern Christians of any name propose to help the negroes, the Southern Christians draw back with a feeling of despair mingled with anger, that God's servants should in wilful ignorance build up the kingdom of evil. I tell you that in most of your efforts you have done harm, and Southern Christians of all churches know it; and hence you can not get their sympathy nor their countenance. Let not our Church repeat this folly. Send no Northern Missionaries down here who barely know a negro when they see him. Work through the Church South, and be not too close handed to do something for your workers also; and then you will enlist those who thoroughly know what they are about, know how to reach the colored people, who love them with the remembrances of childhood and youth and manhood as strangers never can learn or grow to care for them; and who know how to deal with their weaknesses and how to encourage their virtues.

Christianity is not dead in the South, nor the spirit of God Most Holy, nor love for the Saviour who died for all races and kindreds, nor sympathy and sorrow for human souls that are perishing. I tell you that many a Southern heart is aching to-day from a sense of duty undischarged. But we are not equal to the task alone. It is harder to build up a race than it is to destroy it. You freed the slaves and then left them on our hands, and it is too great a burden for us. Blood and trouble have come of it so far and for this you of the North are largely to blame. You must help us if anything is to be done ; and so we call upon you in God's great name, and for Christ's dear sake, to come now and come quickly with aid commensurate to the greatness of the task.

When you have built up one parish in the way I have suggested, take another. I can find you a succession of them. Ask of our Bishops, they know. By the time that you have finished with two or three, you will find fifty more awake to the fact that something can be done, and that a way has been found to do it.

But do not imagine that you are conferring a favor upon such a parish, for you will be in reality laying a heavy burden upon it, heavier than you know or can imagine. Do not think that such a parish ought to be grateful to you. If you give in such a spirit, keep your money; I know of no Southern parish that wants it. Grateful we ought to be in one sense, but not as for a bounty. If we are willing gratuitously to work for you among the negroes, for you as well as ourselves, at a cost to ourselves, of recoil overcome, of time given, of anxieties assumed, of weariness and doubt and discouragement and discomfort and suspicion of personal ends—in such case the gratitude should come from the other end of the line.

Trust us, brethren; have some sympathy for us in the very greatness of the task before us; trust us and you will meet with a response of thanksgiving and gratitude and love from both races that will astonish you.

And may the Almighty Father, Who bends in loving pity over all His children, to whom the negroes are lifting up ignorant hands beseeching Him to have mercy upon them, worshipping Him and desperately sinning against him in one breath—may He, Who is wise and gentle, loving and tender, teach us how to lead poor Africa to the Throne of God.

ENDORSEMENTS.

——o——

LETTER OF THE

REV. ISAAC McCOY WILLIAMS,

A COLORED CAMPBELLiTE MINISTER OF JACKSON, MISS.

——o——

"The Relations of the Church to the Colored Race," is the heading of a speech delivered by the Rev. Dr. Tucker, in the "Congress" of the Episcopal Church, held in Richmond, in October, 1882; a speech which has had its full share of criticism, for and against it, North, South, East and West. With many it seems impossible to be true; and to others that if true perhaps it would have been best not to have said it, at least not so strong. "May he not do more harm than good to himself as well as to the colored people?"

This very important question, the relations of the Church to the colored people, demands the serious and prayerful attention of Christians and citizens of the whole country; for it is a grave, deep and momentous point that the Nation's God lays a suffering Lazarus at the door of every white congregation in the land. I know that a very large portion of professed white Christians stultify and silence the labor of their own consciences, persuading themselves that "I have nothing to do with the colored race," and in vain try to drive the matter from them. But it still comes, and forms no small part of mind matter; and it is the will of God that it shall be so until the Church enables the colored race to care for themselves. And that cannot be until the negro is made capable of the trust, by an intelligent christian morality, growing out of just what has been said by Dr. Tucker, viz: Good and well managed free schools, that will be open to all, and an intelligent Christianity which alone can lead them to know their duty to God, to themselves, and their neighbors.

101

To properly understand this grave question it will be well to do as has been done by Dr. Tucker, in going to the root of the great evil to combat it. And no one or ones can act wisely in the premises, who stop short of that task and labor, of finding out what are the true needs of the race, to learn thereby what becomes the humane duty of the Church.

Now it is true that the speech uncovered and made bare to the eyes of that assembled body, startling facts, that no other man has had the Christian manhood to touch, no, not with his little finger. Yet it will take but little study to learn that it is true; shame as it is on American civilization and its religion that from five to six millions of citizens, so made by hasty legislation, to-day are in ignorance and are left in ignorance of their true manhood; and but few know how to handle that sacred, God-given right the ballot, with which they have been entrusted. When we were made citizens we should have been taught how to be good ones.

I need not say that slavery kept us in a semi-barbarous condition, for no one will deny that. The only thing slavery needed was a strong and able body. Knowledge was at war with slavery and laws were made against educating us, and at this time we have but few well educated men or women of the colored race.

It may be asked, is the country safe from misrule and bad government with such a state of things existing? It cannot be. The few men who have made themselves leaders are led themselves by the men known to be politicians, and all that politics wants is the vote, but cares nothing beyond that, or what becomes of the man who casts the vote. In this it is like slavery and has no use for knowledge or true manhood. It seems to me that the colored people are in a hard case. Slavery used their bodies and politics uses their votes; and the one cares as little as the other that they are full of wounds and bruises and putrefying sores. So first the South and now the North roll them into the ditch, and pass by on the other side.

The Church can see the condition of the heathen when they live abroad, and hundreds of thousands of dollars are annually sent away to convert them. To this no one should object. But should not more be done for *us* to make this in fact a Christian country, by following what has been said by that true friend of the colored people? We need schools and true churches and a pure religion, and young men at study to by and by fill our pulpits. Schools to teach trades also, and educated men to help us up to a true and dignified manhood.

I thank God that the attention of the Church has been called to this matter, and firmly believe that God has put it into the heart of His servant to speak the truth, and stand what may come. Some colored men are offended at his utterances, and some white men, who must either be blind or have some object, deny the truth. But it will in time be seen that he not only spoke truthfully, but has made a base of action which no one has done before, for those who only wanted to know how to do. Let the Church awake to its responsibility, and stand ready to receive and use what the people will give to build up the machinery for the elevation of the colored race; and it will be seen in our country in good fruits, in peace and prosperity and the blessing of God; in the negroes out of politics and into good citizenship, based upon sound principles of integrity and morality.

This speech reveals humiliating facts, so truthful, yet hard to acknowledge. Not one of our social circles, if we can be said to have any, are clean morally. They are full of base, downright hypocrisy and falsehood, and full two-thirds of the whole are members of the Churches. Moral character is not the standard. Crimes that should cause a blush on fair cheeks assume a front of brass, and defy you to speak of or talk about them. Some of them are school teachers. Public opinion among the colored people is not up to the task of duty they owe themselves and their children. Many of our people will not join any of the colored churches on the sole account of the bad lives of the members; and the ministers cannot make them any better. A colored man only a few days ago, contended with me that the negroes were right in certain of their practices, because the Lord Jesus Himself said that seven women should lay hold of one man. We have no Church that cares for its sick, old and poor. Many such are now on the streets begging bread and suffering with cold; and not unfrequently fill a pauper's grave.

I close this for the present by saying that *the half* has not been told. Our youth have no restraint upon the *worst* of passions, and are strangers to good manners. Our boys and girls curse. Boys go to Sunday Schools with weapons on them, and draw on each other as soon as out on the streets.

The remedy can only come through the Church of Christ. Oh send over and help us! The colored people are very tired of the past. The Bibles, Prayer Books and Catechisms are doing a good work, but so much more might be done with more to do with.

ISAAC M'COY WILLIAMS.

——o——

We fully concur in the foregoing letter of Bro. Isaac Williams, having personal knowledge of the facts. We were slaves ourselves, and are now Ministers of the Gospel in Mississippi and Louisiana. Our acquaintance extends over from seven to ten thousand colored people, concerning whose lives we know the truth; and that truth is set forth, without exaggeration, in Dr. Tucker's speech. There are exceptions, but the general truth is stated exactly as it is. We agree also, that he has only given hints as regards many things of such a nature that only hints were possible. We are trying to teach our people better, but we are poor and don't know so much as we wish we did. We agree further that we don't know why anybody should deny these facts, since everybody who lives South knows them to be true—except the politicians who may want to flatter the negroes for their votes. We have met several colored preachers who told us that the speech was all true, but they were afraid to say so, because the politicians would make it hot for them. After talking it over we have determined, for our parts, to acknowledge the truth and take the consequences. The Lord, we hope will take care of us, if our own race do turn against us. The facts stated are true. The colored people mostly have a system of religion that does not influence their practical lives. Reader, will you pray for us that our faith fail not. Now, O Lord, help us, when our own race say that by writing this we have joined the whites against them. Give us intelligent Christian leaders who will fear Thee more than men; that guided by thy word we may grow up to the full measure of men; through Jesus Christ, our Lord, Amen.

REV. W. R. PARKER,
Point Pleasant, Tensas Parish, La.
REV. DANIEL JACKSON,
Redick Station, Jefferson Co., Miss.
REV. R. J. WERMINGTON,
Port Gibson, Miss.
REV. J. N. HOWARD,
Point Pleasant, Tensas Parish, La.

I believe the statements of the Rev. Dr. Tucker, with regard to the native character and disposition and present condition of the negro, to be true; while yet I would not impute the same to many of that race, now amongst us, who have so largely been benefitted by their association with the whites. Of these exceptions, however he has sufficiently spoken.

Dr. Tucker's arduous labors and untiring zeal in behalf of that race and his large experience with them, entitle his statements to the full belief, and his efforts to the charitable aid, of all who feel for their spiritual need.

W. M. GREEN,
Bishop of Mississippi.

———o———

Dr. Tucker has read to me the foregoing address, an expansion of some remarks made by him before the Church Congress held in Richmond, in October last. It will strike many who read this address that he has given a very sad and gloomy picture of the moral condition of the negroes of the South, and it may be inferred that it is almost a hopeless task to undertake to improve that condition. But sad and gloomy as it is, it is not overdrawn. He speaks the truth plainly and emphatically; and I, who have lived among the negroes of the South all my life, and have given much time and labor to their instruction, both as slaves and as freedmen, know whereof he speaks, and am forced sadly to concur in all that he has said.

J. T. PICKETT,
Priest of the Diocese of Mississippi.

———o———

Responding to your request for my opinion of the justness of the views of your late speech in Richmond, of the aspect of the negro race in the Southern States, I now express my concurrence, both as to the actual general facts of their condition, and, in the sympathy and concern for them manifested in that speech, as well as in your daily life.

5

These docile people present all the characteristics which a closet philosopher would predict from thousands of years of barbarism, succeeded by a long period of slavery—inherited instincts not to be spoken away by man, nor expunged by proclamations.

Superstition, modified by mere animal religion, jealousy of former owners born of fear, strangely mixed with a filial confidence in them born of habit, a generous kindness of heart dominating even morals, dishonesty, hypocrisy, present indulgence without providence, no economy, no acquisitiveness, indifference of marriage obligations, obliviousness of moral accountability, a ready imitation of the exteriors of virtue with no conception of its springs, quickness to receive the superficials of education without comprehending reasons, facility in acquiring the vices of their superiors while understanding only the forms of their virtues, concealment, hypocrisy—all these are the natural results of long ages of savageism combined with bondage.

Such features are quite common in the white race which has always been free. It is not surprising the negroes should exhibit them as ordinary traits, and in much greater degree. It is surprising that he is not worse than he really is. Like causes would produce like effects in our own race with yet another, worse than all—ferocity.

My observation is that perjury is the most common of all crimes with both races; but while, with the whites, self-interest induces the false oath, with the blacks kind feeling is enough.

Good nature, kindness of heart and a careless generosity; quick and strong, though momentary, sympathy; powerful though rapidly subsiding, enthusiasm; these are the leading good qualities of the Southern negro; and his future is entrusted to the intelligent philanthropy of our whole people.

His re-generation is not to be expedited except by combining the efforts of the intelligent thinkers of his own race, with the capital, and well pre-considered philanthropy, of ours. By himself he will hardly maintain his present plane and will never achieve a higher position.

He stands to-day in equal danger from the flattery of *bad* men, who would use him, and from the prejudices of *narrow* men, who would ignore him. His real dependence is on the active sympathy of honest men who know what he *is*, and what he *needs* and who speak to him *truth*.

S. S. CALHOON,

[Ex-Circuit Judge.]   Jackson, Miss.

Of all things heretofore written or said on the "negro question," the views presented in your pamphlet are the most satisfactory, because you have struck at the root of the matter. I wish you could have been heard through at the Congress, and yet it may be that your views will be the more speedily spread amongst the much larger constituency—the whole Church. God grant it. I was a Union man through the war, but I was born and lived in the South to manhood, and am perfectly qualified to endorse your pamphlet as being the truth, the whole truth, and nothing but the truth, so far as it is safe to give it utterance.

LOUIS P. TSCHIFFELY,

Rector of Grace Church, Louisville, Ky.

Yours of the 25th inst., is before me together with a copy of your speech in Richmond upon the relation of the Church to the colored race. At your request I write a "short letter" before leaving home.

I regretted that you did not have time to give your speech in full, but I suppose under the rules of the Congress this was unavoidable. You made a good *diagnosis* but had no time to give us your prescription and this left you open for the time being to misconception. I will confine myself as you wish me to do, to your *diagnosis*. I agree with you that the case is very, *very* grave; so grave as to elicit the sympathy and the exertions of all who wish well to the country and the souls of men. I do not think however the case of the negro to be quite as desperate as you do, at least here in South Carolina. Perhaps slavery was more patriarchal with us than in the South-western States which drained us of the sea-board. Moreover, in South Carolina before the war Christians of all denominations devoted a great deal of time, attention and money to the religious instruction of slaves, which bore fruit in genuine Christian character; and in some places in this State, at the close of the war probably saved th. whites from massacre. Slavery was a schoolmaster to the black man, but when the school master was turned out of doors and there was no longer any fear of his rod, there very naturally came along with the first years of emancipation a return to many of the vices which belonged to a recent barbarism. I think we had to look for this. But there is a factor at work for the improvement of the negro which must not be over-looked though it is not often considered. I refer to the laws of the States and their proper administration. These now stand to some extent where formerly the master did. The negro is beginning to learn that citizenship has duties as well as rights. Though he will not pay respect to Moses yet he will to the law which says, that a man who is guilty of stealing his neighbors' cattle shall not have a vote. There is more force in such a law than in sermons. Schools must do their part, the Church must do its part, but there will be great moral power in the State holding the negro to the responsibilities of citizenship. Now then as to some of the points brought forward in your address in regard to character. Of course we both speak of the negroes in mass and especially where intercourse with the whites is very infrequent.

Stealing.—As I go over the State I hear of definite improvement in this regard, on the part of the colored people. Stealing is nothing like as common as immediately after the war. Then stock was not safe hardly beyond the owner's call. Not unfrequently men watched their crops by night to prevent cotton and corn stealing. This has in great measure ceased, I think, owing as I just suggested to the administration of law. The negroes respect the white man's crop, and each other's crop.

Suppression of the truth.—Probably color with the ordinary negro is stronger than truth. The Judges of our Circuit Courts could give information here. My own impression is that much the larger part of the testimony borne in court by negro men and women does not count for much.

One point more only, or I shall make my letter too long. I make all due allowance for the many colored preachers and leaders, and other church officers, who to the best of their abilities, are humbly doing their work for Christ's sake, but I am under the impression that in many colored congregations remote from towns, and having little or no intercourse with whites, a preacher would sooner lose his influence by being a democrat than an adulterer.

In conclusion, I quite agree with you that the co-operation of the Southern whites should be enlisted in all church-work among the colored people; and to bring this about, so that the one shall give and the other receive instruction, having due regard each for the other as servants in the same vineyard, *hic labor, hoc opus est.* But all things are possible to them that believe, and the love of God can bridge the chasm between them. The deeper the moral degradation of the mass of the blacks at the South the louder the call upon the whites both North and South to come to their aid.

W. B. W. Howe,
Bishop of the Diocese of South Carolina.

I have read with great interest your very able speech delivered before the Church Congress in Richmond, Va., last October. I thank you for your kindness in sending it, and fully concur in your belief in regard to the status of the negro, both as to morals and religion. I write this (as you spoke that) in all kindness to the colored race. I have been much interested in the negro population since the war, both as to their prosperity and intellectual acquirements. I offered, soon after the war, to teach a number of them gratuitously, but not one came to be taught. I do not believe for a generation or so there will be much improvement in the race. The old must die before the young will improve intellectually or morally. I believe the best plan would be to establish Normal Schools for them, (such as we have at Hampton, Va.,) where the young can be educated to teach others. Had we many such schools, there would no doubt be much improvement, even in this generation. I am glad to see one man bold enough to speak the truth in regard to the negro. I am sure you have the good of the race at heart, and I know I have.

Isaac White, M. D.

Shawsville, Montgomery Co., Va.

I have read your discourse on the "Relations of the Church to the Colored Race" before the Church Congress at Richmond, Va. The picture which it presents of the moral condition of the negro race, deplorable as it appears, is not overwrought. That the discourse has provoked resentful criticism in the North is not surprising. The illusions which most completely blind the judgment and which are the most difficult to dispel, are those which minister to our vanity and pride. The Northern people are proud of emancipation; the world applauds the achievement. Not content with a just and rational appreciation of it, the Northern people have sought to magnify it by investing the negro with virtues and capacities which he does not possess; and the white master with odious and repulsive vices, from which, in a great measure and in a great majority of cases, he was free. It may be that what are illusions now were not illusions at the begiqning. There was a time when it was deemed politic to deprive the Southern people of all sympathy abroad. People easily impose belief on themselves. Voltaire said of Mahomet that he began by imposing his religion on mankind and ended by imposing it on himself. The discourse was a rude shock to illusions which had created a cherished ideal. It seems to diminish the value of the achievement. It is nevertheless a truthful exposition of the subject.

W. P. Harris,

Jackson, Miss,

What you have said can be verified, but there are other things also true. You have a type of negro beyond us, and you have the vast mass of them,

As Churchmen, having much to do which we cannot touch yet,

110

we deal with those who are inclined to accept our ways and teachings. We cannot get down into the depths where we have no force or money to deal with the hard problems. The query which suggests itself to me practically, since we are not going to be able to take hold of all the situation at once, and since there is certainly a great amelioration in many aspects of the case of late years, from mulattoes, more owning of parcels of land, more money in the savings banks, etc.,—is it wise to give such fearful accounts as would paralyze effort, and cause the Church to say, "There is no use; they are beyond help."? Yet it would not be wise, of course to give a rose-colored view of the situation. Your methods of help suggested are wise and correct, and founded on your experience.

C. F. ROBERTSON,
Bishop of Missouri.

As the result of my own personal experience and observation, I am thoroughly satisfied that the statements made by Rev. Dr. Tucker in his recent pamphlet, concerning the present religious condition of the colored population in the South, are abundantly warranted by facts; and, in my opinion, the means proposed by him for remedying this most deplorable state of things, is the very best one yet proposed, which has come to my knowledge.

R. A. COBBS,
Rector of St. John's Church, Charleston, W. Va.

I have read your address with a feeling of deep interest, with a painful sense of the truth of every one of your statements, and with great admiration for the courage with which you have told us all the truth; and the ability with which you have presented it.

I endorse *ex animo* everything you say, and I pray that God may open the minds of men to receive the true impression of the case as you present it, and endow us all with wisdom and ability to meet it in all its painful details.

To two classes of men your *expose* will be exceedingly unpalatable—men at the North, who know little or nothing of the negro, and men at the South, who, forced to admit the truth of your statements, yet do not wish that truth to be so plainly stated. But is it not better for all that the truth should be known? If the Church has to grapple with the problem of the negro's moral and religious education, ought she not to know all the terms of that problem? Can the case be met, save with an intelligent apprehension of the material on which she has to work, and an equally intelligent application of the means necessary to reach the desired end?

In view of the great issues introduced, I thank you with all my heart for your true and fearless statement of the case.

W. T. DICKINSON DALZELL,
Rector of St. Mark's Church, Shreveport, La.

I have read with great interest your article on the negro race and their religious status. I concur in all your statements and am cognizant of many of the circumstances referred to and know them to be accurately correct. Your theory of unconscious hypocrisy is a new idea to me and the more I think of it the more I am convinced of its truth. I have done for thirty years a large practice, and a majority of my patients have been negroes, and I am satisfied that your portrayal of the negroes' character is more accurate than any I have seen in print and is calculated to do good. THOMAS H. MAYO, M. D.
Deacon of Columbus Baptist Church.

I have received your "Speech," and can endorse your statements made concerning the moral condition of the negroes of the South as being, in my opinion, substantially true.

FRANCIS M. WHITTLE,
Bp. P. E. Ch. in Va.

So far as my observation goes the morality or rather immorality of the negro is as you picture it. That is a question of fact which does not admit of contradiction. As to the reason why, there is abundant room for many hypotheses. There are a good many unpalatable truths in your pamphlet; and my experience in preaching writing and talking unpalatable truths lead me to think that the Northerner will abuse you for abusing the negro, as he will think, and the Southerner will abuse you, because he will think you are reflecting upon him and his ancestors by calling the sin of slavery by its ugly name.   WM. C. McCRACKEN.

Rector of All Saints Church, Grenada, Miss.

By the experience of twenty year's labor among the colored people, I am obliged to endorse the general position taken in your paper. I have long entertained the view expressed in ¶2 page 3, as to God's purpose in bringing the negro to this country. Your view of the effect of Christian teaching upon the African mind may be mainly correct, I had never thought of that, and to them and their immediate descendants the passage on page 7, may possibly have applied, "the great mass of the negroes did not know that they were hypocrites." The rest of the sentence I can not agree with, "and do not yet know it." The gradual improvement of succeeding generations, alluded to on page 8, negatives it, at least in those parts where the Gospel has been truly and extensively preached. I have never been in Mississippi, it may be you are correct as to the masses there. I have heard from friends that the spiritual condition of slaves there was far below those with whom I have been thrown, and I know that there is a wide difference in sections here. Stealing, page 9, too true. Lying is natural to a sinful condition. The epistles show us that both lying and stealing were common among owners, as well as slaves; but slavery no doubt tended to foster both, especially lying. I have read that the Emperor of Russia is the only Russian who does not lie habitually, and he only because there is no necessity or call for it. There is no doubt but that the negro listened to the teachings of *truth* and *honesty* under the suspicion that it was an interested teaching on the part of owners, but I can not agree that there was

6

the same ground of suspicion in regard to chastity. I do not think that either rebellion against the religion of their masters or the *example* of their masters, had any appreciable effect in shaping their morals in regard to marriage. It is true there are *absolutely* many mulattoes, but on the plantations they were relatively few, and they knew this was the result of disloyalty to Christian teaching on the part of men who made no profession of religion; it was not the result of Ministers' guilty shame nor of impiety on the part of white women. Here the looseness of nature fonnd ready vent on the part of both men and women, for the lash was seldom if ever, administered for this crime. That slavery greatly fostered it as well as the other vices is too true, and that too many masters were the guilty participants is too true, but to my mind the great tendency of slavery to foster all these vices lay in this: there was no loss of social position by the commission of these crimes. If a man stole or lied or a woman was unchaste, it did not affect their position as workers; they lost no caste with masters or fellow slaves. Look around you, my dear, sir and I think that you will find that the pressure of social standing is the control which keeps nine-tenths of non-christian people in the path of morality, and I am afraid a large proportion of professors also. The slave had no social position to lose, and the negro has scarcely any more to-day. I think, sir, that you argue incorrectly when you lay so much stress upon their feeling the injustice of slavery and through rebellion against the master's religion learned to be and play the hypocrite. They never, even in Africa, knew anything but slavery, and by nature knew what it was to lie and steal. Chastity is the only thing perhaps they really were ignorant of. There is not a shadow of doubt that they mixed up the heathen ideas and superstitions of their old country with Christian doctrines. No shadow of doubt that in the mass they deceived themselves with the idea, that their prayers and shouts were sufficient to satisfy God for their immoralities. This is not a race peculiarity as so many of our people say. Israel of old was guilty as a people, Jer. vii: 9–10, and xxiii: 11–14. Too many of own race are guilty to-day. How many Romanists are doing the same thing under a different guise. The greater part of their false views of religion was due under slavery to a real lack of teaching, and is due to the same cause to-day. In many portions of our land, especially upon large plantations, sermons by enlightened ministers were few and far between. Their own leaders were their chief teachers; this was the only way open for rule and authority, and therefore in the great majority of cases the grandest rascals were the preachers. Since freedom the whites have felt their release from responsibility and the colored people have b. en left entirely in large sections, to these same leaders, now made preachers. No wonder their religion is what it is under the ban of their color; and so debarred from social position among the whites, it will take generations before they can get up a social status among themselves and their white neighbors, sufficient to counteract the natural tendency to immortality fostered by the influences of slavery.

As a whole, your picture is too true, but the preaching of the Gospel has not been in vain. About four years ago I was conversing with a gentlemen on Cooper River. He had lately come there. He remarked to me: "These people (the colored) are almost heathens, compared with our negroes. I have brought some of our people here and they are shocked at the morals here." He came from a section where the Gospel had been faithfully and widely preached to the slaves for years, by a succession of earnest ministers. In the section where he then was, considerable work had been done, previous to the war, though nothing comparative to that of his section, and nothing had been done by white preachers since, or scarcely anything. About half an hour later I met another planter, also lately removed to Cooper River, but from another section of large plantations. He remarked in conversation; "Sir, the negroes of my section are perfect barbarians compared to this people. I could never return to plant in my section of country again." The remarks of these two gentlemen showed the relative amount of Christian work that had been done in the several sections. Now, sir as, to the remedy. You are right in the statement that something must be done by the whites. It has taken generations and centuries, with all the advantages of

115

social standing sustaining and restraining the unchristian, to bring us where we are; we must be the teachers of this people—part of our national being. You are eminently right in two things; *Southerners* must do the work, and we must "concentrate efforts." Your plans are most excellent, but can you carry them out? The Episcopal Church in this State had brought many hundreds, even thousands under her influence. With emancipation she relaxed her hold and they drifted into other denominations, though I know that many held on. unorganized, waiting and hoping in vain for organization from the church.

In 1875 I entered the Reformed Episcopal Church and was put in charge of a work among these people. I began with two men who had been under my ministry for ten years, four others I took for daily instruction, they could scarcely read; it was slow work but after about four years, I had some six or seven at work, radiating from a centre. I now have twelve ordained men of good moral character, of good report from all around, with nineteen organized congregations and about fifteen hundred communicants. All in these congregations, are not, of course, models of Christian propriety, now and then some fall, but on the whole, there is a wholesome influence emanating from every congregation. I mention this to illustrate two points; first, white influence and control must be exerted. Second, this must be mainly impressed upon colored ministers, who can reach their own people and impart to them the truth first impressed upon themselves by constant, daily prayerful exposition of God's word.

P. S. STEVENS,

Bishop of the Ref. Epis. Ch.

Concerning Bishop Stevens as an authority on this question Mr. Benj. R. Stuart, Principal of the Charleston Classical School, says as follows: "Before the Rev. Mr. Stevens became a Bishop of the Reformed Episcopal Church, and since, he has labored more unremittingly and usefully and devotedly to christianize the blacks than any man in the United States. In my judgment he is the very highest authority we in South Carolina possess upon religion among the colored people. I wish you to know from an unpreju-

diced witness what manner of man, I, who would not unite with
the Reformed Episcopalians for any consideration, believe the Rev.
Mr. Stevens to be."

I have read very carefully and with deep interest the speech of
Rev. Dr. Tucker, on the "relations of the Church to the Colored
Race," materially enlarged since its delivery.

It is the most striking and convincing statement that has appeared since the war; and the many points, especially those of
the moral deterioration of the colored race and some of their distinguishing traits cannot be controverted. As to this, my own
observation, and the admissions made by intelligent and reliable
men of that race, are confirmatory throughout.

In the unqualified denunciations, so often expressed, of the
evils of domestic slavery, or in its being an unmitigated curse to
either race, I do not concur. It brought its benefits and blessings
no less than evils, as Dr. Tucker has unanswerably shown. This,
however, is a question which does not affect the correctness of his
views of the present status and of what should now be done. As
to the best mode of elevating the colored race at the South, morally and religiously, in and through the Church, for we know no
other, I still adhere to the position taken by me in the House of
Bishops, in October, 1874, that it can only be most effectually
done by a suffragan, a white man of Southern birth and experience in that work, with the general control and counsel of the
Bishop of the Diocese.

The questions that would necessarily arise with the progress of
such an organized effort, in its unity and catholicity, under the
Bishop—questions as to schools, Parochial organization and representation, requirements for candidates for Orders and a rapidly
increasing colored ministry—it would be quite time enough to
settle with the growth and development of the work. Wisdom
would be given, for the Holy Ghost would be with the Church in
that auspicious and long hoped for time of renovation.

Adequate support would have to come mainly from the Church
in the North. Should that not be fully extended, the Church in

the South would be forced to struggle on then feebly and slowly to the distant consummation. ALEX. GREGG,
Bishop of Texas.

———

I have been accustomed to the colored people all my life in Maryland and Virginia—especially the latter State; not however, on the large plantations where they formed communities of their own, but in the towns and cities, and in some cases on the smaller farms.

My experience therefore necessarily differs somewhat from yours. I recognize, however, in the picture you draw, the fuller developement of what I have myself seen in my life. To sum it all up in a word, the natural outcome, the luxuriant growth under favorable circumstances, of the plant we have in Va., is i. e: The divorce of morality from religion.

The remedy you suggest seems eminently practical and full of promise. I pray God to put it into the hearts of some to give it a trial. GEO. W. PETERKIN,
Bishop of West Va.

———.

I have read your speech carefully. It is able, candid and fearless. Do you think if Canon Farrar's new book on Early Christianity had fallen under the eyes of the Pagan world of the age he describes, it would have been believed by them? Do you think that the negroes will recognize their own condition as you have described it? or do you believe that where there is so much pronounced opinion at the North, that you will get credit for your statements? I fear you will antagonize rather than conciliate. It is not known that you are by birth a Northern man, and it will be regarded as a Southern man's prejudices.

Your assertion that "the great mass of the negro race in the South, professing religion, have a form of Christianity without its substance ; and further, that they have no comprehension of what that substance ought to be—" is as true as anything in Holy Writ. * * How is it to be expected that it should be otherwise, considering the history of the negro? It has taken over a thousand years to produce the man of our own race to-day; and, God knows, there is hypocrisy, deceit, lying, stealing and impurity, and a form of godliness without the power thereof, among our own race—enough to call down the wrath of heaven. What wonder that a people whose ancestors 150 years ago were naked savages in Africa, should not have had those traits which they brought with them·eradicated under the tutelage of slavery among us? If the world knew as we parish priests know of the immorality of men, of the accepted and recognized habits of youths and young men of the white race, they would not doubt that the negro as a race is all that you have described him. I join issue with you, however that slavery made him thus. Thank God we are now free from that burden of slavery which our fathers left upon us, and which was put upon them when they could not help it.

I am now 55 years old; at 21 I inherited from my grandfather's estate a gang of negroes, among whom were five, still living, whom he had bought as naked savages from Guinea ships. They were tattooed, and spoke to their death, the last of them in 1856, an unintelligible language. All the rest of my gang were the immediate children and grand-children of those who had come from Africa with all those traits deeply rooted in them, such as you have described. Had they not in God's Providence been brought here as slaves, they would never have been permitted to land on our coasts. What people could have permitted thousands of such savages to have come among them as free men? Would life or property have been safe? In slavery they were gradually raised. Among them I have myself met Christians of the deepest piety, of the most beautiful traits of character, of truth, honesty and virtue—rare, but actual. Our friends at the North thought that we had done so much for them in slavery as to transform the barbarous Africans into enlightened citizens, fit for the Senate and the House, for Judgeships and Treasurerships; and that we had made their children the equals in intellect and morality of the children of those who had a thousand years behind them of civilization, education, freedom and Christianity, fit to be educated in the same schools. We who live among them know better. We know that the immoralities and sins and traits of character which came with them were not eradicated; and it is not only philosophy, it is hard common sense to know that the statements you have made are in a general application strictly true. Slavery was bad enough, but do not let us lay to our doors more than we deserve. A friend from the North, now living in Florida, joins issue with you as to the training of slavery in the matter of the relations of the sexes. Knowing the condition of the Sandwich Islanders, he says that the facts you set forth are the normal condition of all colored races, so that he thinks it is not just to charge the immorality of the negroes to the influence of slavery.

Your plan is a good one; it seems to me that it is the best plan for the whites as well as for the negroes. * * Your speech is unpalatable; it will not be believed by thousands; but those who are earnest in their interest in this race, which possesses many of the finest natural traits found among men, those persons will hear you; they will think and they will pray, and the best thing to be done they will do. God grant it. My heart yearns to see the Church in earnest, doing its duty to these people, whom I believe are the destined missionaries to Africa.

A. TOOMER PORTER,
Rector of the Church of the Holy Communion,
Charleston, South Carolina.

I have just completed a second reading of your address on "The Relations of the Church to the Colored Race."

At the first reading I was startled, and my whole nature recoiled at the fearful scene it presented of the moral condition of our colored population,—not because it revealed anything that I had not known before,—but because I had never had the question brought before my mind so forcibly, and palpably, and in such a concentrated form. But to-night I sat down pencil in hand, prepared to note down anything which I thought too highly colored, or from which I might dissent, and the result is, that after a second careful and dispassionate perusal, it is my deliberate judgment that your address as published in the pamphlet before me, contains the truth,—and nothing but the truth,—in describing the present moral condition of the negro race. This conclusion is reached after thirty-five years experience with the race in question.

H. SANSOM,
Rector Christ Church, Vicksburg, Miss.

In reference to the speech, I am of the opinion that it presents the fullest exposition of the subject I have seen, and so far as the correctness of its statements are concerned, I see nothing incompatible with any knowledge I have on the subject from observation, experience or otherwise.

I am fully impressed with the belief that much good will be done if the plan you propose be acted upon and carried out in the spirit which dictates it.

L. HAUGHTON,
Chancellor 1st. District, Miss.

I have had the pleasure of hearing read and carefully considering the speech of the Rev. Dr. Tucker, on the relations of the Church to the Colored Race, and do not hesitate to express my full concurrence in the entire truthfulness of the facts set forth and the general views so forcibly stated. Reared and educated in the South, intimately acquainted with the character and habits of the colored race for years before and ever since the war, I believe Dr. Tucker has rendered invaluable service to both races, and that his weighty words should excite deep interest and move to sympathetic action all parties of the Union.

O. H. MARSHALL,
De Soto Parish, La.

I have read very carefully your speech delivered before the Church Congress in Richmond, and write to say that it has my unqualified approval in every particular. In the first instance, the moral condition of the negro race is in my opinion such as you describe it, nay even *worse*. Secondly, you have pointed out very clearly the only possible way for their evangelization. I need scarcely add that you are at liberty to use my name as endorsee.

H. STRINGFELLOW, JR.,
Rector of St. John's Church, Montgomery, Ala.

7

I have read your speech with very great care, and wish to say, first of all, that I do thank you from my heart for having written, spoken and printed these words. I believe that the circulation of them must do good, for you have spoken the truth plainly and forcibly, as nobody to my knowledge has done upon this subject before you. In the main I agree to the truth of all that you have said. Certainly I agree that the system of slavery was efficacious in intensifying the condition of "unconscious hypocrisy." I say "intensifying," for I believe that slavery did not produce it, but found it already in the African when brought to this country. Yet do not understand me as finding fault with your statements in reference to the system of slavery. I have none to find.

But I cannot endorse the whole of your speech; chiefly I can not at all agree to what you so earnestly plead for; namely, that the white people of the South must be helped in the same way and the same manner as the negroes. I am sure that you speak wisely and well when you say that only through the agency of Southern white people can the negroes be christianized, and that the efforts made in disregard of their advice and opinion and personal co-operation have been worse than none. But I do not think it true that their own receipt of corresponding benefaction is the condition precedent to their willingness to aid in this work; and I fear that your appeal will be hindered by this statement.

Wishing you God-speed in your noble work and praying, always that our Church may be aroused to "come down" ere this poor race shall die. I am, etc.,   T. U. DUDLEY,
                         Assistant Bishop of Kentucky.

Cordially endorse every word.   T. T. MEADE, M. D.,
                                  Brookhaven, Miss.

Your printed speech on the "Relations of the Church to the Colored Race" just received. My personal knowledge of the negro, in Kentucky, Tennessee, North Carolina and Virginia, enables me to endorse your statements concerning his moral condition. I am convinced that the only way of making the negro a sincere Churchman is to educate him in the Church from his infancy up.   C. B. HUDGINS,
                                    Henderson, Ky.

122

In regard to your statements respecting the colored race, I may say that so far as my observation has extended, which has not been great, you have spoken accurately in regard to the lack of honesty and truthfulness in the negro race—as a rule. I think, too, that the tendency in the past has been, and is largely so now, to separate morality from religion. At the same time I must say that I think there has been some improvement in the race's moral and religious condition during the last few years; as much, perhaps, as the peculiar circumstances of the case would admit of.

M. M. MOORE,
Rector of St. Peter's Church, Oxford, Miss.

I have received and read with interest your speech, part of which was delivered before the Church Congress in Richmond.

Having lived among the negroes for many years and having had every opportunity to study their character I am compelled to say that your statements are, alas, too true. I believe that you have suggested the only feasible plan by which the condition of the negro can be ameliorated. And I believe that many intelligent negroes will endorse your sentiments, and while they deplore the facts, will acknowledge them to be true.

STEPHEN H. GREENE.
Rector Church of the Redeemer, Elgin, Ills.

·I received your speech on the "Relations of the Church to the Colored Race," yesterday; have read it carefully and with great interest; and have no hesitation to say that my observation of something more than eight years in this city enables me to say that I think you but state the truth very kindly and discriminatingly. J. L. TOWNSEND,
Rector Church of the Incarnation, Washington, D. C.

I have just read your speech on the Colored Race, and take pleasure in endorsing it. I have practiced medicine for thirty years among them and know them thoroughly.

GEO. N. SMITH, M. D.,
Pass Christian, Miss.

123

I have read Dr. Tucker's speech upon the "relations of the Church to the Colored Race," and to the best of my knowledge and belief his statements of the present moral condition of the colored people in the South, especially in the country districts, is in the main correct.

Considerable allowance must be made for many exceptional cases of veracity, honesty and morality; but with this proviso, the general facts of the case are, I believe, as Dr. Tucker states them.

ALEX. MARKS,
Rector of Trinity Church, Natchez, Miss.

I endorse every thing you say, and you have permission to use my name if you wish to do so. I endorse it from personal knowledge and experience, and could say much more than you have as to their improvidence. J. W. CHAMPLIN,
Yazoo City, Miss.

We fully and heartily endorse your exposition of the African Race in the Southern States. W. P. BROWNE,
Rector of Emmanual Chnrch, Winona, Miss.
J. C. PURNELL,
FRANK HAWKINS,
Wardens.

I have read your address in relation to the Colored Race. From forty years residence in the South and pretty extensive observation of the race, I fully endorse the statements of the address and highly approve the remedy proposed. You are at liberty to use my name if you see proper. WILLARD PRESBURY,
Kirkwood, Miss.

I have read your forcible and graphic pamphlet on the "Relations of the Church to the Colored Race," with unusual interest, and in general with full concurrence in the truthfulness of the picture you have presented.

I do not agree with you that the negroes, when enslaved, had (as stated on page 6,) "the traditions of former lives in freedom as guides," &c. With few, if any exceptions, they had never been free, either in Africa or in America, and therefore could have had no traditions of freedom.

Nor do I think that the slaves had any lively perception of "the monstrous wrongs of slavery," as intimated on page 11, and perhaps in some other passages. That they felt it as an evil, and were galled by it, is unquestionable, but it was pretty much as they would have felt the misfortune of a club-foot, or any other providential infliction. The ethical view of it, as a wrong, was (as I take it) taught them from without—first, by their own white masters and mistresses, who, fifty years ago, were almost universally abolitionists in sentiment, and afterwards by the political agitation of the question. With these and possibly a few other minor and merely incidental exceptions, not affecting the general statement of the case or the essential and practical questions involved in it, my own views are heartily in accord with yours. It is one of the most vitally momentous of subjects that demand the consideration of the men of this generation, whether regarded in the light of Christianity or statesmanship. I wish that your admirable presentation of it could be in the hands of every thoughtful and intelligent reader in every part of the country.

W. T. WALTHALL,
Biloxi, Miss.

I thank you for giving me the opportunity of reading your pamphlet on "The relations of the Church to the Colored Race."

From a personal observation of about forty years in ministering to this people, four years as Rector of your present parish and the balance in the State of Maryland, I must pronounce your speech to be as thoughtful and true an exhibition of the case as the nature of the case admitted and I pray God that it may lead Churchmen, instead of criticizing, to "consider their ways," and remedy the evil which, I thank God, He enabled you so truthfully and ably to bring to our attention. MEYER LEWIN,
Upper Marlborough, Md.

Your admirable address on "the Relations of the Church to the Colored Race," delivered before the late Church Congress in Richmond, Va., I have read with great pleasure, and I have no hesitation in saying that every thought in that address receives my hearty endorsement, as being true in letter and in spirit. In saying this, I speak as one having a right to speak on this great subject, inasmuch as I have for three and thirty years been a presbyter of this diocese. I have mingled with the colored people a great deal. I have baptized, catechized, and preached the Gospel to them by day and by night, and were it necessary I could intensify much that you have truly and faithfully stated in your address, but it is unnecessary. Your statements will stand, for they have truth for their foundation, and the Church in the near future will act upon them.   GEO. MACAULEY,

Rector of St. Marks Church, Dalton, Ga.

I have read with care your speech before the Church Congress on "The Relations of the Church to the Colored Race."

What you have said will, I am persuaded, have the effect to "wake up" our brethren at the North, and set them to thinking; even if your words should prove to be somewhat distasteful to some of them. There is a good deal of sentiment indulged, but too little of real practical thought, in connection with this grave question throughout the Church; and for this reason, I am glad you had the boldness to speak as you have done

While I am not prepared to endorse *everything* in your speech, yet I do unhesitatingly and entirely approve and endorse what you have said about the "effect of freedom" upon the negro; his "progress"—rather, his "advance backward," his moral degeneration—"since the war," and the "plan of work" suggested by you for his true emancipation, moral and spiritual, which is far worse than it was before the war.

The charge that the Northern people are largely responsible for the present moral and religious status of the colored man in the South, cannot, I think, be successfully refuted; and I fully agree with you that a very grave responsibility rests now upon them to furnish out of their wealth the means that shall be abundantly sufficient to enable the Church in the South to discharge faithfully and successfully the obligations of the whole Church to this race.

These I conceive to be essential points in your speech, for which you ask my endorsement. JNO. F. GIRAULT,
Rector St. Anna's Ch., New Orleans.

I endorse the statements made by Dr. Tucker concerning the moral and religious condition of the negroes and have no objection to his using my name for that purpose. His statements as to their moral and religious condition are, according to my judgment and observation, literally true.

There are other things in his address from which I dissent.
H. A. BARR,
Oxford Miss.

The above is from one of the leading lawyers of the State, and a most zealous member of the Presbyterian Church.

You are at liberty to use my name as endorsing *in the main,* your address which strikingly presents the indisputable fact that religion and morality are wholly dissociated in the minds of the bulk of our negro population. H. H. CHALMERS,
Jackson, Miss.
[Chief Justice Supreme Court State of Mississippi.]

I have read with much interest the address concerning the colored people, and the accompanying comments added since it was delivered; the gravity of the subject having occupied a goodly share of my reflections from the date of emancipation to the present hour.

I assure you that it is a matter of gratification to realize the fact, that I have not been alone in trying to mature some plan inviting concert of action on the part of our own people, whereby both races might be benefitted morally, materially and politically. For my feeble efforts in that direction, I have been the victim of a subsidized press, more or less a target of an uninformed and high-

ly prejudiced public opinion, and I might add, a sort of scape-goat
for the delinquencies and short comings of a class of politicians,
who, for the purpose of advancing their own aggrandizement, are
wanting either in moral courage or practical knowledge to deal
with the question on other than demagogue issues.

Your straight forward, manly, conservative, non-partizan discussion of the subject comes at a more opportune time; a period,
I hope, when disagreeable memories will have less to do with its
solution; and the remedies you suggest intrusted to the keeping
and administering of the more thoughtful, more discriminating,
and less passionate of all concerned. Indeed, I feel so encouraged
in reading your address, as to invite the fond hope that both of
us may survive long enough to realize the fruits of your patriotic,
christian undertaking. The ice had to be broken in the spirit
you have manifested; the responsibility of paternity to some definite plan had to fall on the shoulders of some one outside the political arena; and I am truly glad the mantle of conception has
fallen to the lot of one who is guided alone by a sense of christian
duty, guided by the fidelity he worthily bears to the high calling
of a minister and servant of a just and merciful, but avenging
God. Trusting that "the bread you have cast on the waters may
be seen many days hence" I am &c., WM. H. VASSER,
Ex. State Treasurer of Miss.

Please accept my thanks for your kind letter and the pamphlet
accompanying the same. I must also thank you for the brave
presentation of the Church's duty to the colored people. However much we and other Christians may differ as to the mode of
action necessary to cure the evil, I think every true, brave
Christian wants to go to the very bottom of that evil
and work up from the solid ground of truth. Everything
else must fail—truth and truth only can do the work. When
they know the truth they shall be free, and when we advance
along the line of truth, we shall more and more aid in giving them
this real freedom; yea, the "glorious liberty of the sons of God."
Whatever dust and clamor we may raise, we must dig down and

unearth these buried souls from beneath the debris of heathenism, slavism, fanaticism and politics, and bring them forth, dress their wounds, pour in wine and oil, and thus by God's help, set them "free indeed."

You have been misled in your idea of the character, or, I should say the knowledge, of the "west coast" tribes. They do believe in a future state. Some of the tribes at least have words of gratitude—the "Veys," have, "issa," for "I thank you." Theft is punished with slavery. Modesty is valued from their stand-point; these are truths I can substantiate, and the failure to recognize them by African travelers I think has arisen from their haste and the superficial study a passer-by gives such subjects. Yea, of necessity must give it, the same thing you complain of in the Northern study of the Southern negro.

I have in my possession a number of African fables which show, beyond doubt, that the native African has the sentiment of immortality, and a true idea of the great characteristics of God; but this knowledge is only in sentiment, not principle; and like all sentimentalized truths becomes powerless as a rule of life and standard of action.

There is another important matter in dealing with the American negro, viz: To separate the negro from the mulatto. The negro is not a white man and does not want to be. The mulatto is part white and wants to be treated as if he were all white. He does not want to be classed among blacks, nor do they want him. This forms the bitter base of discord in Liberian politics, and any system which attempts to treat all as one will certainly prove defective.

Again, I do not think the slavery of America produced the deceptiveness of the negroes here; it may have intensified, but did not produce it. This is born in the life of a heathen, and I think has tended to multiply languages in Africa, even until there are tribes who have a whistle language to use in the presence of strangers when necessary. So this deception forms one of the Missionary's troubles and trials there.

The great stumbling block to the mulatto is he cannot have

8

129

social equality. This is the real tug of war after all is said and done; and here we must draw clear lines and conditions and have a full and unmistakable understanding on this point. They must know how far they can come, and by what steps and under what conditions they can gain the highest standard of social respectability. We must define this clearly and truly. If the simple fact of color is to forever and inevitably debar them from the full realization of their hopes in this matter, the sooner they know this fact the better—so that they may form a new aim in life. At present, this is causing them great soreness and increasing bitterness of feeling to the white man—North as well as South. (Yea, he feels nearer to the Southern than he does to the Northern man when they are brought in actual contact.) And it is this supposed cruel injustice on the part of whites that causes the negro as he becomes more educated also to become more miserable and discontented. He wants recognition, appreciation and position. He does not want to be driven away from, but to become the equal of the white man, and be so recognized.

Now, we as Christians, are bound to recognize their good as fast as it is demonstrated and give it the appreciation it deserves, if we would encourage them and help them to rise. Our own moral and spiritual welfare are wrapped up in theirs. To treat them less than Christians is to be less than Christian ourselves. Can any human soul rise to the fulness of its moral status without appreciation? But I am writing too much. Let me say, however, that I think the most natural, true, ready and speedy solution of this matter is for every Christian minister to treat the negroes as real parishoners without any cant or patronizing; but go in and out among them as a Christian man among suffering men, and insist on every communicant doing the same, and keeping the Golden Rule; and the less outside help and organization you have the better, seeing these will tend to hide your kindness of heart from those to whom you minister. They will give the money received and the organization credit and no gratitude to you. An alms house does not make a good Church atmosphere. My work and study among these people convince me, that the more directly

130

the individual can minister to the individual, the better. The Church and the family are God's two great organizations, and it is a question how far charitable institutions, supported by distant helpers and conducted by paid hands, develope true charity in either giver, doer or receiver. The great needs of the negro are man's sympathy and God's grace. I believe he, by proper management, can be made to supply most of the money needed to educate him.

Such are my views hurriedly expressed. Again, let me thank you for bravely and truly showing the negroes' real state, and giving our people a more clear and definite idea of what is before them.

May God grant us all grace to press forward in this matter until we reach the mark Jesus has set before us, is the prayer of,

C. CLIFTON PENICK,
Bishop Cape Palmas, etc., W. Africa.

In response to a second letter Bishop Penick writes as follows:

1st. I have long felt the inadequacy of words to convey accurate meaning, and especially when used away from the scene and life you would speak of. Words are all conventional and do our best others will not truly read us. Even Jesus himself had to put his life back of his words, and commanded a missionary to stand ever behind the gospel as a living dictionary.

2nd. Negroes consider their safety dependent on deception, and try to deceive strangers; all strangers in every thing, so far as my observation goes; and they argue, "We don't know what use the stranger will make of his knowledge to harm us." One of the easiest, most agreeable and most profitable ways of deceiving is to find out the kind of truth the stranger wants to get and tell him a corroborative lie.

3rd. Gratitude.—The point I wish to make here is not one of degree, but of capacity or fact, i. e. that the West Coast negroes have in them the capacity for gratitude though as yet it is but rudely developed. It is a rare thing to meet with gratitude for your efforts, among that people; but I doubt if any rarer than among our forefathers before Jesus came with His "good will to men" and "cup of cold water" motives. I believe the vitalizing of all these instincts depends on the gospel power directly or indirectly touching them. Suppose we say instead of, "no idea of gratitude," "their ideas of gratitude reach but little deeper than outward formality."

4th. "Theft punishable with slavery." I believe their law demands that you or any robbed person should say what punishment the thief shall have. But at the same time the whole tribe would try to defend him against your charges. Admit the guilt and they give the penalty; but there as here they do what they can to cover up guilt, if a fellow of their own. Here as with gratitude I only claim to demonstrate their "idea" of the thing and not the degree of vitality in the idea.

5. Modesty.—Here it is far more difficult to convey my meaning. Of course most of them wear very few clothes and much of the person is necessarily exposed. But it is a very rare exception to find a young woman or man by look or gesture conveying an immodest impression. So one may walk through a heathen town full of almost naked people and see less immodesty than in some of our most fashionable streets in some of our best cities. They have an idea of what they call impropriety, which they are careful to observe. To them virtue is secondary to getting money, and at the bidding of parent or husband they give it up, ofttimes, it may be, without their bidding. But here as in the other points named they certainly have an idea of the right and wrong of the matter and violation of these rights cause most of their wars and law suits. The "high Priest" of a tribe would be degraded from his office for adultery. Yet so mixed have they got things that it is a common matter for a man to hire out his wife, or parents their daughter, provided she is not betrothed. I am afraid I am not making my meaning clear, it is so hard to do where all the surroundings are so different. It is a very rare thing to see a native man or woman do an immodest act, or say an immodest word.

6th. The Veys have a very strong word for "liar," Epharwe," also words for lazy," "thief," "virtue," and "gentleness," though

132

I do not know the words for each. I do know the things signified are common themes of conversation. They are an exceedingly polite people though I can not say their gratitude is very deep. Every time a Vey asks after the health of your household and you reply, "he is well," he replies "I thank you;" and his protestations of gratitude are often profuse.

7th. Slavery is very complete among them and in some cases the master may kill his slaves, but superstition and fear lest the spirit of the departed should return and witch the murderer, is a tremendous restraint. This, by the way, is proof positive of their belief of life after death, if not immortality.

I have tried to throw what light I could on your questions, but feel that it has been imperfectly done. The subjects are so vast and carry in them what at first sight appears so many contradictions that I have refrained from publishing anything directly on the subject. Of course indirectly, these things crop out in many ways from my letters. But though I have been a very close observer and at least a moderate student of the African for years, I am by no means as confident of his real character as I would like to be before publishing anything directly on this head. Yet information true and clear is a "*sine que non*" for successful work among them. Africa is to-day the great problem of civilization. What God has wrapped up in the African race we can not divine, nor have we yet struck the type of civilization which seems likely to develop the fullness of their capacities. It is very chafing in this break neck age to be compelled to go on gathering fragments without being able to put them together in the shape of positive and clear cut result. But I am sure that patience in our searches into the nature of the African people is after all real haste. But by patience do not for one instant infer I mean inaction. God knows we have had by far too much of that already. Surely if we will do the things nearest to us now, we will find ample occupation and get more and more light. Do not let us generalize too far on too small a stock of experiment, but keep experimenting.

9th. I am frank to say that the best specimen of African manhood and culture I have ever met came by bringing the African in contact with and putting him under the supervision of white men. So far I have seen nothing that indicates their greatness as an independent people; but certainly their mental, moral and material progress seems most rapid when and where they are coupled with the white race.

Finally, don't get discouraged; you have struck a good and brave blow in what I consider the right direction. That you should be attacked by some and questioned much by others, only indicates that you have made progress.   C. C. Penick,
     Missionary Bishop of Cape Palmas, Africa.

You have stated clearly and as candidly as public print would allow, one of the most difficult and delicate questions now face to face with the American people: the negro enfranchised, his political and moral status and the relation and duty of the people and Church toward him.

For the past ten or twelve years I have had under my control and supervision a large number of negroes and have interested myself in their moral and educational advancement, and can testify with a feeling of deep concern that the truth is but half told in your statements regarding their moral condition or their conception of moral living and acting.

The plan you suggest for their gradual enlightenment is probably the best that can be devised. Young men and young women of their own race must be elevated to a higher standard and then go out and do the work among their people, but for long years to come under the guidance and support of good men who will do this trying home missionary work.

I trust that your plain statements of these facts, appallingly true, and of the trying position of the Church in the South, will rouse the Church throughout the country to grapple this common duty, and that good work, even in our day and generation, may give hope or the moral enlightenment of this race.   F. S. Shields,
     Natchez, Miss.

134

I have read the speech very carefully, and it has not only impressed me with the conviction of your earnest sincerity, but has
strengthened the opinion I have for years entertained, that the
problem arising out of the moral and religious condition of the
negroes of the South, is one of the most serious and difficult of solution, in our immediate future; and that very grave responsibilities and most solemn duties, in connection with its wise and safe
solution, are imposed by God upon the Christians of an entire
country, and especially upon those of our own Apostolic and
Conservative Church.

In my judgment, the Protestant Episcopal Church is specially
called upon to extend its strong hand for the rescue of the colored
race from influences which now tend to degrade their morals and
paralyze their spiritual capacities; and thereby to guard against
most serious dangers, which threaten the social and civil welfare
of the entire South.

Since my youth, I have resided in the valley of Virginia
where the colored population has been about one-fifth of that of
the white. With us, the colored people have been more intelligent, better trained, and being under the more direct and personal
influence of the superior race, have been of better morals, than
those of many portions of Eastern Virginia, and of the planting
districts of the South.

I can not, therefore speak with such personal knowledge as
others, of those *dark regions,* in our "Sunny South," in which ignorance, vice, superstition and a grossly perverted Christianity,
are so sadly commingled. But from my knowledge of you, and of
your earnest devotion to the best interests of the colored people,
I am persuaded, that the pictures, reluctantly drawn by you, of
the moral and spiritual state of the colored masses of the South,
who have been under your observation, have been conscientiously
and truthfully portrayed. Indeed, I am satisfied by information
derived from other sources, that the moral and spiritual evils
which you describe, do, more or less, exist in all those portions of
the South, in which the negroes are densely massed together.
And I will add, that your analysis of the causes, traceable back

135

to Africa and to the conditions of slavery itself, which have produced such deplorable effects, is not only logical and satisfactory, but is well calculated to excite deep sympathy with, and interest in, a race suffering not only from the taint of original sin, but from the slavery of habits of thought, emotion and action, which it will require wise and heroic efforts to break through so as to bring them unto "the perfect liberty of the children of God."

I will further state, that even in my own most favored region, the currents of moral and spiritual influences, which affect and control the colored people, are wholly distinct from those which govern the whites—they flow in separate channels. The colored people have their own churches, their own spiritual instructors, and their own methods of moral teaching and church discipline; and, so far as any direct influence of the whites upon the religious instruction and training of the negroes is concerned, (except in a few feeble and inefficient Sunday-schools,) the two races might as well be separated by a wall reaching from earth to Heaven. True, where the whites constitute a controlling majority of the community, the refracted rays of their higher moral and religious culture and the light of a more elevating public opinion, may, and doubtless do reach them, and to some extent guide them aright. But, thus far, that is all; as suggested, the races have practically almost nothing to do with each other in respect to the worship of God and the cultivation and growth of the moral and spiritual attributes of a common humanity.

And the great question for the Church is, how shall *its* light be turned upon the colored masses in the South, to enlighten, purify and guide them unto all truth? How (as they would express it) shall the *"white people's* religion be made *theirs?"* How shall they be led not only to see, believe, and shout for joy in believing, the truth, but also be taught to do what God demands, "to *work the works of God,"* as a matter of conscience and daily duty; in a word, to understand and to do what, in its sublime simplicity, the catechism teaches in respect to duty—duty to God and duty to man.

A satisfactory solution of the suggested difficulties, I am persuaded, can never be reached (to use a military phrase) by a direct assault; for their works are guarded with sleepless jealousy and suspicious alertness. The only hope of success will be found in some such movement as you suggest, which will withdraw them from their defences; win them to us ; and make them, by degrees, submissive and obedient prisoners of Christ and true soldiers of the Cross.

Allow me in conclusion to say, that I have a warm affection for and interest in the colored race. I was born in the midst of slaves, was nursed and cared for by them in my childhood; grew up with them; and I owned them until emancipation came to *them and me!* and I cannot throw off the associations of my life connected with them, or fail to remember and be grateful for their marvellous behavior, during the war, when our old men and helpless women and children were, in many places, left to their care ; and as far as I know or have heard, no violence or wrong was done in any single instance by them to those thus entrusted to their keeping. They are a docile and an affectionate race of people; they can be led by the soft hand and gentle, loving voice, a long way; and I have full faith that they can and will in time be thus brought into the fold of the Church, and that by God's grace and by the guidance of the Holy Spirit such efforts as yours will be crowned with success. And if Churchmen, nay, Christian men and Christian women all over our land shall wake up and realize that "the dark districts," of which I have spoken are, in truth, the most important fields for missions in the world—fields for wise and liberal expenditures of money, through local church agencies in the South; and shall act and give as large hearted and godly men should, I can not doubt that the colored people will be gathered into the church, and taught to lead sober, righteous and godly lives; and so be made true men, good citizens and practical christians.   HUGH W. SHEFFEY.

Staunton, Va.

———

I have read the advanced sheets of your pamphet very carefully. Feeling the deepest interest in this matter of the present condition
9

of the colored people; as anxious as you are that the whole truth
may be brought out and emphasized in every possible way, I am
going to make a suggestion to you. You have taken hold of a
subject about which a great many worthy people, North and
South, are naturally very sensitive, and they look with suspicion
upon whatever seriously touches their life-long prejudices and
feelings in regard to the negro race. You have discussed your
subject with entire frankness and fearlessness. Under such circumstances, as a matter of course, you been already grievously misunderstood, your motives have been misconstrued, and by interested parties you have been and will still further be grossly misrepresented. The best answer to be given to what has been said
and will be said and done by your opponents, to break the force of
your fearful array of facts, is to make a faithful statement of your
own true relations to the colored race. That statement will put
the matter in such a light, that at least it will be impossible to
misunderstand your motives in what you have said upon the subject. Unless you do make such a statement, so terrible are the
true conditions you reveal, even the unprejudiced and kindly reader may not understand you. I have taken the pains therefore to
inform myself of what you have done and are now doing in the
interest of the negro. In the first place, although a very young
man and of Northern birth, you were a faithful soldier in the Confederate army during the war between the two sections. For
sixteen years since the war you have had the closest and most intimate contact with the colored people, In the years 1866–67, as
a planter you had large numbers of them in your employment, and
that, in what is called "the black belt" of Mississippi; you know
all about that, in some respects the darkest side of the matter,
about which very little is known by most of those who write and
speak upon this subject. Your interest in the race then, was manifested in the organization of a school, which, although a planter,
you yourself taught. You have seen and known them intimately
in the city of Columbus, where you lived for several years and
where you were ordained both Deacon and Priest. You taught
several of them in private while you were a Candidate for Orders.

Afterwards in Christ Church, Rochester, New York, you had several of them of Northern birth in your Sunday School and under your pastoral care, and since you have been Rector of St. Andrew's Church, Jackson, Miss., as the head of a colored school and at a great sacrifice for the past five years, you have been daily, almost hourly in the closest contact with them. So then both as planter and voluntary teacher you know thoroughly the plantation negro in the ugliest phase of his life. You know the city negro South, and the free born negro North, have taught both, and I take it few men of your refinement and cultured tastes and intelligence and and keenness of perception have ever enjoyed the same opportunity of knowing the negro character. It is from that stand-point and for the good of the negro you have patiently and prayerfully studied this matter. It is from that stand-point you have spoken frankly and fearlessly.

Now then, as to your work in Jackson. In what you call the Unique School, held in your own Church, under your own eye, where you yourself play the organ for them, and where you lead in training them, you have five hundred colored children taken from every social plane among the colored race. In West Jackson you have a class numbering one hundred; at China Grove, an outcome of your work and under your influence there are one hundred and fifty. At White Rock, one hundred and twenty-five. At Hope Spring, one hundred, making in all nine hundred and seventy-five colored children under your influence and in a measure under your eye. And now, to reckon the number to whom those children give you access, you have at least four or five thousand colored people looking towards you and leaning more or less upon you and your instruction. I should say you had some right to speak by authority upon such a subject, and I take it men will listen to a man who so speaks.

A single word more. In your treatment of the subject of the present condition of the negro, it was of course impossible for you to avoid a reference to his condition as a slave. Whether slavery worked good, and only good to him, or evil and only evil, or how much good and how much evil are open questions, and

about which men differ very wid··ly.   If those questions could in
any way be eliminated from your discussion of the subject, I believe no intelligent Southern man would withhold from you his
unqualified and emphatic endorsement of what you say in regard
to the present condition of the negro.   WM. MUNFORD.
> Rector of St. Paul's Church, Columbus, Miss.

From the Kentucky Church Chronicle, Feb. 1883.

WORK AMONG THE NEGROES. —Much has been written recently
upon the subject of Church work among the negroes, but we have
seen nothing that gives so true a presentation of this difficult
problem, as the speech of the Rev. Dr. Tucker, of Mississippi,
delivered at the Church Congress in Richmond. This question
has been too much involved in politics for an unbiased discussion.
Prejudice and sentiment have warped the judgment of most writers, while ignorance has prevented a clear comprehension of the
problem, even by those most deeply interested in its solution.   In
Dr. Tucker's speech, however, we have a fearless presentation of
the awful facts of the case.   Facts gathered from a long experience in patient, faithful work among the negroes, and prayerful
and intelligent study of the whole question.   No one who is
familiar with the negro of the South can read this speech without
the conviction that it is the product of one who, laying aside all
fear, prejudice, and sentiment, has calmly spoken the words of
truth ; and we would urge all who would have definite, accurate
knowledge of the religious condition of the Southern negro to read
this speech.   There has been too much profitless work among the negroes leading to discouragement, because it has been ignorant work.
These words of Dr. Tucker show us clearly the condition of the
negro race, and suggest a simple, feasible plan of working among
them, that will, under God, bring forth much fruit.   This is a
work for the whole Church, which will require workers and money.
The South will furnish the workers, men and women, cleric and
lay, black and white, if the North will supply the money.

From the London "Spectator" (Oct. 14th, 1882,) on the Portugese Expedition to West Africa.

No writers place so low an estimate upon the West-African tribes as Ivens and Capello, who gave the following account of the Bihenos, natives of one of the richest tracts of territory in the interior of Africa, and much superior to those tribes whom they afterwards encountered: —

They live in a beautiful country, where there is nothing ugly but mankind, in a delicious climate, so that they need not guard against either heat or cold, on a soil so fertile that they need never dread want; and—these writers tell us—the pigment of an African negro is a perfect protection against the electrical influences which disturb the European in those climes. The writers confidently assert that the Behenos have no notion of the existence of a Creator, and no idea of a future life; fetishism has no relation to such ideas, but is merely concerned with the present. They are ready, handy and business-like. The women do almost all the field work; the men exercise certain mechanical arts, work in iron and even manufacture steel. The usual routine of difficulties about porterage, desertions, loss of bales in fording rivers, thefts, quarrels, intervals of illness, disgusting spectacles, hideous dances, exquisite scenery, beautiful skies, and wonderful vegetation makes up the travelers' narrative. The Luimbe people with wonderful head-dresses, inhabit a wilderness of monkeys, where "huge leguminous plants, whose fruit measures fourteen inches in length, with thick foliage, the trunk covered with a layer of cork, and long, pendent, vermillion flowers, constitute the superior flora." The Sovas are rather monotonous, being invariably dirty, cruel, and mean; but N'Dumba Tembo of Cangombe, is a pleasant variety. He came to the audience granted to the travellers mounted on the shoulders of one of his vassals, a stalwart and nimble negro, who, curvetting and prancing, bore him into the open space severely testing his Majesty's powers of horsemanship. All the "assistance" danced and bawled an accompaniment to the drums, and the Sova's nephew, in command of the advance guard, from time to time rested the palms of his hands upon the ground and threw his heels up in the air, like Dickens's Tom Scott.

From the Southern Churchman.

DR. TUCKER'S ADDRESS.—We have received the speech, which Rev. Dr. Tucker, of Mississippi, delivered in part before the Church Congress, on "The Relations of the Church to the Colored Race." It is a document which should have the widest circulation.   *   *   *   *   Nothing has ever been printed which will show so well how great the work is, and how important.

Dr. Tucker calls attention to a matter which Northern men have never understood, These go among the blacks for a brief space and witness their wonderful religious spirit; then come to the conclusion, there never was such a *religious* race!   And it is true; but their religion does not change their "character;" it is a "religion" which affects the emotional and not the moral nature; and hence Northern men in the general, have not the slightest knowledge of the work to be done.   On the contrary, they think all that is to be done is to give them school instruction, for their religion is well nigh perfect.   Yet in the vast majority of cases, they have no *Christian* religion at all; and need to be taught, here a little and there a little, over and over and over again, what be the very first principles of the religion of Christ.   In a long conversation the writer of this had with a most excellent Northern clergyman who had visited Brunswick county, we could not convince him that their religion was not the most perfect he had ever witnessed in his life!   We gave last week some testimony on this subject, which we found in our Baptist neighbor, the *Religious Herald*.   This paper recurs to it again and we read this other testimony endorsed by the *Herald* as coming from "a venerable and distinguished Doctor of Divinity" who says:—

*Dear Brethren—*Brother Becker has given you some "truth about the South."   I will tell you some more.

Near me they have held a "praise meeting" for years, frequently keeping me awake till after midnight.   Much of the time is spent in "shouting."   Sometimes they all stand in a circle, take hands and sing, keeping time with feet, head, hands and body. Again, they shout in pairs.   A man and a woman stand a few steps apart, when one says:—

"Bam, bam, bam." The other replies:

"Who comes dah?"

"Sinner."

"What sinner want?"

"Confess."

"Confess to who?"

"Confess to Mary Jones" or "John Smith."

Then they take hands and shuffle around, saying, "fol lol diddle lol." This is "fol dol shout."

Again, they walk slowly and solemnly past each other, saying, "Dem——Geor——gy——rabbit." Repeating this three times, they take hands and dance around, saying, "come bouncing along, bouncing along, bouncing along." This is "Georgy rabbit shout."

It will be hard for some of your readers to believe that this and such as this is a large part of the religion of the negroes in Lower Carolina, but it is true.

A MYSTERY.

Missionaries tell us that when a heathen, whether in Africa, China, or elsewhere, becomes a Christian, he at once becomes truthful, honest and chaste—in a word," a new creature in Christ Jesus." These people have had that same gospel preached by white and black, Northern and Southern, yet in *nine cases out of ten*, if not more, it exerts absolutely no influence on their lives. They believe theft, adultery, and lying to be sins, but they fully believe that if they "pray," especially "in de wilderness, "after each sin, it is as good as if they had not committed it. Hence, theft is almost universal; adultery—they are almost as common as goats. Lying is, of course, a concomitant of the other two.

Why has not the gospel the same transforming power here as in foreign lands? I have preached to them, taught them and their preachers "at my own charges," as I could, ever since I began to preach, and yet I see almost no fruit of my labor.

As you go into the interior of the State, where they are fewer and more in contact with the whites, you find them better in every respect. But how those of the low country are to be civilized and Christianized, I know not.

But will not education elevate them? As far as my observation extends, this simply makes them vain, idle and vicious. But would not higher education than they get in common schools improve them? I do not believe that "a little learning is a dangerous thing." I think it would be better if all our people knew the "three R's—readin', ritin', rithmetic," than if we had only two classes, collegians and utterly illiterate. I do not know what effect higher education might have on the colored people, nor is it possible to make the experiment. I speak only of what I have seen.

What, then, is to be done with and for them? Well, we must continue to preach the gospel to them, but in doing so "we walk by faith," certainly "not by sight." W. B. CARSON,

Appleton, S. C.

We need hardly say how very, very sad this state of affairs is; how this statement agrees with that of Dr. Tucker; and what a work is before us in the South, to elevate this race from their darkness and abominable living. And how the religion of this people is misunderstood by Northern Christians is a mystery. They do not appear to have the slightest knowledge; or rather their knowledge is wrong and consequently their efforts misdirected.   *   *

Extracts from the N. Y. "*Guardian*" of Jan 20t⁴, 1883.

A Layman at the South, an intelligent gentleman, long time a resident there, and thoroughly familiar with the subject on which he writes, sends us a communication which we give in full. * *

The sudden emancipation of the Negro imposed new responsibilities upon both races, which were understood by neither; and least of all by our Northern brethren.   *   *   *

The statements of Dr. Tucker, of Jackson, Miss., at the Church Congress in Richmond, are entirely true; for one I thank him for the public declaration of facts as they existed.   *   *

In the days of slavery, the master watched with a vigilant eye the intercourse between the sexes, as he had a direct pecuniary interest in it; but when the safeguard is abandoned and there are no moral instincts to interfere, the results are painful to contemplate. Even the marriage relation is not appreciated, and it may well be doubted whether any people can be Christianized or advanced to any extent in civilization, who do not hold this relation as sacred.

The improvement of the negro race is a National question; and was so admitted by the late lamented President in his Inaugural, and the wisdom of the Christian philanthropist and statesman must be invoked.

The race is already more numerous than the entire population of the United States at the adoption of our Constitution, and is constantly increasing; while the area of territory suited to him is restricted by nature. He has been entrusted with the ballot; and in this country where there have ever been, and probably will continue to be, two political parties of nearly equal strength how long will it be, if indeed it is not now the fact, before the negro will hold the balance of power; and vice and immorality sap the foundations of the greatest Republic of the world, and destroy the hopes of mankind?

The negro must be elevated and educated. I use the term elevated first; because I insist that he can not be educated without the elevation of his moral nature; and if he could be, it would be an injury, rather than an advantage. The ground must be prepared before planting.

I suggest, then, that our school houses be closed, and the books locked up for the present; that the teachers be at least doubled in numbers; that they lay off each county into small districts; and in these districts give a lecture every night; to which both adults and children should not only be invited but urged to attend.

Let the lecturer take a single subject, and lecture upon it night after night : until he shall find that it is understood; then take another subject, and so on until he shall believe that the minds of the negroes are prepared for what we call book education.   *

A NATIVE OF MASSACHUSETTS.

(The remedy suggested above is a curious one; but the fact that such a plan could be seriously proposed by an intelligent gentleman, is an evidence that the problem is a most difficult, perplexing, and even confusing one.   J. L. T.)

10

145

From the Popular Science Monthly, Feb. 1883.

THE AFRICAN IN THE UNITED STATES.—The future of the African in the United States is, in the judgment of many, the gravest question of the day. It must, from its nature, swell in volume and thrust itself forward more and more; and though the evils as depicted in these pages be in their worst forms comparatively remote, yet, if there be real grounds for them, the time for action in seeking and applying a remedy lies in the present. The far-reaching and critical character of the subject demands that it should be approached without political bias, and treated solely from the point of view of the national welfare.

(The writer then enters into an elaborate examination of the census returns, from which he deduces that according to the present ratio of increase, in ten decades the whites of the United States will number three hundred and thirty-six millions and the blacks one hundred and ninety-two millions. While in the Southern States the whites will number ninety-six millions against the one hundred and ninety-two millions of blacks.) The second factor in our argument is the impossibility of fusion between the whites and the blacks. The latter have been, and must continue to be a distinct and alien race. The fusion of races is the resultant from social equality and intermarriage, and the barrier to this here is insurmountable.

    *   *   * The factors in our argument are; 1st. That the black population is gaining on the whites; 2d. that the former is and must continue to be a distinct and alien people.

     *   *   *   *

But what will the upshot be, when the black population, advancing on the white finally outnumbers it? The outlook is most serious. It is a repetition of the Israelites in Egypt, a lower and laboring class gaining in population on the upper, and, as a distinct and alien race, causing apprehensions to the Egyptians. There is a point at which mere numbers must prevail over wealth, intelligence, and prestige combined. Unless relief comes, when that point approaches, woes await the land. This dark, swelling, muttering mass along the social horizon, gathering strength with edu-

cation, and ambitious to rise, will grow increasingly restless and
sullen under repression, until at length conscious, through numbers, of superior power, it will assert that power destructively,
and, bursting forth like an angry, furious cloud, avenge, in tu-
mult and disorder, the social law broken against it. (After a
statement that the blacks will probably always vote together, the
writer says:) We regard it as a mistake both for the country and
for the interest of the Republican party, that the enfranchisement
of the blacks followed immediately upon emancipation. * *

It was a mistake, we conceive, to have given this privilege to a
people just freed from the bonds of slavery, and still characterized
as a whole, by profound ignorance ; and, that no greater harm has
resulted, is because white intelligence has been able to exert a controlling influence and shape legislation. Certainly, while the
whites were disfranchised and the blacks politically supreme, the
state of the South was intolerable. * * * The ignorance and inexperience of this unlettered mass, fresh from slavery,
were immensely unequal to the science of enlightened governing.
To the whites it was a matter of life or death. They became a
"solid South," as any other people, similarly circumstanced, would
have become. Wealth and intelligence gave them the victory, as
it ever will, where numbers approach an equality—a victory which
does not mean injury to the blacks, but is the pledge for good government and order—the proof whereof is the present peaceful and
prosperous condition of the Southern States, for the blacks no less
than for the whites, compared with their state of wretchedness,
under negro political rule, in the days immediately following
upon the close of the war.

We must again ask the question : What, from this stand-point,
will be the upshot when the blacks numerically will so far exceed
the whites as to overcome the vantage that the superior
wealth and intelligence of the latter now give them? The
outlook here is no less serious. ⁃ * Who can doubt
that, when this day comes, the blacks will obey a race instinct
which all their surroundings will have powerfully tended to develop, and vote blacks alone into office? Thus they have done wher-

ever the power existed. Kept, as they are, a distinct and alien race, no other issue is reasonably conceivable. And who can doubt that, under this state of affairs—an inferior and incompetent race completely dominating. by mere numbers, a superior one—the worst disorders would ensue? The whites would not submit, and a violent and disastrous conflict of races must follow. * * The incompetency of the negro to provide legislatively, for the manifold and complex interests of an advanced civilization, would arrest its activiti⸳ s, paralize its trade, and spread a decline throughout the entire country. These are real and gigantic evils gradually looming up, and they merit the immediate and best attention of American statesmen. [The remedy proposed in the article is colonization.]

I insert this letter as showing the impression made upon the mind of a Northern man, by the negroes of the South Carolina Sea Coast.

From the New York Sun.]

St. Helena's Island, Dec. 15, '82.—This island is about twen·y miles long and from two to seven miles wide Its area is about eighty square miles. It is estimated that there are 8,000 inhabitants living on the island, or about 100 negroes to the square mile. There are no towns. The population is strictly agricultural, and is more dense than in any agricultural country I have ever seen. The people are, almost without exception, pure blacks. I have gathered my information about these people, first from the negroes; second, from the white men who trade with them—Republicans these; third, from the Bourbon Democrats; fourth, from the Independents. I have allowed for the prejudices of race and caste, and I have sunk my political belief and studied these people, honestly trying to understand the questions that arose before me.

These black people are without religion, and I greatly doubt if they have sufficient capacity to understand the principles that underlie the Christian faith.   *   *

These blacks are thoroughly dishonest. I do not believe this is the direct result of slavery. I have never seen an Indian who was not a liar and a thief, and I hold that dishonesty is a quality of the blood of all uncivilized people. There is no pretence of honesty among the blacks, one to the other, when by themselves. When talking to a white man they all, without exception, claim to be honest, to be the one negro "ole massa" trusted with the meat-house key. No negro is disgraced by having been imprisoned for stealing. The actual feeling among the negroes is that it is not a sin to steal. The crime consists in being caught. They habitually put sticks and stones in cotton bags. They sand their cotton. During the rush of business, when the weighing-room is crowded with negroes all clamoring for their cotton to be weighed next, they will salt cotton, hoping that it will pass unnoticed in the hurry of trade. Salting cotton ruins it. The salt attracts the moisture, and the cotton cannot be ginned. To obtain five and a half cents per pound for twenty pounds of salt, they will cheerfully, yes, eagerly, ruin $15 worth of cotton.   *   *

In the stores the clerks cannot take their eyes off their black customers without some small article disappearing. One clerk must watch the negroes. In some stores an iron rod runs along the outer edges of the counter, some ten or twelve inches above it. This rod is put there to protect the goods, that if the counters were low, could be reached by dishonest negroes. A new clerk is an irresistible attraction to these people. They fairly flock to the store to trade with a white man who has any confidence in their honesty. His confidence in the honesty of negroes is promptly destroyed. The first raid cures him of his folly.

One gentleman told me that several years ago he engaged in the enterprise of raising Irish potatoes for the Northern market. He employed a gang of twenty negro women to dig and gather the potatoes. He was called from the field to the gin house to attend to some business. He was absent from the field for a couple of hours. On his return he passed through a patch of weeds and stumbled over an apron filed with a bushel of selected potatoes. He emptied the apron, and, calling to the line of women who were digging potatoes, he waved the garment aloft and asked who had lost her apron. All the women but one turned

and shook their aprons at him. They jeered and taunted the
thief for the rest of the day. That evening when they quit work
the apronless woman stood under a tree until all the other women
had left the field, every one of them taunting her as they passed.
When they were all out of sight she walked up to the white man
humbly asked for her apron and got it. Then she made the white
man promise not to tell, not to betray her to the other negroes,
and on his passing his word to her, she showed him where the
nineteen honest women had buried twenty bushels of potatoes
while he was absent.   *   *

The ambition of the young black men who are playing at going
to school is to become preachers or members of the Legislature,
or clerks or storekeepers. The little education they receive unfits
them for field work. To educate a negro is to spoil a plough
hand.   *   *   I think it unwise to teach boys and
girls higher branches of education until they have a foundation of
elementary education on which to build. This these negroes do
not possess. I was strongly and unfavorably impressed by the
pretence of knowledge made by the black youths and by their
self-satisfied air.   *   *

I judge from what I have been told that the black race is devoid
of the sense of gratitude. They can be fed when they are starving, clad when they are naked, nursed when sick, protected from
assault, aided in all conceivable ways, and the negro who has been
so benefitted will rob his white benefactor on the first favorable
opportunity. Of course there are exceptions to this broad statement; but the assertion that the race, as a race, is devoid of gratitude is true. As house servants they are the most aggravating
creatures in existence. They are slow, stupid, and thievish. All
provision must be locked up, or they will steal it and carry it
home. The custom in South Carolina is to have the servants employed in the house go to their homes to sleep. They are not allowed in the house over night; indeed, they refuse to stay, much
preferring to go to their cabins. A family of blacks who have
one of their number employed as a cook in a white family or in a
hotel, are provided for. The cook will steal enough food to sup-

port the family. One gentleman, a rich planter, told me that he bought a cow, a most excellent cow—indeed, quite a wonderful cow—that actually gave two gallons of milk per day. He paid $40 for this vaccine phonomenon. His cook, an old servant who had been in the family for years, milked the horned wonder of Beaufort Island. Under the manipulations of the colored cook, the yield of milk steadily shrank. At the end of a week this most excellent cow gave but a quart of milk per day. The cook solemnly swore that the cow was a "no 'count beast." One morning the gentleman arose before his usual hour and gazed pensively out of his back window, which was open. Below him, with her head thrust into the cow's flank, was the faithful cook milking the cow. She lingered long at her task. She was evidently doing her best to prevent the cow from going dry. It took a long time to draw a pint of milk. When the cook had finished milking she stood up and beckoned with her hand. From behind a live oak tree, a small boy who carried a large pitcher in his hand, stalked forth. The faithful cook who had been in the family so long, poured seven-eighths of the milk into the pitcher; then wiping her hands on the woolly head of her son, she bade him be a good boy and not spill the milk on his way home. This gentleman quit housekeeping.

In my opinion the determining factor in the problem offered for solution by these Sea Island negroes is their morals. This is a delicate subject, but it must be understood, so as to comprehend the difficulties that beset the advancement of this people. As I have said, they are liars and thieves, and I now add that almost without exception, the women of these islands who have negro blood in their veins are impure. It is absolutely no disgrace for any black girl to have children before she is married. These people are devoid of shame. Their personal habits are so filthy, that I suspected that venereal disease was widespread among them. On inquiry of the physicians who practice among them, I found I was correct in my inference. The negroes are saturated with this deadly taint. This being the case, and free love in its vilest sense being practiced among them, it can be readily seen how widely diffused this ineradicable poison must necessarily be. As in the well-known case of the almost total extinction of the natives of the Hawaiian Islands by syphilis, and the diseases that spring from it, a similar fate is in store for these negroes. They will probably be exterminated by their licentious habits. FRANK WILKESON.

From the Nyanza, Great Basin of the Nile; and Explorations of the Nile Sources, by Samuel White Baker, London, Macmillan & Co., 1866 —From Chap. VIII, Page 194, *et seq*.

The black man is a curious anomaly, the good and bad points of human nature bursting forth without any arrangement, like the flowers and thorns of his own wilderness. A creature of impulse seldom actuated by reflection, the black man astounds by his complete obtuseness, and as suddenly confounds you by an unexpected exhibition of sympathy. From a long experience with African savages, I think it as absurd to condemn the negro in toto, as it is preposterous to compare his intellectual capacity with that of the white man.

It is unfortunately the fashion for one party to uphold the negro as a superior being, while the other denies him the common powers of reason. So great a difference of opinion has ever existed upon the intrinsic value of the negro, that the very perplexity of the question is a proof that he is altogether a distinct variety.

So long as it is generally considered that the negro and the white man are to be governed by the same laws and guided by the same management, so long will the former remain a thorn in the side of every community to which he may unhappily belong. When the horse and the ass shall be found to match in double harness, the white man and the African black will pull together under the same regime. It is the grand error of equalizing that which is unequal that has lowered the negro character, and made the black man a reproach.

In his savage home, what is the African? Certainly bad: but not so bad as white men would (I believe) be under similar circumstances. He is acted upon by the bad passions inherent in human nature, but there is no exaggerated vice, such as is found in civilized countries.

The strong takes from the weak, one tribe fights the other—do not we perhaps in Europe? These are the legitimate acts of independent tribes, authorized by their Chiefs. They mutually enslave each other. How long is it since America and we ourselves ceased to be slaveholders? He is callous and ungrateful. In Europe is there no ingratitude? He is cunning and a liar by nature. In Europe is all truth and sincerity? Why should not the black man be equal to the white? He is as powerful in frame, why should he not be as exalted in mind?

In childhood I believe the negro to be in advance in intellectual quickness, of the white child of a similar age, but the mind does not expand. It promises fruit, but does not ripen; and the negro man has grown in body, but has not advanced in intellect.

The puppy of three months old is superior in intellect to a child of the same age, but the mind of the child expands, while that of the dog has arrived at its limit. The chicken of the common fowl has sufficient power and instinct to run in search of food the moment that it leaves the egg, while the young of the eagle lies helpless in its nest; but the young eagle outstrips the chicken in the course of time.

The earth presents a wonderful example of variety in all classes of the human race, the animal, and vegetable kingdoms. People, beasts, and plants belonging to distinct classes, exhibit special qualities and peculiarities. The existence of many hundred varieties of dogs cannot interfere with the fact that they belong to one genus: the greyhound, pug, bloodhound, pointer, poodle, mastiff and toy terrier are all as entirely different in their peculiar instincts as are the varieties of the human race. The different fruits and flowers continue the example ; the wild grapes of the forest are grapes, but although they belong to the same class they are distinct from the luscious "Muscatel;" and the wild dog-rose of the hedge, although of the same class, is inferior to the moss-rose of the garden. From fruits and flowers we may turn to insect life, and watch the air teeming with varieties of the same species; the thousands of butterflies and beetles, the many members of each class varying in instincts and peculiarities. Fishes, and even

11

shell-fish, all exhibit the same arrangement, that every group is divided into varieties all differing from each other, and each distinguished by some peculiar excellence or defect.

In the great system of creation that divided races and subdivided them according to mysterious laws, apportioning special qualities to each, the varieties of the human race exhibit certain characteristics and qualifications which adapt them for specific localities. The natural character of those races will not alter with a change of locality, but the instincts of each race will be developed in any country where they may be located. Thus the English are as English in Australia, India, and America, as they are in England, and in every locality they exhibit the industry and energy of their native land; even so the African will remain negro in all his natural instincts, although transplanted to other soils; and those natural instincts being a love of idleness and savagedom, he will assuredly relapse into an idle and savage state, unless specially governed and forced to industry.

The history of the negro has proved the correctness of this theory. In no instance has he evinced other than a retrogression when once freed from restraint. Like a horse without harness, he runs wild, but, if harnessed, no animal is more useful. Unfortunately this is contrary to public opinion in England where the vox populi assumes the right of dictation upon matters and men in which it has no experience. The English insist upon their own weights and measures as the scales of human excellence, and it has been decreed by the multitude, inexperienced in the negro personally, that he has been a badly treated brother; that he is a worthy member of the human family, placed in an inferior position through the prejudice and ignorance of the white man, with whom he should be upon equality.

The negro has been and still is, thoroughly misunderstood. However severely we may condemn the horrible system of slavery the results of emancipation have proven that the negro does not appreciate the blessings of freedom, nor does he show the slightest feeling of gratitude to the hand that broke the rivets of his fetters.

His narrow mind cannot embrace that feeling of pure philanthropy that first prompted England to declare herself against slavery, and he only regards the anti-slavery movement as a proof of his own importance. In his limited horizon he is himself the important object, and as a sequence to his self conceit, he imagines that the whole world is at issue concerning the black man. The negro, therefore, being the important question, must be an important person, and he conducted himself accordingly; he is far too great a man to work. Upon this point his natural character exhibits itself most determinedly. Accordingly he resists any attempt at coercion. Being free, his first impulse is to claim an equality with those whom he lately served, and to usurp a dignity with absurd pretensions, that must inevitably insure the disgust of the white community. Ill-will thus engendered, a hatred and jealousy is established between the two races, combined with the errors that in such conditions must arise upon both sides. The final question remains, Why was the negro first introduced into our colonies, and to America?

The sun is the great arbitrator between the white and the black man. There are productions necessary to civilized countries, that can alone be cultivated in tropical climates where the white man cannot live if exposed to labor in the sun. Thus, such fertile countries as the West Indies and portions of America being without a native population, the negro was originally imported as a slave to fulfil the conditions of a laborer. In his own country he was a wild savage, and enslaved his brother man; he thus became a victim to his own system; to the institution of slavery that is indigenous to the soil of Africa, and that has not been taught to the African by the white man, as is currently reported, but that has ever been the peculiar characteristic of African tribes.

In his state of slavery the negro was compelled to work, and through his labor, every country prospered where he had been introduced. He was suddenly freed; and from that moment he refused to work, and instead of being a useful member of society, he not only became a useless burden to the community, but a plotter and intriguer, imbued with a deadly hatred to the white man who had generously declared him free.

Now, as the negro was originally imported as a laborer, but now refuses to labor, it is self—evident that he is a lamentable failure. Either he must be compelled to work, by some stringent law against vagrancy, or those beautiful countries that prospered under the conditions of negro forced industry must yield to ruin under negro freedom and idle independence. For an example of the results look to St. Domingo!

Under peculiar guidance, and subject to a certain restraint, the negro may be an important and most useful being; but if treated as an Englishman, he will affect the vices but none of the virtues of civilization, and his natural good qualities will be lost in his attempts to become a "white man."

———

We are satisfied that the description of the immoral condition of the colored people in the South, as given by the Rev. J. L. Tucker, D. D., in his published speech upon the subject, is substantially correct.

J. N. CARPENTER,
JOHN RAWLE,
A. W. RAWLINGS,
GEO. W. KOONTZ,
Natchez, Miss.
J. B. T. THORNTON,
Yazoo City, Miss.

———

The following send their names as endorsing the statements of the speech. T. T. LAND,
Member of the Shreveport Bar, and Ex. Judge of the
Supreme Court of Louisiana.
J. C. MONCURE,
Judge of Court of Appeals, Shreveport, La.
J. LEWIS JAYTON,
District Judge, Shreveport, La.
J. S. JOHNSON,
Rector of Trinity Church, Mobile, Ala.
JNO. B. LINN,
Rector of St. John's Church, Corsicana, Texas.

In illustration of the difficulty of working for and with the negro race. I append the following resolutions passed by a meeting of colored people held on the 25th of January. They probably contain all that can be said against my statements and are valuable for that reason. I sincerely wish I could believe the resolutions true and myself mistaken; no one would more heartily rejoice than I should at proof to that effect:

Whereas, In a speech upon the "Relations of the Church to the Colored Race," delivered by the Rev. J. L. Tucker, of Jackson, Miss., before the Church Congress at Richmond, Va., October, 1882, certain statements as to the intellectual and moral condition of the colored people were made, and these were of a character so sensational and misleading, that the speech was cut short in the Congress, and not heard to the end, and the local newspapers and the religious press, in different places North contradicted the truth of the representations made in said speech, and severely criticised the same as being unjust and without foundation in fact; and,

Whereas, Since the adjournment of the Church Congress, the Rev. J. L. Tucker, has had published a pamphlet, setting forth what he intended to say, as his speech to the Congress, enlarging the original speech, and adding an "Appeal" thereto, and has distributed this pamphlet, asking that the names of both white and colored men of prominence be given him, as endorsing the extraordinary assertions made therein by him in reference to the colored race; and,

Whereas, This pamphlet, in our judgment, contains charges and declarations against the colored race that demand answer, denial and condemnation in a public manner; therefore, be it

Resolved, By the citizens of Jackson, Miss., in mass meeting assembled, That the speech of Rev. J. L. Tucker, as delivered and as explained and published in pamphlet form, contains assertions and statements in regard to the moral condition of the colored people that have no foundation elsewhere than in the prurient imagination of their author.

Resolved, further, That the representations as set forth by Rev. J. L. Tucker, in said speech and pamphlet touching the domestic, religious and public customs and habits of the colored people, are grossly malicious and utterly at variance with the true condition of the affairs of the race, either South or North, as they now are or have been heretofore.

Resolved, further, That a minister of the gospel who has the brazen effrontery to insult the intelligence of his fellow men by

such statements as ' That out of 500 negro families only a few
dozen are legally married;" "That the proportion of marriage
licenses issued in a Mississippi county (where the colored people
are in the majority) were as 300 for white to 3 for colored marriages;" "That the negroes will steal from each other while at prayer
in church;" "That the freedmen steal and kill more cattle in one
year than was lost or destroyed during the late civil war;" "That
they lie from instinct," and more of the same sort.   That such a
minister justly merits the contempt of those whom he has tra-
duced, and we thank with heartfelt sincerity the "two or three
Southern clergy who spoke good words in our defense, at the time
these slanders were uttered.

Resolved, further, That it is with regret we acknowledge having in
the past accepted the Pharisaical teachings of one whom we
thought was a true friend to the youth of our race; one that we
hoped was rigorously following in the footsteps and continuing the
good work founded and fostered in Saint Andrew's Church for
their benefit by his revered and lamented predecessor; and we feel
that we have been "betrayed in the house of our friends" simply
to gratify the desire for notoriety of one who is ambitious to "pose"
before the public in the character of a reformer, with views
unique and methods sensational.

Resolved, further, That a copy of these resolutions be forwarded
to the "Northern Bishops and Clergy," and to every colored newspaper in the country, and that the papers of our State be re-
quested to publish them as the sentiments of the colored people and their white friends in this community.

There were present at this "mass meeting" about fifty men, the
rest being women and children.   This pamphlet had not then been
published and but three or four of those present had any idea of
what the speech really was.

A few weeks later the following was handed me for publication :

We, the undersigned, colored citizens of Jackson, have seen with
regret the action of a meeting of colored people in this city, attacking with virulence the address of the Rev. Dr. Tucker on the
relations of the church to the colored race.   We think that meeting did great injustice to him and to our race, in being led by passion rather than by reason.   We are agreed as to the following
statements.

1st. We regard Dr. Tucker as a friend to our race; one who
from the standpoint of Christian philanthropy, has spoken the
truth in an effort to arouse the Christians of the whole country to

the magnitude of the work demanded of the Church. We recognize in his speech a careful essay having but one object, viz: the welfare of the colored race; and we see in the plan proposed an intelligent system whose successful operation would result in great good to our people.

2d. While vice and immorality exist in all races and while the sins described in the address are quite common among the white people, yet it is not surprising that they should be more common with the masses of our race, when our youthfulness in freedom is considered. We regard the speech as, in truth, a defense of our people concerning their present condition, as well as an effort to better that condition. We understand it to be general in its application, and to recognize and thank God for those exceptions among us, who are alive to our situation and are struggling hard to better it. We therefore thank our friend for his humane and unselfish effort to obtain help for us from the North, as we thank him for all his labor in the past.

3d. We concur fully in the suggestion that Southern white men, of standing and influence, be entrusted with the guidance and direction of any work begun for us. We know them and can trust them as we could not trust strangers, and they know us; and as citizens in the same community, are interested in our welfare and improvement.

MARCH WILLIAMS,	EDWARD HICKS,
SAMUEL HILL,	WILLIAM LEWIS,
PETER DUNBAR,	OLIVER SAN FRANCISCO,
WILLIAM MYERS,	RICHARD BROOKS,
JOHN BRANDON,	SIMMONS GILES,
ABRAM ROBINSON,	BENJAMIN GOODLOE,

LONDON JACKSON, JOSEPH AILS, ROBERT AUSTIN.

Over fifty names are in my possession to add to the above, and others are being handed in daily.

I add to the foregoing an article taken from the *Richmond Whig*, of Dec. 1st.

LET US BE JUST.—The Rev. Mr. Tucker, of Mississippi, has become rather a famous man, not as a member of the Episcopal clergy, but as one of that class who are still asking "Can there any good thing come out of Nazareth?"—that prejudiced class who still are doubting the virtue dwelling in the lowly. It was he who boldly, in the Episcopal Congress in Richmond, characterized the negro race as "liars, thieves and adulterers." If all men are liars, then, too, is the negro; but if there be truth, the heart of the negro holds it as well as the white. If there be honesty, the white man has no monopoly of it. As for adultery, oh! ye gods,

that the white man should have the audacity to point the finger
of scorn at any race!   And this, too, from a Southerner who
knows that the South went to battle strong in the knowledge that
the chastity of its wives and daughters would find protectors and
not seducers in the faithful slaves around them—those downtrodden slaves whose wives and daughters must yield though all
unwilling, to the lustful passions of their masters.   Pray who has
filled the land with unmarried mothers and illegitimate mulatto
children?   The white man—who knows no law save self-indul-
gence, no continence save satiety; who sees in weak chastity not
something to be sustained and upheld by his example and precept, but to be brought low from its high though frail estate to
minister at whatever cost to his selfish pleasure; who considers
himself justifiable in tempting any woman who will listen to the
voice of the tempter, whether through blind love or gaunt starva-
tion, or through passion like unto his own; who knows no self-con-
trol, no s lf-respect, and therefore no honor, for weak or unpro-
tected woman.

Ah! one among ten thousand only is there who is true to himself, and therefore true to all womanhood, whether strong or weak
whether high or low; but he is found quite as often among the despised negro race as among the arrogant white.   I wonder the negro does not long for its oppressor, its seducer, to be but "one
head that it may be struck off at a single blow;" but this is a patient, tender-hearted, long-suffering people, whose day cometh
slowly.   As for its women, the highest types of womanhood I have
found among this people—not for culture, but for moral worth;
the most honest, the most christian, the most chaste under foulest
temptation.   Are there many among them, alas! *so many* fallen
now?   And why ?   Because it is found that honest wages for
honest work is but a shadow, and that the only commodity that
will sell at all times and under all circumstances is woman's virtue;
that for this, and this alone, lustful man will pay.   The mother
once seduced, ruined, deserted, her moral faculties benumbed and
deadened, how can the daughter be otherwise?   Truly adultery
and seduction do stalk through the land at this the noonday of
our civilization and no man bids them halt.   For the polygamy of
the West we may indeed frame laws, but the terrible blight of
the East holds unmolested sway.   But when Mr. Tucker speaks
of "adultery, fornication, and all uncleanness," let him look his
own race straight in the face and say "thou art the man."   Let
him preach the gospel of continence, purity, chastity, and when
he can persuade his own race to follow this ideal he will not find
the negro slow to follow where virtue leads.   And when men,
high and low, rich and poor, young and old, married and unmar-

ried, have accepted and fashioned their lives upon this model and up to this standard, then will this be a goodly land; then, and not until then, will men be worthy the boasted name of "woman's protector;" then, and not until then, will the sins of the father be lifted from the children; and then, ah! then shall "sorrow and sighing flee away." I. G.

———

I call attention to the fact that the assertions I have made with regard to the negro race, are virtually admitted to be true in the above article, written, as I understand, by a negro, while the whole blame is thrown upon the white race. That some measure of blame is undoubtedly the just due of individuals among the white race no one will deny, yet to refute the sweeping nature of this negro's condemnation it is only necessary to ask two questions:

"Suppose there had been no slavery and that the negroes in this country had remained in Africa, what would have been their condition?"

"If the negroes now in this country are .in a better condition and have a better future before them than the negroes in Africa, to what domestic institution, to what race, and to what portion of that race do they owe this advancement?"

And I would like to add———

"Had there been no slavery whose head would you desire to cut off in revenge for being native and naked African savages?"

I quote this negro's "Let us be just," and urge that the justice be not one sided. In this article mention is made of the fidelity of the slaves during the war, as if that had been a peculiar evidence of race virtue. Also, one of the speakers at the Church Congress alluded to it as if in some way it refuted my statements regarding their moral condition. Let us therefore be exactly just as regards this also. All Southern men recognize the docility and kindly feeling which led the negroes to remain quietly at home while their masters were away during the war; and they also recognize that no white race or red race would have been thus easily controlled. Yet both the masters and the slaves knew that an insurrection would have been perfectly hopeless. There were few parts of the South where the sound of the cannon was not heard.

12

Every little town had its Provost Marshal and guard. There were soldiers and armed men and occasional bodies of Cavalry everywhere. Had the negroes been disposed to rise they would not have dared to do so from the display of force on every side, knowledge of which spread by rumor to the remotest plantations. Had such a rising occurred, it would have been remorselessly and instantly crushed. The negroes were not armed and could have made no resistance whatever. The negroes knew this; and both the fact and the knowledge of the fact should be taken into consideration by any one who aims to be "just." The white men went away without an atom of fear for their families; and this confidence was founded in knowledge of the negro character, intimate knowledge of particular negroes, confidence in the affection of their servants, and confidence in their own strength.

Why this should prevent us from telling the truth about the present moral condition of the negroes, in order to awaken the nation, or a part of it, to the duty we owe that race, I do not comprehend. But it is easy to raise a false issue and fight over that rather than the true one.

———

In closing this pamphlet and giving it to the public I have a few final words to say.

When I spoke in Richmond I had no conception of the stir that would be created by my brief address of only twenty minutes. The severity of criticism and the overwhelming volume of correspondence which poured in upon me, forced me to the step I have taken in publishing this pamphlet. It seemed to me that the devil himself entered the lists and measured swords with me, determined to defeat any effort to shake his hold upon the negro race. I was not aware, before, how much abuse could be heaped upon one man, not a politician or candidate for office, whose sole object was the good of others; nor was I aware how such abuse could hurt. I notice one conspicuous fact, that among all the attacks and denials that have reached me, not one of my critics undertakes to furnish proof that I am wrong. I suppose it is the devil's method of combat, to throw dust and obscure the main issue.

I am Rector of a fairly prosperous white parish, and there is no obligation that I know of resting upon me more than upon other Southern men, to labor for the negroes. It is a hard and difficult work in itself, and is made doubly so by the suspicions of the negroes and the cavils and criticisms which the devil stirs up from the white race. The difficulties are so many and so great that but few Southern people have had the courage to engage directly in the work of teaching colored schools or classes, and still fewer to persevere in the work when once engaged. For myself I have only to drop my own Mission work to have a large accession of peace and comfort. If I could reconcile it with a sense of duty I would gladly dismiss our colored scholars, close our Mission, and leave the colored people to shift for themselves so far as I am concerned. My experience has been such that I would hesitate a long time before beginning a similar work in any fresh place. I cannot, however, undo what has been done, nor throw off the negro families who look to me as their leader, guide and friend; nor do I think it right to destroy the opening which exists here for greater things. But I want it to be understood that I and my parish are perfectly independent in the matter. Our mission will go on, no matter who likes or dislikes, as long as the colored people come to be taught. Should they stay away so that we can be blameless for closing the Mission, it is an open question as to who would regret it least. To do any greater things we need help We cannot make our Church into a cathedral and open a transept for the colored people, or build schools for them, without money and a good deal of it. If any one asks the direct question, "Do you desire to do this?" we must answer candidly, "For our own sakes, no; for Christ's sake, yes." To those who can understand this mixture of motives and who desire to aid, we extend a hearty welcome. But we want no man's money who has any doubts about our opinions, our methods, our motives, or ourselves.

J. L. TUCKER,
Rector of St. Andrew's Church,
Jackson, Mississippi.

THE NEGRO AMERICAN CITIZEN IN THE
NEW AMERICAN LIFE.

BY REV. A. D. MAYO, A. M.

During the past ten years of a Ministry of Education among the Southern people in all the Southern States, I have been often challenged to formulate my opinion concerning the present condition and future outcome of the Negro. My invariable answer is: I have come to this portion of the country as an out-and-out advocate of the universal education of the heart, the head, and the hand possible for all orders and conditions of the American people. I believe the Christian religion, as it lay in the mind and shone forth in the speech and life of the great Teacher and Saviour of man, includes this idea of education. All the progress this world has seen out of old pagan conditions of race, caste, society, and government, has been the work of this mighty regenerating influence. I hold it the deadliest treason and revolt against the Christian civilization, a backing down into paganism, or a worse lapse into the Slough of Despond of absolute atheism and secularism, to impeach the power of this divine agency to cure all our American ills.

I began my present Ministry of Education ten years ago, in the Southern States, in full faith in this gospel of the reconstruction of the whole republic from "the remainder of wrath" that still vexes its progress and looms like a black despair over its least advanced portion. And, although I cannot pretend to have converted or convinced anybody, I have seen with what an uplifting of the soul the better sort of the Southern people welcome any man who, in honesty of purpose, love of country and of all his countrymen, endeavors to get down to the bottom facts of the situation, with a just appreciation of the position of all true men, and with an invincible hope and a holy obstinacy in standing by the bright side of God's providence in American affairs. The fact that one man can go through all these States, among all classes, everywhere testifying to the grandeur of the full American idea, and urging the people to live up to the vision of the Fathers, with all but universal acceptation, so that the discords in this ministry have hardly been enough to emphasize the harmonies, is to me an assurance that the same line of work, assumed by a greater man, and finally adopted by the influential classes of our people, will shape the highway out of the present complications.

My only recipe for the solution of all these problems that still divide the country is the putting on of that judicial and resolute Christian attitude of mind that insists on looking at all the facts of the case, setting them in their proper relations, all the time searching for the elements of progress which are the vital centres. It seems to me that a great portion of the misunderstanding and conflict, at present, is the result of a practical inability in the masses of the people to rise to this position and the mischievous pertinacity of too many leaders of public opinion everywhere, in keeping the national mind engrossed with the temporary and unessential facts of the case. With no disposition to misrepresent or misunderstand anybody, I respond to your call to tell my experience as an observer of the Southern situation, especially as it concerns the Negro citizen in the sixteen Southern States of the Union, as I have seen him during a virtual residence in these States for ten years past.

It would seem that thoughtful Christian people might at least endeavor to realize the simple gospel rule of "doing as they would be done by" in the judgment of each other, in an affair so momentous, where mistakes are fraught with such mournful possibilities as in this great discussion. It is easy to see how much of the difficulty comes from this inability to "put one's self in the place" of his opponent.

Would it not be possible for a larger number of our foremost Southern leaders, in Church, State, and society, to try to appreciate the motives and temper of the loyal people of the North in the great act of conferring full American citizenship on the Negro, after his emancipation, twenty-five years ago? I do not defend any injustice, tyranny, reckless experimenting with government itself, that followed that act. No thoughtful man defends such things to-day. But I do hold that no true conception of this matter can be had by any man who honestly believes that this exaltation of the Negro to full American citizenship was either an act of sectional revenge, a narrow and ferocious partisan policy or the reckless experiment of an excited sentimentalism. If ever a people, in a great national emergency, acted under a solemn sense of responsibility to God, humanity, patriotism, and republican institutions, I believe the conviction of the loyal Northern people, that shaped the acts of reconstruction, is entitled to this judgment, and will so abide in history. It was the most memorable testimony of a national government, just rescued from desperate peril, solemnized by the death of its venerated leader, to its faith in popular institutions, recorded in the annals of mankind.

But it must be acknowledged that the very nobility of the act that conferred the highest earthly distinction of full American citizenship on a nation of newly emancipated slaves, of an alien race, involved the penalty of great injustice to its object. It was inevitable that the nation, having committed itself to this daring experiment, would watch its success from an ideal point of observation. So, for the past twenty years, one misfortune of the Negro citizen has been that the portion of the country that won his freedom and lifted him to this proud eminence could do no otherwise than judge him out of its own lofty expectation, piecing out its almost complete ignorance of any similar people or situation by repeated drafts on a boundless hope, an almost childlike trust, and a deep religious faith, proven by the cheerful giving of fifty millions of dollars and the sacrifice of the service of noble men and women of priceless value, in the effort to realize the great expectation of the nation.

Again, is it more than plain justice that the leading mind of the loyal North, that saved the Union to nationality and freedom in 1865, should endeavor to represent to itself the actual point of view of the Southern people concerning this act of reconstruction, then, and, to a great extent, in the present time? I know that the most painful lesson of history is the difficulty of such comprehension of an aristocratic form of society by a people for a century trained in the school of a proud and successful democracy. Not one educated man in a thousand in the United States can put himself in the place of one of the great Tory leaders or scholars of Great Britain, or listen with anything but impatience to the account that any European government or the Catholic Church can give of itself. How much more difficult for the average New England or Western citizen to understand the attitude of mind with which an old Southern planter or a modern Southern politician must contemplate this sudden and portentous upheaving of five millions of freedmen to the complete endowment of American citizenship at the close of the great war.

For, surely, at first sight, no body of five millions of people could be imagined less qualified by its past to justify such expectations than the Negro freedmen. Three hundred years ago the Negro was a pagan savage, inhabiting a continent still dark with the shadow of an unrecorded past. A hundred years ago the ancestors perhaps of a majority of the seven millions of Negroes now in the United States were in the same condition. Of no people on the face of the earth is so little known to-day as of the African ancestors of the American Negro. Of various tribes, nationalities, and characteristics, perhaps with an ancestry as varied as the present inhabitants of the European nationalities, these people were cast into a state of slavery which confounded all previous conditions, and only recognized the native ability of each man or woman in "the survival of the fittest," in the struggle for existence on the plantation and in the household.

Once more: it has never been realized by the loyal North, what is evident to every intelligent Southern man, what a prodigious change had been wrought in this people during its years of bondage, and how, without the schooling of this era, the subsequent elevation of the emancipated slave to full American citizenship would have been an impossibility. During this brief period of tutelage, briefest of all compared with any European race, the Negro was sheltered from the three furies of the prayer book,— sword, pestilence, and famine,— was brought into contact with the upper strata of the most powerful of civilized peoples, in a republic, amid the trials, sacrifices, and educating influences of a new country, in the opening years of "the grand and awful time" in which our lot is cast. In that condition, he learned the three great elements of civilization more speedily than they were ever learned before. He learned to work. He acquired the language and adopted the religion of the most progressive of peoples. Gifted with a marvellous aptitude for such schooling, he was found, in 1865, further "out of the woods" of barbarism than any other people at the end of a thousand years. The American Indian, in his proud isolation, repelled all these beneficent changes; and to-day the entire philanthropy, religion, and statesmanship of the republic are wrestling with the problem of saving him from the fate of the buffalo.

I find only in the broad-minded and most charitable leaders of our Northern affairs any real understanding of the inevitable habit of mind which the average Southern citizen brings to the contemplation of the actual condition or possibilities of the Negro American citizen. With a personal attachment to the Negro greater than is possible for the people of the North; with habits of forbearance and patient waiting on the infirmities, vices, and shortcomings of this people, which to the North are unaccountable and well-nigh impossible of imitation; with the general willingness to co-operate, as far as the comfort and the personal prosperity of its old slaves are concerned,— is it strange that this act of statesmanship should appear to him as the wildest and most reckless experiment in the annals of national life? Even the most intelligent and conservative parent finds it difficult to believe his beloved child is competent to the duties of manhood or womanhood, and only with a pang does he see the dear boy or girl launch out on the stormy ocean of life. What, then, would be the inevitable feeling of the dominant Southern class, to whom the Negro had only been known as a savage slowly evolving into the humbler strata of civilization, as a dependent chattel, when, at the end of a frightful war, it found itself in a state of civil subjugation to its old bondmen? No subject race ever reveals its highest aspirations and aptitudes to its master race; and it is not remarkable that only the most observing and broad-minded of the Southern people, even yet, heartily believe in the capacity of the Negro for civil, social, or industrial co-operation with any of the European peoples.

Now, say what we will, this obstinate inability and sometimes unwillingness to put one's self in the place of the opposition has been the most hopeless feature of the case, the real "chasm" between the leading mind of the North and the South. So to-day, while even partisan politics seems to pause in uncertainty on the steep edge of a dark abyss, when noble and humane people all over the country seem to be falling into despondency, when an ominous twilight, threatening a storm, is peopled by all the birds of ill omen, and "the hearts of men are shaken with fear," I am glad that we have been summoned here to look things squarely in the face, to bring a varied experience to bear on a new and more careful consideration of the whole matter, and by the guidance of a Christian insight endeavor to see the hopeful elements of the situation. We do not need to rehearse our separate knowledge of the shadow side of the new South. The shadows we have always with us, everywhere. But, if we can locate the centre of the new "Sunny South," we may go home with the conviction that, while the shadows in human affairs are always on the move, the sun shines on forever, and is bound to bring in God's final day of light.

The pivotal question on which this vast problem turns is, Has the Negro, in his American experience, demonstrated a capacity for self-developing American citizenship? I leave out of the estimate, at present, the exceptional people of the race, and look for the answer to the average Negro, as I see him in the Southern States. For I suppose nobody believes that full American citizenship is possible, as the permanent condition of any people destitute of this capacity for self-dependent manhood and womanhood. The child race must be cared for by a paternal organization of society, and that element of paternalism is just what every good American citizen declares he will not have in his government. In lieu of that, an extemporized or permanent social public opinion, or an unwritten law, will take its place and do its work.

If the Negro, as so many Southern people believe, is only a perpetual child, capable of a great deal that is useful and interesting, but destitute of the capacity for "the one thing needful" that lifts the subject of paternal up to the citizen of a republican government, then the thing to do is to leave him to the care of his superiors in the South, who certainly know this side of him far better than the people of the North, and, whatever mistakes on the side of occasional severity may be made, will, in the end, do the best for his permanent estate. In fact, nothing seems more evident to me than the practical inability of the national government to essentially change the status of its seven millions of Negro citizens, except through national aid to education. There is no power at Washington that can hold up, for a series of generations, any people in the permanent state of illiteracy in which the majority of the Southern Negroes are at present found. This illiteracy is simply a mixture of ignorance, superstition, shiftlessness, vulgarity, and vice. The general and State governments, aided all the while by private benevolence and missionary zeal, can surround these people with an environment of valuable opportunities. Indeed, in many respects, they are now environed with such helps and encouragements as no race, of European lineage, has enjoyed at a similar stage of its history. But the test question is, Has the Negro, on the whole, during his entire life of three hundred years on American soil, indicated his power to appreciate and use such opportunities for full American citizenship as are now vouchsafed to him by a gracious Providence?

To my mind he had vindicated his capacity for indefinite improvement in this direction even before he received the precious boon of citizenship of the American republic. Remarkable as his progress, in some ways, has been during the past twenty-five years of freedom, I would be content to refer to his two centuries of slavery for proof of a remarkable aptitude for civilization. The best evidence for such capacity is a certain unconscious tact, a habit of getting on in a tolerable way under unfavorable circumstances, the turning his sunny and adaptive side to a hard bondage, the eager adaptation to and taking on of all helps to a better state of living. Contemplate, for a moment, this people, landing from an African slave-ship on our shores. Contrast the status of the American Negro, with all his imperfections, in 1865, when he appeared, the last comer that has stepped over the threshold of the higher civilization and begun the upward career. How can that amazing progress in practical ability, in adaptation to the habits and manners of civilized life, reception of a Christian faith, be accounted for on the theory of perpetual childishness, as a race characteristic? Did any people, under a similar strain, realizing, as the Negro did, the awful issues of the mighty Civil War amid which his closing years of servitude were involved, ever bear itself with such personal fidelity to present duty, with such remarkable wisdom and tact, with such complete reliance on Providence for the result?

Bishop Haygood says the religion of the Negro accounts for his bearing during these tremendous years, when the home life of the South was virtually in his hands. That a race, less than two centuries out of the jungle of African paganism, was found so imbued with the central element of Christianity, is evidence that it is not the perpetual child of humanity. Grant the failure of the Negro, during the fearful years that followed the war, to govern States rocking in the throes of a defeated rebellion, exasperated to the death by all the passions that wreck the souls of men and communities. Still, what a display of ability of many sorts, the practical faculty of getting a living, often the higher faculty that has thrown up thousands of shrewd, successful people, there was! Radical that he is, the Negro has shown himself the most politic of peoples in his endurance of what could not be overcome, and his tactful, even crafty, appropriation of all opportunities. He has pushed in at every open door, listened at the white man's table, hung about church and the stump, taken in the great public day, looked on when he did not vote at the election. He has been all eyes and ears, and every pore of his skin has been open to the incoming of his only possible education. Deprived of books and the ordinary apparatus of instruction, he has used all the more eagerly the agencies of God's supreme University, human life,—used them so much better than several millions of "the superior race" that, in proportion to his opportunity, he has made more out of the Southern American life than any other Southern people.

On the eve of the day when the great assembly of Confederate veterans at Richmond solemnly buried their old cause in the unveiling of the statue of their great military commander, I sat on a platform, before a crowded congregation of Negro citizens, in the city of Washington, gathered at the commencement exercises of Wayland Seminary. Eighteen young men and women, all from Virginia, received the diploma; and ten of them appeared in the usual way. As I looked over that audience of well-dressed, well-mannered, appreciative people, and listened to the speeches of those young folk, so marked by sobriety of style, soundness of thought, practical views of life, lofty consecration of purpose, and comprehensive patriotism; as I read their class motto, "Not to be ministered unto, but to minister," and remembered that, only two hundred and seventy years ago, the first cargo of African pagan savages was landed on the shore of the Old Dominion, and all this was the outcome of that,— I wondered where were the eyes of men that they did not behold the revelation of Divine Providence in this little less than the miraculous evolution of the new citizenship of a State destined yet to praise and magnify the ways of God in American affairs. Say that this only demonstrates his "power of imitation." But what is this mysterious faculty of "imitation," that everybody says the Negro has to the last degree, but another name for a capacity for civilization? Nine-tenths of our human education is imitating what a superior person does, from the child repeating its mother's words to the saint "putting on the Lord Jesus Christ."

It may be granted that, in one respect, slavery was a help to this progress. It protected the Negro from his lower self, on the side of vagrancy; and that is "the terrible temptation" of every people in its rudimentary years. He was protected against vagrancy, laziness, drunkenness, and several temptations of a semi-tropical clime which are too much for thousands of his betters. But here has been a sore obstacle to his success in his new estate of freedom. A great wrong that has been done him during these years has been the neglect to enforce order, decency, and industry, along with the observance of the common moralities of every-day life, by the people among whom he has lived. What would be the condition of New England to-day, had her people tolerated, in the multitudes of foreign-born peasants who have landed on her shores, the vagrancy, laziness, shiftlessness, dependence on common charity, with the perpetual violation of the minor morals, which confront the observer, from every part of the civilized world, in his travels throughout the Southern States? Here was the place for the Anglo-Saxon to assert his superiority, by insisting on the common observance of the common order, decencies, and moralities of life, in and out of the household, by the freedman. For lack of this, the vagrant class has been left virtually at large, like a plague of frogs and lice over all the land, choking up the towns and villages, making good housekeeping, for the Southern woman, the most trying human lot, and surrounding childhood, of every condition and class, with such temptations as no people can permanently resist.

If the well-disposed class, the majority, could have been aided by the law of the land and public opinion to move on unhindered by this intolerable impediment, the last twenty-five years would have told a far different tale. Of course, the white people of the South do not realize this. Slavery was a police that made vagrancy impossible, and the lower slave element was securely locked up under the Argus eyes of the old-time system of labor. I am not here to defend any denial of the suffrage, or social or industrial disability, inflicted on the Negro citizen; but I give it as my deliberate conviction that all these things have not been so harmful to the Negro as this strange neglect of the Anglo-Saxon South to enforce the recognized policy of all civilized lands on its vagrant colored and white class, at the very time when this race specially needed the primary lessons of sobriety, obedience to law, every-day morality, and of that hard work without which "no man shall eat." Yet, spite of this drawback (and only an observer from a differently regulated community can appreciate what a drawback), the better-disposed class of the Negroes has signally vindicated its capacity for civilization within the limitations of personal and race impediments, and in the use it has made of its opportunities.

I observe, also, in the average Negro, an amiability, a patience and forbearance, a capacity for affectionate devotion, sacrifice, and unselfishness, that separate him decisively from the savage and the savage side of civilized life. What an element of civil, social, and industrial lubrication this may become, has already become, in our grating, pitiless, ferocious Anglo-Saxon greed of power, gain, and all kinds of superiority, any man can realize who sees the working of it in a thousand ways. I can understand why the Southerner feels a certain loneliness amid the splendors and well-ordered regulations of our higher Northern life. He misses the atmosphere of kindliness, broad good-humor, real belief in human nature, that the Negro always diffuses around himself. I feel it the moment I touch a Northern city on my return from every annual visit to the South; and I thank God that the Negro "man and brother," especially the woman and sister, were sent by heaven to teach our proud, restless, too often inhuman civilization some of the amenities that outlive the inhumanities and finally bring in the kingdom of God.

Another quality the Negro displays, of great promise in the future, though so often turned to his disadvantage in the present,— a love of approbation, self-possession, and an ability to "put his best foot foremost" and show for all he is worth, the perpetual assertion that he is going to be somebody some time. "Why did you sell that corn you promised to me?" said a white parson to his Negro "brother in the ministry." "Well, boss, I got a bigger price for it." "But was that honest?" "No, it warn't that." "Why did you do it?" "Because, boss, I warn't the man I took myself to be."

It is well to "take yourself to be" a man of parts and character, even at the peril of disappointment. And that persistent pushing to the front, crowding in at every open door, "claiming the earth," which now makes the life of the most sensible and considerate white citizen of the South often a weariness, sometimes a despair, in his dealing with the Negro, is the prophecy of an aspiration for better things and a loftiness of manhood and womanhood of vital importance.

Along with this is the eagerness for knowledge, that is still a characteristic even of the ignorant classes, though less apparent now than in the years following the war. Spite of the neglect of the proper conditions and the means of gaining this precious boon for the children, the average Negro, in humble estate, believes in the school with a vigor that in the lower European classes is not developed, more than in the corresponding class among the Southern whites. Discontent with a low estate is the movement power of American civilization, and no class in America is less content with its own infirmities than the better sort, the majority of the freedmen.

Another valuable characteristic is the good taste, love of beauty, native capacity for ornamental art, which always appear in the Negro, when suitably encouraged. The handwriting in the colored schools is often remarkable, the drawing uniformly respectable, the taste in dress, the arrangement of flowers and ornaments, above the average of any corresponding class in the country. In the Negro, the new South has its most valuable deposit of "raw material" for the best operative and mechanical class for that clime and country. Already he is domesticated in all these mechanical and operative industries, with the exception of the cotton mills, where the labor is still monopolized by the poorer white class, greatly to its own advantage. Here is a great work being done by the numerous mission schools, of the higher sort, supported by the Christian people of the North, in the organization of industrial education. In this important branch of schooling, the superior class of Negro youth has, so far, enjoyed greater opportunities than the corresponding class of white youth. And, although the graduates of these schools will not be day laborers or servants, yet, as teachers, housekeepers, and general leaders of their people, they will exert a prodigious influence in the years to come. The introduction of a simple and practical annex for industrial education, for both sexes, in the school system of the South, especially for the Negro children, would be a movement of incalculable value to the whole people of that region, so much in need of intelligent and skilled labor in the uprising of its new industrial life.

All these qualities tell in the steady progress of large numbers of these people toward a more comfortable, wholesome, and respectable way of living. This is evident especially to a regular visitor, not involved in the wear and tear of seven millions of freedmen getting on their citizen legs, as are our Southern white brothers and sisters. I see, everywhere, every year, a larger number of well-looking, well-dressed, well-churched, housed, well-mannered colored people. One reason why our Southern friends are not so impressed with this upward movement is that, as soon as a colored family gets above the humble or vagrant class, it somehow disappears from the ordinary view. One inevitable result of the social boycott that shuts down on every Negro family that attains respectability is that its white neighbors are put out of connection with this class, and left to the tender mercies of the class beneath, where their patience is worn out, and, too often, the impression taken for the whole race. The estimate of the increasing wealth of the Negroes is often disputed; but, at the most reasonable figure, it is a significant testimony to the growth of practical enterprise and steady improvement in the upper strata of the whole body.

While the acknowledged vices of the race are still a terrible weight on the lower and a constant temptation and humiliation to the better class, it is not certain that any of them, save those "failings that lean to virtue's side," are especially "race defects." A distinguished physician of Alabama has shown that the illegitimate births among the Negro population of the black belt of that State are in the exact per cent. of the Kingdom of Bavaria. Certainly, the vices of the lower class of the south of Europe people, that are now swarming the shores of the Gulf States, are not less common, and far more dangerous, than those of the Negro. Human nature, in its lower estate, especially when shot out from its barbarism into the devil-side of civilization, is fearfully deficient in its appreciation of the ten commandments. But I believe no people of the humbler sort are making more progress in overcoming the weakness of the appetites and getting in sight of the Christian moralities than the better sort of the Negroes. In the church, the home, and the school, I see the growth of a self-respecting manhood and womanhood that in due time will tell.

Though differing from many whose opinions and experience I respect, I do not regard the temporary isolation of the Negro in the

Southern church, school, and society, so much an evil as a providential aid in gaining the self-respect and habit of self-help absolutely essential to good citizenship. Spite of the hard side of slavery, the Negro has not had his fair share of the rough training that brings out the final results and the determination that tell in history. A habit of dependence, even to the extent of servility, in the lower orders, is still one of his most dangerous temptations. He has also been greatly tried by being, for a generation, the romantic figure of American life, — the especial object of philanthropic interest in Church, State, and society, everywhere outside the sixteen Southern States. It is well that he should be relieved for a while from these temptations. In company with the white boy, the Negro boy, on the same school bench, would all the time be tempted to fall into his old position of an annex to the white man, and, in the Church, would be under a strain that would sorely tax his manhood. Where he is, he grows up with a wholesome confidence in himself. His own best people are teaching him, with no hindrance, the law of responsible manhood and womanhood. The result is that, when he emerges into active life, if he has well appropriated his training, he is in a position to treat with a similar class of white people on terms that insure mutual respect.

I am struck with this feature of Southern society,— the constant "working together for good" of the better class, especially of the men of both races in all communities. The outrage of a drunken rabble upon a Negro settlement is published to all the world; while the constant intercourse of the respectable classes of men of the two races, that prevents a thousand such outbreaks and makes Southern life, on the whole, orderly, like the progress of the seasons and the hours, goes on in silence. It is not necessary to project the social question into the heart of communities in this state of transition. The very zealous brethren of the press and the political fold, who are digging this "last ditch" of social caste, away out in the wilderness, half a century ahead of any present emergency, may be assured that nobody in the United States will ever be obliged to associate with people disagreeable to him, and that, as Thomas Jefferson suggested, "if we educate the children of to-day, our descendants will be wiser than we, and many things that seem impossible to us may be easily accomplished by them." At present, the office of colored teacher and preacher is the noblest opportunity for general usefulness granted to an educated, righteous, and able young man or woman in any land. That teacher or preacher becomes the man or woman of all spiritual work to a constituency singularly appreciative; if instructed in industrial craft, all the more valuable. I am amazed at the assertion of some eminent people that the superior education of the Negro youth has been a failure. If the destiny of the Negro is only that of a child-peasant forever, this is true; but, if his range of possibility is what we believe, no such result of even a modified form of the secondary and higher education, with industrial accompaniments, has ever been seen in Christendom, as is evident to any man who regards this side of the life of this people with open eyes.

All that I have said bears on a fundamental truth concerning the uplifting of the American Negro citizen. The Northern white man, especially if a philanthropist, regards the Negro as an annex to the Northern, the Southern white man regards him as an annex to the Southern white citizen : but the Negro is anything but an annex to anybody. He is an original element, providentially injected into American civilization,—the only man who did not come to us of his own will. It may turn out, for that reason, that he is to be the "little child that shall lead them," and finally compel a reconciliation of all the distracting elements of our national life. Every race that has any outcome finally demonstrates its capacity by throwing up a superior class by which it is led, stimulated, and gradually lifted to its own highest achievement of civilization. Tried by this test, the Negro is not behind.

I have spoken so far of the average man and woman of the race. But that observer must be strangely blinded who does not see the evidence of the formation of a genuine aristocracy of intelligence, character, industry, and superior living among these millions. I do not refer to that unfortunate class who assert a superficial superiority by separation from their people and an uneasy longing to be recognized by their white superiors. I mean the growing class that is trying, under a solemn sense of gratitude to God, love to the brother, and consecrated patriotism, to lift up its own race. Among the seven millions of this people in the United States, there must be several hundred thousand of this sort. They are found everywhere, all the way from Massachusetts to Texas. They already form a distinct society; and the most American of all our great newspapers, the Cincinnati *Commercial Gazette*, has already recognized the fact by the prominent "Colored Society Column" in its Sunday morning issue. This class is becoming a distinct power, and its influence on the classes below is one of the most important elements of the race problem. It is already on good terms with the corresponding class of white people, though differing in politics and often grieved by what it regards public, social, and industrial injustice.

One significant fact in this connection is that now the Negro is the most determined Southerner. The young Southern white man, relieved from the attractions of the old aristocratic position of slaveholder, like all American young men of parts, is on the lookout for the main chance. The South is less and less to him a name to charm with. His own State no longer seems to him a "nation" which claims his uttermost devotion. A million of these young men, it is said, have left the South for the North and North-west since the war. Whole regions of these older States are as steadily drained of this important population as the older portions of the North-east. The Southern young woman will follow as soon as her call is heard. At present she is the "main-stay" of the rural South, the good angel of its coming civilization, getting more education and having more to do with the upper story of Southern life than her average male companion who stays at home. But the Negro loves the sacred soil, the old home, the climate, and its surroundings. In due time he will become the dominant occupant of large portions of the lowland South. He has no more idea of going to Africa than the Southern Jew of going into business in Jerusalem. He will move about as he becomes more intelligent and understands his own interests ; but he is the Southerner of to-day, and all persuasion or threats that would dislodge him are vain. As the political issues of the past fade into the distance, he will more and more act in all public affairs with the leading race, with whom his companionship and interest belong. He must be educated where he is: and, as the years go on, he will rise to the call of his own superior class and find his own place,—a great and beneficent place in our wonderful American family.

Education is the lever that will raise this great mass of humanity to the high plane of full American citizenship. I believe it would be a great blessing to the whole South, could the suffrage, educational, labor, and vagrant laws of Massachusetts be incorporated into the legislation of every Southern State. Protection to the child, suppression of vagrancy, enforcement of industry, an educational test of suffrage, better churching, improvement in the home, reading of good books, all the influences that are so potent in any respectable Northern community, will in good time achieve the success of every class and race of the American people. For the Negro, two-thirds of this education must be, for a generation, outside the school-room, in the broad university of the new Southern American life. If we only knew it, this is one of the richest educational opportunities God has ever vouchsafed to any people.

What a call is this opportunity for missionary service, in its broadest and loftiest aspect, to the whole American people. Every theory of despair on the race problem proceeds from a pagan or atheistic estimate of human nature and destiny, and leads down to despotism or anarchy. Without the blessed gospel of Christ, our American race problem would be too awful to contemplate. Thank God, it did not come to us in an age of pagan darkness, of mediæval violence, in a land crowded with people, in a civilization cursed by the bitter results of a long and stormy past. It came to us in an opening age of light, when all the celestial forces are at an upward slant, when the Church is getting itself together to work for man while God takes care of the creeds, in a country so large and bountiful that hundreds of millions would not crowd it, and "every man may sit under his own vine and fig-tree, with no one to molest and make afraid."

As I am borne through the vast spaces of our marvellous Southern land, and stand in amazement before its revelation of resources, hitherto unknown, I ask myself ;— Is this only to become the theatre of a greater greed of gain, "a hazard of new fortunes," its only outcome a semi-tropical materialism, an inevitable temptation to a dismal era of "booms" and "syndicates" and "trusts," with a new insanity for the almighty dollar, so powerless to satisfy the deeper need of the humblest human heart? May it not, rather, be God's summons to such an awakening of our overworked and materialized American people as will compel them, in sheer self-defence, to give mind and heart and hand to that lifting up of the lowly, and that preaching the gospel of self-help to the poor, which is the end of Christian charity? I look for the day when the divided churches of our three great Protestant denominations will be brought together by the growing sense of this "home mission" claim, and the whole Church and the adjacent realm of the world be polarized in one supreme effort to solve this old caste puzzle of the nations and ages, by showing that the simple gospel of Christ means peace on earth and good will to all men.

But now comes the final question, on which not so much the destiny of the Negro citizen as the very existence of Southern American civilization depends. Will the Anglo-Saxon Southern people, at present nine-tenths of the entire white population, in due time appreciate this opportunity, and join hands with all good men and women, at home and abroad, in this, the grandest crusade of all the ages?

I have no doubt that the race problem will finally be solved, in the South, largely through the agency of the Southern Anglo-Saxon people,— not over their heads, but with their thorough co-operation. I see already, amid superficial indica:'⌐ns to the contrary, the converging lines of this tendency, and, below hostile theories, the inevitable drift of the common life of all these great commonwealths towards the American type of society.

I see the positive indication of this great convergence of opinion, especially in what may be called the Educational Public of the South. By this, I mean that portion of the Southern people, of all classes and both races, which within the past twenty-five years, amid difficulties and complications almost unconquerable elsewhere, has quietly and persistently laid the foundations of the American system of universal education in every State, county, city, and neighborhood in these sixteen commonwealths.

The common school is so much the habit and unquestioned postulate of republican government everywhere in the North that we have never done half justice to the people of the sixteen Southern States for this, by all odds, the most significant movement of the past generation this side the water. That a people, in 1860 the most aristocratic in organization of its society upon earth, who fought through a bloody war and only fell in "the last ditch" of the absolute ruin of their old social order, should have risen up from this awful overthrow, cleared the ground of rubbish, and, with scarcely any aid that they could use, of their own will have planted on the soil the one institution that is the eternal foe of everything save republican government and democratic society, is the wonder of the age, and the complete vindication of the essential Americanism of the Southern people. It would be well for our cynical scholars and self-confident politicians, who dilate on the imperfections of this system of education, to remember what Massachusetts was, fifty years ago, when Horace Mann drew his sword, what Pennsylvania was, thirty years ago, when Wickersham took command, what even to-day some portions of the older Atlantic States are declared by the testimony of their own educational authorities to be. Doubtless there has been exaggeration of the achievement of the South in popular education, partly through ignorance, more in the way of home advertisement, most in the interest of the defeat of the Blair Bill. But, with all this drawback, the Southern people have taken "the first step that costs," and established the free school, for all classes and both races, unsectarian, but practically one of the most potent moral and religious forces of this section, growing all the time, already beyond the peril of destruction or serious damage from its numerous enemies ; and it "has come to stay." True, the educational public has not half converted the average Southern politician, for whom, as General Grant said, " there is too much reading and writing now." It has not yet entirely swung the Southern clergy and the Church over to its hearty support, as against the old-time Protestant parochial and private system of instruction. It is still a social outsider in some regions ; and, through vast spaces of the rural South, it is so poor that it seems to have hindered more than helped the better-off classes who shoulder its expenses. But it has for the first time gone down into the basement story of the Southern household, bearing that common schooling to the lower orders and the " plain people," which means modern civilization and progressive Christianity, involving the full committal to the new American order of affairs. It is a wonder that the leading classes of the North — the press, the political organizations, the industrial leaders, even the philanthropists — are still so imperfectly informed concerning this, by all odds, the most vital and significant end of Southern life. The splendid mission work of our Northern churches, which, indirectly, has so greatly aided the growth of the schools for the Negroes by training their teachers, has sometimes obscured the magnitude of the home work. But this, with the remarkable rally of the whole secondary and higher education, is a demonstration that the South has no intention of remaining permanently in any second place in the great educational movement of the time. Imperfect as the common school is, the Negro has been the greatest gainer therefrom ; for, through it and all that goes along therewith, he is laying up a steady increase of self-respect, intelligence, and practical power, which will astonish many good people who still go on repeating the parrot cry that education has only demoralized the younger Negro generation for the industrial side of life. But it is not what the common schools have done, but what the Southern people has failed to do to re-enforce them, that still holds thousands of Negro youth in the bonds of a vagrancy, shiftlessness, and debasement that deserve all things that can be said against them. The cure for this is more and better education, re-enforced by the policy of every civilized land in the suppression of the devil-side of society, that will ruin the greatest country under the sun.

But, below and beyond this open and evident work of education, I see more clearly, every year, that the logic of the new Southern life is all on the side of the final elevation of the Negro to the essential rights and opportunities of American citizenship ; and, beyond, to the generous co-operation with the nation in aiding him to make his own best use of that supreme opportunity. We at the North are constantly misled by the press, which is a very poor representative of this most important element of Southern life. We hear the superficial talk and read of the disorder that is the inevitable accompaniment of States in the transition from a great civil war to their final adjustment to the national life. An eminent educator of the South writes me : " Ask a hundred men at the street corner what they think about the education of the Negro, and seventy-five of them will demur, and some of them will swear. The next day every man of them will vote for the higher school tax that gives the Negro a better school-house and the permanent establishment of his education." Our Southern friends are no more logical than other portions of the country, and the superficial life of all countries is constantly adjusting itself to the logic of its undertow. I can see, in more ways than I could explain, even to a Northern community, that these people are "in the swim ". whose tide can only drift them off into regions of life which seem almost impossible to them to-day.

The test of this drift is that, spite of all obstacles and embarrassments, there is, in every respectable Southern community, no real hindrance to an intelligent, moral, industrious, and prudent Negro family getting all out of American life that anybody expects, save that social and, in some localities, political recognition, that are the last achievements of long periods of social evolution in national affairs. In all essential respects, the Negro citizen is better off in the South than in any Northern State. The outward opportunities for full association with the white population in the North are, after all, of little value in comparison with the substantial opportunity for becoming the great laboring agricultural class and of capturing the field of mechanical and operative labor. It will be his own fault if he permits the insolent naturalized foreign element that now dominates our Northern industrial centres to elbow him off into a peasantry or a menial and subordinate laboring population.

As I look at the way in which these seven millions of people are gaining all the vital opportunities of life among the twelve millions of their Anglo-Saxon neighbors, I am amazed at the way they seem to go on, only half-conscious of what the rest of the world is saying about them, "working out their own salvation" by the power that is in them, in the only way by which an American people can finally succeed. The only fit symbol of this mighty movement is the Mississippi River after it has become "the inland sea" of the Southland. States and their peoples, Congress and the nation, scientists and cranks, debate and experiment on the way to put the "Father of Waters" in harness, to tie up this awful creature that holds the fate of ten millions of people in its every-day whim. But all discourse, legislation, and experiment, at last run against the question ;—What will the Mississippi River do with us next week? So, while the Southern people and the nation are wrestling with what they choose to call the "race problem," this inland, Southern human ocean, searching and spreading and pushing into every nook and corner of the low-land, is going on its way ; and every deliverance of the scientist, the socialist, and the statesman, brings up against some new and unexpected thing that the Negro has really done. "How are you getting on with your neighbors down here ?" said I to a deputation of fine-looking colored men, who stepped out of a carriage and presented me with a well-written address of welcome to the city of Vicksburg. "Well, we used to have trouble ; but we have finally concluded the white man has come to stay, and we adjust ourselves to that fact." The white man has indeed come to stay all over the United States of America ; but he will stay, not always as the white man proposes, but as God Almighty disposes. And, wherever he abides, he will finally be compelled, by the logic of American events, to stay in peace and justice, in freedom and order, in Christian co-operation with all the great elements of republican society, shaped from all the peoples that a beneficent Providence has called to abide together in this, God's morning land.

SOME ASPECTS

...OF...

THE RACE PROBLEM
IN THE SOUTH

A PAPER BY

REV. ROBERT F. CAMPBELL, D. D.,

Pastor of the First Presbyterian Church,

ASHEVILLE, N. C.

ASHEVILLE:
ASHEVILLE PRINTING COMPANY, PRINT.
1899.

PREFATORY NOTE.

On Christmas day, 1898, the writer preached a sermon in the First Presbyterian Church, Asheville, on Our Duty to the Negroes. The congregation was composed of persons representing the four quarters of the Union, many of whom have asked that the sermon be published. A condensed report appeared in the columns of The Asheville Daily Citizen, and this report excited considerable interest among those who had not heard the discourse.

Several of the negro pastors in the city have expressed a desire to have copies of the sermon for circulation among their people. In addition to these requests, there comes one from the Rev. D. Clay Lilly, Secretary of Colored Evangelization for the Southern Presbyterian Church, for fifteen hundred copies, to be issued by the Committee having this work in charge.

These requests coming from so many independent sources, and from so many classes of persons supposed to have divergent views on the subject treated, seem to indicate that some good might be accomplished by the publication of the substance of what was said. The sermon was preached from outline notes and could not be reproduced in the exact form in which it was delivered. It has seemed best in preparing it for publication, to alter its character somewhat, and to send it forth as a paper rather than as a sermon. The points discussed are the same, but the proportion of the parts has been changed, much more space being given in the paper to the historical and sociological setting. Use has been made of some material that has appeared since the sermon was delivered.

When the writer was a boy thirteen and fourteen years of age he taught during two scholastic years a night school for colored men. He was for several years a teacher in a Sunday school for negroes and afterwards superintendent of the school. From his boyhood he has been interested in the advancement of the negro race.

R. F. CAMPBELL.

Asheville, N. C., March 23, 1899.

Some Aspects of the Race Problem in the South.

Though the present generation is not responsible for the existence of the race problem, it is responsible for its solution. In the providence of God, this great problem has fallen to us as part of our inheritance, and we must settle it according to the eternal principles of truth and righteousness.

The fact that this question has been made a rallying point for sectionalism has been the greatest obstacle in the way of its peaceful solution.

It is high time that the two sections, so long and so unhappily divided by strife over the negro's status in this country, should join hands as a token of peace and a pledge of mutual helpfulness in all that concerns the solution of this question in its present phases. It should be remembered that while geographically the problem is largely a Southern one, historically both sections are responsible for its existence, and the interests of both are involved in its settlement. It is the purpose of this paper to call attention to some aspects of the race problem, with reference to the past history, the present status, and the future prospects of the negro in this country, and the white man's duty to his brother in black.

I. The responsibility for the negro's former status as a slave in this country rests equally on both sections of the Union.

The first cargo of Africans was landed in a half starving condition on the shore of Virginia by a Dutch man-of-war in 1620, and bartered to the colonists for food. The seed of African slavery, introduced into America by accident so far as any previous intention on the part of these colonists was concerned, soon took root, and the institution spread with the growth of the country.

Mr. Geo. H. Moore, librarian of the Historical Society of New York, and corresponding member of the Historical Society of Massachusetts, has shown that Massachusetts was "the first community in America to legalize the slave-trade and slavery by legislative act; the first to send out a slave-ship, and the first to secure a fugitive slave-law."*

In 1776 slavery existed in all the thirteen colonies, and what Mr. E. B. Sanford says of Connecticut in his history of that State is true of the North generally: "The cause of the final abolition of slavery in the State was the fact that it became unprofitable." †

Mr. Hamilton W. Mabie says: "All the Northern States abolished slavery, beginning with Vermont in 1777, and ending with New Jersey in 1804. It should be added, however, that many of the Northern slaves were not freed, but sold to the South. The agricultural and commercial conditions in the North were such as to make slave labor less and less profitable, while in the South the social order of things, agricultural conditions and the climate, were gradually making it seemingly indispensable "‡

Even after the abolition of slavery in New England, "the slave-trade in New England vessels did not cease." §

In 1769 the Virginia legislature enacted that the further importation of negroes, to be sold into slavery, should be prohibited. ‖

Six years later Massachusetts followed Virginia's example. The action of both colonies was rendered null and void by the British government, which, for the sake of gain, fastened the traffic in slaves on the American colonies. **

In the Federal convention (1787) New England voted with South Carolina and Georgia, against the sturdy opposition of Virginia, for the prolonging of the slave-trade for twenty years ††

Though all the foremost statesmen and many of the planters of Virginia were from an early date opposed to the continuance of slavery, the question of emancipation assumed a

---

*Moore's "History of Slavery in the Massachusetts," cited by Thomas Nelson Page in "The Old South," pp. 292-296.

† John Fiske, "The Critical Period of American History," p. 73. Sanford's "History of Connecticut," p. 252.

‡ "The Story of America," by Hamilton W. Mabie and Marshal H. Bright, p. 282.

§ W. B. Weeden, "Economic and Social History of New England," Vol. 2, p. 835.

‖ John Fiske, "The Critical Period of American History," p. 72.

** Ibid., p. 72.

†† Ibid., p. 264.

much more serious phase in the South than in the North, because economic conditions had caused a natural gravitation of the negroes southward. *

"The number of African slaves in North America in 1756 was about 292,000. Of these Virginia had 120,000, her white population amounting at the same time to 173,000." †

By the census of 1790 there were only 40,370 negroes at the North, while the South had 657,527. "In that (the Northern) part of America," wrote Mr. Jefferson, who was a vigorous opponent of slavery, "there are but few slaves, and they can easily disencumber themselves of them."

The statement of these historical facts should allay rather than exasperate sectionalism. They show that the responsibility for slavery in this country rests on both shoulders of the body politic, and therefore "the right hand cannot say to the left, I have no need of thee." One hand needs the help of the other in bearing the great burden which, as we shall see, has been shifted but not removed by emancipation.

II. The negro could not have existed in the early stages of his career in this country except as a slave, and there is reason to believe that slavery accomplished more for him than could have been accomplished under any other system of labor whatsoever.

That the negro could not have found or kept a footing in this country except as a slave is too obvious for proof. The Chinaman tried to get in, but was met at the threshold by an act of Congress to the effect that this is "a white man's country," or, at least, not a yellow man's country. The Indian, who equally with the negro has "rights which a white man is bound to respect," has been driven westward, and is "fast being removed by powder, rascality and liquor." ‡

Would the black man, under the same conditions, have fared any better than his brother in yellow or red?

The Rev. Dr. H. B. Frissel of Hampton Institute, Va., says, "When Indian and negro are placed side by side in the school-room and work-shop at Hampton, it is very clear that slavery was a much better training school for life alongside of the white man than was the reservation." §

And Dr. Frissel's great predecessor, Gen. Armstrong, an-

* John Fiske, "The Critical Period of American History," p. 73.
† J. E. Cooke's "Virginia," p. 367.
‡ Dr. A. L. Phillips, Presbyterian Quarterly, Oct. 1891, p. 537.
§ Proceedings of the First Capon Springs Conference for Christian Education in the South, 1898, p. 4.

other of those noble men of the North who came South to give practical aid in the solution of the race problem, said, "We can see that while slavery was called 'the sum of all villanies,' it became, as it was called by a clever Virginian, 'the greatest missionary enterprise of the century.' " *

Senator Vance was simply stating a patent historical fact when he declared, "The negro has made more progress in one hundred years as a Southern slave than in all the five thousand years intervening from his creation until his landing on these shores."†

The highest tribute ever paid to the institution of slavery was the conferring of the laurel wreath of citizenship upon its graduates by the government of the United States. The negro came to this country a savage, but was civilized and elevated to such a degree by the training he received in the homes and on the plantations of the South that he was deemed ready, without any further preparation, for the highest civic responsibilities known on earth.

III. The hope for peaceful relations between the two races in the future lies along the line of the adjustment established between the negro and the white man through these years of slavery. If the negro is driven to the wall before the stronger race, it will be because the friendly relations of the past shall be entirely, as they have been partially, disrupted by selfish and malicious demagogues, or by well-meaning but misguided philanthropists.

The kindly feeling that existed between the two races under the institution of slavery has been written in indelible characters, and no amount of misrepresentation, whether prompted by malice or flowing from ignorance, can obliterate the record. That there were instances of cruelty and wrong connected with the relation of master and slave, no one will deny; but that the slaves of the South were as a class kindly treated by their masters is proved by their conduct during the civil war, "wherein the negro was ready to take sides with his alleged oppressor against his self-appointed champion."‡

* Proceedings of the First Capon Springs Conference for Christian Education in the South, 1898, p. 4.
† Dowd's Life of Vance, p. 253.
‡ Henry Alexander White, "Robert E. Lee and The Southern Confederacy," p. 85.

Senator Vance in a lecture delivered in Boston before a post of the Grand Army of the Republic,—a lecture which was enthusiastically applauded by the brave and magnanimous veterans who heard it,—spoke of this remarkable fact as follows: "Here permit me to call your attention to the conduct of the Southern slaves during the war. You had been taught by press, pulpit and hustings, to believe that they were an oppressed, abused and diabolically treated race; that their groans daily and hourly appealed to heaven, whilst their shackles and their scars testified in the face of all humanity against their treatment. . . . . . How was this grave impeachment of a whole people sustained, when you went among them to emancipate them from the horrors of their serfdom? When the war began, naturally you expected insurrections, incendiary burnings, murder and outrage, with all the terrible conditions of servile war. There were not wanting fanatical wretches who did their utmost to excite it. Did you find it so? Here is what you found. Within hearing of the guns that were roaring to set them free, with the land stripped of its male population, and none around them except the aged, the women and the children, they not only failed to embrace their opportunity of vengeance, but for the most part they failed to avail themselves of the chance of freedom itself. They remained quietly on our plantations, cultivated our fields, and cared for our mothers, wives and little ones, with a faithful love and a loyal kindness which, in the nature of things, could only be born of sincere good-will. . . . . . These facts are significant. That they are complimentary in the highest degree to the black race no one doubts; do they not also say enough for the Southern whites, in regard to their rule as masters, to justify you in thinking better of them than perhaps you have been accustomed to do? According to well known moral laws this kindly loyalty of the one race could not have been begotten by the cruelty and oppression of the other."*

Concerning the happiness of the Southern slaves Thackeray wrote, after a visit to the United States: "How they sang; how they laughed and grinned; how they scraped, bowed, and complimented you and each other, those negroes of the

* Dowd's "Life of Zebulon B. Vance," pp. 449-450.

cities of the Southern parts of the then United States! My business kept me in the towns; I was but in one negro plantation village, and there were only women and little children, the men being out a-field. But there was plenty of cheerfulness in the huts, under the great trees—I speak of what I saw—and amidst the dusky bondsmen of the cities. I witnessed a curious gayety; heard amongst the black folk endless singing, shouting and laughter; and saw on holidays black gentlemen and ladies arrayed in such splendor and comfort as freeborn workmen in our towns seldom exhibit."*

Much has been written by New England poets on the horrors of Southern slavery. Here is a picture of the relation of master and slave drawn by the poet of the negro race, Paul Laurence Dunbar:

Dat Chrismus on de ol' Plantation. †

It was Chrismus Eve, I mind hit fu' a mighty gloomy day—
Bofe de weathah an' de people—not a one of us was gay:
Cose you'll t'ink dat's mighty funny twell I try to mek hit cleah
Fu' a da'ky's allus happy when de holidays is near.

But we wasn't, fu' dat mo'nin' Mastah'd tol' us we mus' go,
He'd been payin' us sence freedom, but he couldn't pay no mo'.
He wa'n't nevah used to plannin' 'fo' he got so po' an' ol',
So he gwine to give up tryin' an' de homestead must be sol'.

I kin see him stan'in' now.erpon de step ez cleah ez day,
Wid de win' a-kin' o' fondlin' thoo his haih all thin an' gray:
An' I 'membah how he trimbled when he said, "It's ha'd fu' me,
Not to mek yo' Chrismus brightah, but I 'low it wa'n't to be.

All de women was a-cryin' an' de men, too, on de sly,
An' I noticed somep'n' shinin' even in ol' Mastah's eye,
But we all stood still to listen ez ol' Ben come f'om de crowd
An' spoke up a-tryin' to steady down his voice and mek it loud:

* Thackeray's "Roundabout Papers—A Mississippi Bubble."
† From "The Ladies' Home Journal," December, 1898, through the courtesy of the Publishers.

"Look hyeah, Mastah, I's been servin' you fu' lo! dese many
    yeahs,
An' now sence we's all got freedom an' you's kind o' po', hit
    'pears
Dat you want us all to leave you 'cause you don't t'ink you can
    pay—
Ef my membry hasn't fooled me, seem dat what I hyeard you
    say.

Er in othah wo'ds, you wants us to fu'git dat you's been kin',
An' ez soon ez you is he'pless, we's to leave you hyeah behin'.
Well, ef dat's de way dis freedom ac's on people, white er
    black,
You kin' jes' tell Mistah Lincum fu' to tek his freedom back.

Wĕ gwine wo'k dis ol' plantation fu' whatevah we kin git,
Fu' I know hit did suppo't us, an' de place kin do it yit.
Now de land is yo's, de hands is ouahs, but I reckon we'll be
    brave,
An' we'll bah ez much ez you do when we have to scrape an'
    save."

Ol' Mastah stood dah trimblin', but a-smilin', thoo his teahs,
An' den hit seemed jes' nachul-like, de place fah rung wid'
    cheahs,
An' soon ez dey was quiet, some one sta'ted sof' an' low:
"Praise God" an' den we all jined in. "from whom all bless-
    in's flow!"

Well, dey wasn't no use tryin', ouah min's was sot to stay,
An' po' ol' Mastah couldn't plead ner baig, ner drive us
    'way,
An' all at once, hit seemed to us, de day was bright agin,
So evah one was gay dat night an' watched de Chrismus in.

Many examples might be given of time's failure to impair
the bond of affection that waxed strong on the old plantation.

Two instances that have very lately come under the personal observation of the writer are selected. They are like the
obverse and reverse of an old coin, whose image and superscription remain clear-cut and distinct in spite of the abrasion
of years.

The first instance illustrates the very common interest felt by former slave-holders and their families in the welfare of the freedmen whom they once owned; the second is a rare manifestation of the no less common gratitude and affection abiding in the hearts of ex-slaves for those whom they still call "Massa" and "Missus."

More than thirty-five years after the Emancipation Proclamation this letter was addressed by the daughter of a slaveholder to the pastor of the First Presbyterian Church, Asheville.

——————, N. C., Dec. 2, '98.

Dear Sir:—May I venture to tax your time and strength to visit a poor sick negro man in Asheville, who once belonged to my father. His mother was our faithful servant, and in his childhood he lived in the family until some years after they were freed. Since then he has led a bad life and now is dying slowly by disease. Perhaps the gospel message might reach his heart now at the eleventh hour and save him at last. I am sure you will rejoice to be the bearer of the precious message to a dying sinner, and may God make it a saving one.

Your sincere friend,

——————————.

Directions were given for finding the poor man and the message was delivered. He said joyfully that he had been trusting Jesus Christ as his Saviour for several months, that "Miss Sarah" had been very kind in sending him money to buy medicine and food, and he sent her word that he would meet her in heaven.

The reverse picture is vouched for by a Presbyterian elder on whose place the ex-slave spoken of now lives. About 1856 the holder of a small tract of poor land, which was worked by a few slaves, died, leaving a widow and two children. The surrender left this little family with only the very poor and worn-out plantation.

In 1876 the son died, and about the same time the daughter married a worthless man and removed to another State. This left the widow alone with no means of support. One of the negroes formerly owned by the family, seeing the condition of his old mistress, came at once to her relief and began to supply her with food purchased with his own wages.

In 1891 he moved to another part of the State, 225 miles from the old plantation home. But before leaving he told one of the leading merchants of the community to see that his old mistress did not suffer for anything, and to send the bills to him. At first bills for food came, but later he has paid for her clothes, too, and all this without the slightest expectation of getting anything in return. She is now over eighty years of age, and her last days are made bright by the gratitude and affection of her former slave. The Presbyterian elder who gave me these facts says of him: "He is quite reticent about it, and I learned of it only about a year ago."

No one will contend that slavery is an ideal system. At best it could be only temporary, not final. But as a matter of fact, there has never been in the world an economic system which could compare with Southern slavery in forging bonds of personal affection between capital and labor, grappling the hearts of the two together with hooks of steel.

Any stable superstructure of good-will between the two races under the new conditions in the South must be built upon the foundation laid in the days of slavery, a foundation that has been shaken but not destroyed by the storms that have beat upon it. This is recognized by the wisest leaders of the negro in both races, notably by that great and good colored man, Booker T. Washington.

My friend, Dr. Thomas Lawrence, now President of the Normal and Collegiate Institute of this city, who spent twelve years of his life in educational work for the negro at Biddle University, has said to me repeatedly, that in his opinion all efforts of Northern philanthropists to help the negro will be in vain, unless conserving the friendly relation between the two races and enlisting the approval, sympathy and co-operation of the best white people of the South.

No graver mistake has been made in dealing with the race problem than the ignoring of this first principle by some of the negro's would-be-friends.

It must not be understood from what has been said of the benefits that came to the negro through slavery that the Southern whites regret the passing away of this institution. It put shackles upon Southern industry and retarded the economic development of states richly dowered with material resources.

"For domestic purposes," wrote Thackeray in the paper already quoted, "it seemed to me about the dearest institution that can be devised. In a house in a Southern city, you will find fifteen negroes doing the work which John, the cook, the housemaid, and the help, do perfectly in your own comfortable London house. And these fifteen negroes are the pick of a family of some eighty or ninety. Twenty are too sick, or too old for work, let us say: twenty too clumsy: twenty are too young, and have to be nursed and watched by ten more. And master has to maintain the immense crew to do the work of half a dozen willing hands."

It was a common saying that the greatest slaves in the household and on the plantation were master and mistress.

That the abolition of this double bondage has been a blessing to the white man, no one can doubt, whatever may be the judgment concerning his brother in black. Though clouds and darkness veil the final issue of the new race problem, we may trust that in pursuing "the right, as God gives us to see the right," clouds and darkness will flee before us. It is the path of the just that shineth more and more unto the perfect day.

IV. And here emerges a question of grave importance because of its bearing on the future. Has the negro improved since emancipation? To those who have given little heed to the history of the freedmen, it may seem strange that this inquiry should be raised. But there are two sides to the question, and, while one side seems very bright, the other is just as dark.

Let us look at the question from several points of view.*

(1). *The Negro and Education.*

"Here," says Bishop Penick, "is one of the wonders of the time." In 1865 a very small proportion of the negroes of the South could read. "Today not less than twenty-five thousand are professors or teachers in colleges and schools. A vast

* For the statistics that follow, so far as based on the Census of 1890 I am indebted largely to the Rt. Rev. C. Clifton Penick, D. D., of the Protestant Episcopal Church, who has made a thorough study of this question, in the light of that Census, in his "Struggles, Perils and Hopes of the Negroes in the United States."

number of well-read preachers, lawyers, doctors, mail agents and clerks are at work."

There are about one hundred and fifty newspapers edited by black men, all established since 1865.

For the school year 1896-'97 there were 1,460,084 negro children enrolled in the public schools. This enrollment is nearly 52 per cent. of the colored school population, as against an enrollment of about 68 per cent. of the white school population. The percentage of illiteracy among the negroes fell from 70 per cent. in 1880 to 56 per cent. in 1890.

According to the estimate of Dr. A. D. Mayo, of Boston, the Southern States have contributed $85,000,000 for negro education, which large sum has been supplemented by $25,-000,000 from philanthropists of the North and the national government.*

Dr. W. T. Harris, Commissioner of Education, says, "It is believed that since 1870 the Southern States have expended about $100,000,000 for the education of colored children." †

(2). *The Negro and the Churches.*

It is well-established, and ought to be well-known, that provision was made in the cities and on most of the plantations of the South for the religious instruction of the slaves, and that large numbers of them were members of the various churches along with the white people. A few examples selected from scores that might be cited will show that white masters were not indifferent to the spiritual welfare of their black slaves.

In 1848 an enterprise was begun for the more thorough-going evangelization of the colored people in Charleston, S. C., under the auspices of the Rev. Dr. J. B. Adger and the session of the Second Presbyterian Church. In 1859 a church building costing twenty-five thousand dollars, contributed by the citizens of Charleston, was dedicated. From the first the great building was filled, the blacks occupying the main floor, and the whites the galleries, which seated two hunderd and fifty persons. The Rev. Dr. J. L. Girardeau, one of the greatest preachers in the South, was for years the pastor of

---

* First Capon Springs Conference, p. 5.
† Report of Commissioner of Education, 1896-97, Vol. 2, p. 2296.

this church. The close of the war found it with exactly five hundred colored members, and nearly one hundred white.

A minister in Natchez wrote to Dr. Charles Colcock Jones in the '30's: "I have committed to me the instruction of the negroes on five plantations, in all about three hundred, the owners of whom are professors of religion. I usually preach three times on the Sabbath, and after each sermon I spend a short time catechising. I have occasional meetings for inquiry . "

Another wrote from the Savannah river: "I visit eighteen plantations every two weeks : catechise the children, and pray with the sick in the week. Preach twice or thrice on the Sabbath. The owners have built three good churches at their own expense, all framed; 290 members have been added, and about 400 children are instructed each week."*

Stonewall Jackson took the deepest interest in the religious welfare of the slaves, and his colored Sunday school at Lexington, Va., has become famous.

"A day or two after the battle of Manassas, and before the news of the victory had reached Lexington in authentic form, the postoffice was thronged with people, awaiting with intense interest the opening of the mail. Soon a letter was handed to the Rev. Dr. White, who immediately recognized the well-known superscription of his deacon soldier, and exclaimed to the eager and expectant group around him: 'Now we shall know all the facts.' Upon opening it the bulletin read thus: 'My Dear Pastor,—In my tent last night, after a fatiguing day's service, I remembered that I had failed to send you my contribution for our colored Sunday school. Enclosed you will find my check for that object, which please acknowledge at your earliest convenience, and oblige yours faithfully,

T. J. Jackson.' " †

These are not exceptional instances. They might be multiplied indefinitely. The Rev. T. C. Thornton, late President of the Centenary College, Clinton, Mississippi, who traveled

---

* Dr. R. Q. Mallard's "Plantation Life before Emancipation," pp. 148-149, 156-157. Those who desire to study plantation life as it really was should read this book, published by Whittet and Shepperson, Richmond, Va.; and also "The Memorials of a Southern Planter," by Mrs. Smedes: Cushing & Co., Baltimore.

† Mrs. Mary A. Jackson, "Memoirs of Stonewall Jackson," pp. 181-2.

extensively through the South, wrote in 1841, "In some places they (the negroes) have large, spacious churches for themselves, as in Baltimore, Alexandria, Charleston; in others they have seats appropriated for them on the lower floor, or a portion or the whole of the galleries of the churches. We do not know in any slave-holding State in the Union, a neighborhood, where a church has been built for any of the orthodox Protestant denominations, in which a portion thereof was not set apart for the colored people, unless they have a church of their own, or other provision in some church in the vicinity." Mr. Thornton estimates that there were at that time at least 500,000 church members among the slaves, or about one-fifth of the negro population, and that 2,000,000 were regular church attendants.*

It was about this date that the Hon. William Jay, of New York, charged the people of the South with "having compelled 2,245,144 slaves to live without God and die without hope among a people professing to reverence the obligations of Christianity." †

On the other hand, the Hon. Henry A. Wise declared in a speech before the Colonization Society of Virginia, of which President Tyler was the chief officer, "Africa gave to Virginia a savage and a slave—Virginia gives back to Africa a citizen and a Christian!" ‡

These facts have been given because the religious history of the negroes since the war cannot be understood apart from them.

"It was fortunate for the negro," says Dr. H. K. Carroll, of the United States census staff, "that while he was the slave of the white master, that master was a Christian and instructed him in the Christian faith." §

Emancipation loosened the tie that bound the negro to his master's church, and he straightway became a church-builder on his own account. In the twenty-five years from 1865 to 1890 the negroes built 19,753 churches, with a seating capacity of 5,818,459, at a cost of $20,323,887. While a large

---

* Rev. T. C. Thornton, "An Inquiry into the History of Slavery, etc.," pp. 110-111.

† Ibid. p. 98.

‡ Ibid. p. 277.

§ "The Religious Forces of the United States," pp. liv, lv.

part of this has been contributed by white neighbors, the negroes have shown commendable liberality and self-denial in this work, sometimes mortgaging their little homes in order to build their churches.

Dr. H. K. Carroll, compiler of the religious census, put the number of communicants in 1890 at 2,610,525 out of a total population of 7,470,000, or nearly one in three.

(3). *The Negro's Material Prosperity.*

Beginning with nothing in 1865, this race has accumulated property whose assessed value is $260,000,000. Many of them own their homes, some are land-holders, and the more thrifty and industrious live in neatness and comfort.

There is much that is encouraging and hopeful in these statistics, and they would seem to indicate that the negro's condition has wonderfully improved. But, unfortunately, there is another side to the question, the facts of which look dark for the future of the race. These facts may be grouped under two heads.

(1). *Vital Statistics.*

From 1870 to 1880 the negro population increased nearly 36 per cent.; from 1880 to 1890 the increase was only a little over 13 per cent. This is about one-half the rate of increase among the whites.

"For the year 1895, when 82 white deaths from consumption occurred in the city of Nashville, there ought to have been only 49 colored, whereas there really were 218, or nearly four and one-half times as many as there ought to have beer It is an occasion of serious alarm when 37 per cent. of the whole people are responsible for 72 per cent. of the deaths from consumption. Deaths among colored people from pulmonary diseases seem to be on the increase throughout the South. During the period 1882-1885, the excess of colored deaths (over white) for the city of Memphis was 90.80 per cent. For the period 1891-1895 the excess had risen to over 137 per cent. For the period of 1886-1890, the excess of colored deaths from consumption and pneumonia for the city of Atlanta was 139 per cent. For the period 1891-1895, it had risen to nearly 166 per cent. . . . . . Before the (civil) war this dread disease was virtually unknown among the slaves. According to Hoffman, deaths from consumption have fallen off 134 in 100,000 among the whites and increased 234 in 100,000 among the blacks since the war."*

When we remember that tubercular and scrofulous diseases are the natural agents that have swept away the weaker races before the onward march of Anglo-Saxon civilization, it would seem that unless the progress of these diseases among the negroes is checked, that race is destined to gradual extinction.

(2). Closely associated with these "vital statistics," and underlying them, is the question of *immorality and crime.* And this is the saddest part of the picture.

Prof. Eugene Harris says in the report already quoted: "The constitutional diseases which are responsible for our unusual mortality are often traceable to enfeebled constitutions, broken down by sexual immoralities. According to Hoffman, over 25 per cent. of the negro children born in Washington City are admittedly illegitimate. According to a writer quoted in Black America, in one county in Miss., there were during 12 months 300 marriage licenses taken out in the county clerk's office for white people. According to the proportion of population there should have been in the same time 1,200 or more for negroes. There were actually taken out by colored people just three. . . . . A few years ago I said in a sermon at Fisk University, that wherever the Anglo-Saxon comes into contact with an inferior race the inferior race invariably goes to the wall. I called attention to the fact that, in spite of humanitarian and philanthropic efforts, the printing press, the steam engine, and the electric motor in the hands of the Anglo-Saxon were exterminating the inferior races more rapidly and more surely than shot and shell and bayonet. I mentioned a number of races that have perished, not because of destructive wars and pestilence, but because they were unable to live in the environment of a nineteenth century civilization; races whose destruction was

---

* Prof. Eugene Harris. Fisk University. Nashville. Tenn., "Report on the Social and Physical Condition of Negroes in Cities," in Report of Commissioner of Education, 1896-97. Vol. 2, p. 2310.

not due to a persecution that came to them from without, but to a lack of moral stamina within; races that perished in spite of the humanitarian and philanthropic efforts that were put forth to save them."

If the cause of the excessive death rate among the negroes be moral rather than sanitary, then, as Prof. Harris says, this fact ought to appear not only in the vital, but in the criminal statistics as well. And there it is found in most appalling figures. Three-fourths of the crimes in the South are committed by negroes. The negroes, constituting about 11 per cent. of the entire population of the nation, furnish 37 per cent. of all its homicides, and 66 per cent. of its female homicides. The statistics seem to indicate that the full harvest is yet to come, for the rising generation far outstrips in crime the generation that is passing off the stage. Of homicides from 50 to 60 years of age, the negroes furnish about one-fifth, which is not quite twice their share in proportion to population; from 30 to 40, they furnish about one-third; from 20 to 30 nearly one-half; and under 20 years of age two-thirds of the homicides are negroes, that is, six times their share in proportion to population.

That this disparity is not due to any prejudice against the negro in the courts of the South is shown by the fact that in the State of Pennsylvania, where the negroes form only 2 per cent. of the population, they furnish 16 per cent. of the male prisoners and 34 per cent. of the female; and in Chicago, which some colored people call the "Negroes' Heaven," while they form only 1½ per cent. of the population, they furnish ten per cent. of the arrests.*

In order to avoid every appearance of prejudice or unfairness that might be supposed to color a white man's portrayal, I have presented the dark side of the picture as painted chiefly by a prominent negro educator who is giving his life to the amelioration of his people. One of the most hopeful auguries for the race is to be found in the clear-sightedness, candor and moral earnestness of Prof. Harris and his compeers.

V. And now, we come to the serious question, Wherein lie

---

* Prof. Eugene Harris in "Report of Commissioner of Education," 1896-97, Vol. 2, p. 2312.

the causes of this appalling increase in immorality and crime?
The main causes are three:

1. The sudden and violent removal of the restraints put upon the negro by slavery and his elevation to a position for which he was not prepared. The New York Voice, which will not be suspected of a bias toward the institution of slavery, said in a recent editorial: "It has been the subject of frequent remark in the last 30 years that these same negroes showed themselves remarkably free from any disposition to commit either murder or rape prior to the civil war, and during the civil war when they were left as almost the sole guardians of the women of the Southland. Where were these primitive instincts then? They were latent, we are told. Why are they not latent now? The question is a formidable one. Doubtless the conditions of freedom, the removal of habitual restraint, the sense of unaccustomed liberty, has had something to do with it."

In slavery the negro was kept under the influence, largely, of the best people of the South. The firm hand of the good master and the gentle ministry of the kind mistress, and the care of little children, made him tender, loyal and affectionate. Since emancipation, "while the good of the land have left him largely alone, the workers of sin have been active to a remarkable degree; the vicious of both races have met and mingled and ripened into criminality, until the land cries aloud."*

The negro was plunged into an environment for which he was not prepared; he was not ready for sudden emancipation, much less for citizenship. The bestowment of the franchise alienated him from those who were his life-long and natural friends, and betrayed him into the hands of those who have proved to be his worst enemies. This is now clearly seen and strongly expressed by some of the wisest leaders of the race.

The Rev. James L. White, a colored minister of North Carolina, in an address delivered before a large audience of colored people in Washington City a few weeks ago, said, as reported in the Washington Post: "Colored men have been marshaled for over 30 years to fight against the interests

---

* Rt. Rev. C. Clifton Penick, D.D., "The Struggles, Perils and Hopes of the Negro in the United States." p. 17.

of the South. This political war in the South will continue as long as the colored men are led by these third-class men. These men have misled the colored people ever since the civil war."

Prof. Booker T. Washington in an address recently delivered in the Old South Church, Boston, said in part: "It was unfortunate that, with few exceptions, those of the white race, from the North, who got the political control of the South in the beginning of our freedom were not men of such high and unselfish natures as to lead them to do something that fundamentally and permanently would help the negro, rather than yield to the temptation to use the negro as a means to lift themselves into political power and eminence. This mistake had the effect of making the negro and the Southern white man political enemies.

It was unfortunate that the negro got the idea that every Southern white man was opposed by nature to his highest friend in the white man who was removed from him by a disinterest and advancement, and that he could only find a tance of thousands of miles."*

The very statesmen of the South who deprecated most earnestly the existence and continuance of slavery saw most clearly the dangers of sudden emancipation.

"Much as I deplore slavery," said Patrick Henry, "I see that prudence forbids its abolition." Chief Justice Marshall declared that abolition would not remove the evils caused by the negro's presence.

Jefferson dreaded the effects of immediate emancipation, and leaned towards colonization as a remedy, with grave doubts of its practicability.

Henry Clay declared, "The evils of slavery are absolutely nothing in comparison with the far greater evils which would inevitably follow, from a sudden, general and indiscriminate emancipation." †

The sentiment in favor of gradual emancipation was beginning to take hold in the South, "when the counter movement of forcible and immediate abolition by the general government was initiated." ‡

* "Boston Transcript," January 9, 1899.
† White's "Lee and the Southern Confederacy," p. 66.
‡ Rev. H. M. White, D.D., "W. S. White and His Times," Chap. 13.

The circulation of incendiary publications intended to instigate the slaves to insurrection put the South on the defensive, and the instinct of self-preservation estopped all plans for the education of the negro with a view to preparing him for freedom.

Our Northern friends who take it for granted that we have safely passed the dangers predicted by the statesmen of a hundred years ago, will do well to ponder recent words of thoughtful men of the North on the race question of today. Theodore Roosevelt writes, in his Life of Benton: "It was perfectly possible and reasonable for enlightened and virtuous men, who fully recognized slavery as an evil, yet to prefer its continuance to having it interfered with in a way that would produce even worse results. Black slavery in Hayti was characterized by worse abuse than ever was the case in the United States; yet looking at the condition of that republic now, it may well be questioned whether it would not have been greatly to her benefit in the end to have had slavery continue a century or so longer."

G. T. Curtis, in the Life of Buchanan, declares: "Emancipation without any training for freedom could not be a blessing. . . . . . .The Christianity and the philanthropy of this age have before them a task that is far more serious, more weighty and more difficult than it would have been, if the emancipation had been a regulated process, even if its final consummation had been postponed for generations."

These sentiments of Northern men sound like an echo of those expressed by Gen. Robert E. Lee, in 1856: "There are few, I believe, in this enlightened age, who will not acknowledge that slavery as an institution is a moral and political evil in any country. It is useless to expatiate on its disadvantages. I think it a greater evil to the white than to the black race. While my feelings are strongly enlisted in behalf of the latter, my sympathies are more strong for the former. The blacks are immeasurably better off here than in Africa, morally, physically and socially. The painful discipline they are undergoing is necessary for their further instruction as a race, and I hope will prepare them for better things. How long their servitude may be necessary is known and ordered by a merciful Providence. Their emancipation will sooner result from the mild and melting influences of Christianity than from the storms and tempests of fiery controversy. This influence, though slow, is sure. . . . . . While we see the course of the final abolition of human slavery is still onward, and give it the aid of our prayers, and all justifiable means in our power, we must leave the progress as well as the result in His hands who sees the end; who chooses to work by slow influences; with whom a thousand years are but as a single day."*

Of course no one deems it either possible or desirable to re-instate the institution of slavery. We must face the situation as it is. One of the greatest dangers threatening the South today is, that burdened with the evils that have grown out of sudden and violent abolition, she may resort more and more to sudden and violent means of relieving herself of these burdens. The shot-gun policy is far from being an ideal one among a civilized people, and political legerdemain is even worse. Any limitation that may be put on the suffrage should not discriminate against the negro as such, but should apply to white and black alike. Let us beware of the boomerang of injustice.

2. The second cause of increased crime among the negroes is the all too common resort to lynching instead of to law, as a corrective of crime.

Within the past fifteen years nearly 2,500 persons have been lynched in the United States. According to a record kept by the Chicago Tribune there were, for the years 1886 to 1895, 1,655 lynchings as against 1,040 legal executions. †

We need not be surprised to find that crime has progressed with rapid strides under the lash of lawlessness. In 1886 there were 1,449 murders committed in the United States; in 1895, by an alarming yearly increase, the record had grown to 7,900.

A large proportion of the lynchings are perpetrated in the South. In the year 1889 there were 117 lynchings in the United States, of which 94, or about 80 per cent. of the whole number, were in the South. Some one may say that this is due to the presence of the negroes among us, and that

* White's "Lee and the Southern Confederacy," pp. 50, 51, 77.
† "Encyclopedia of Social Reform," p. 694.

under the same conditions lynchings would be just as prevalent at the North. This may be true, and if we were answerable only to Northern newspapers, the reply might suffice. But it will not satisfy a healthy conscience. Much less will it adequately meet God's awful question, "Where is thy brother?" Verily, our brother's blood crieth against us from the ground.

The prevalence of the terrible crime against womanhood does not excuse us. Unless we can find a way to deal with this exasperating evil by process of law rather than by the fury of the mob, we shall be overwhelmed by the lawlessness that lawlessness begets. "Lynch law as an epidemic will never be suppressed," says Dr. E. L. Pell, "by ignoring the conditions which keep the atmosphere infected with the germs of the lynching fever. Briefly stated these conditions are: (1). The prevalence of crime among the blacks and (2) the prevalence of race prejudice among the whites. A serious difficulty which has confronted the student of the problem from the beginning is the popular disposition to ignore one or the other of these conditions. For a long while the friends of the negro at the North saw nothing to account for the infected state of the atmosphere but race prejudice, while the average Southerner could see nothing but negro crime."

As to the proper attitude of North and South respectively to this question, Dr. Pell makes a most valuable suggestion. He recommends that the two sections exchange texts. That Northern preaching, which is most influential with the negro, should be directed against negro crime, and that Southern preaching, which is most influential with the white people of this section, should be directed against lawlessness and race prejudice.*

The trouble has been that the thrusts of North and South have been against each other rather than against lynching and the crime that provokes it. The result has been an endless logomachy that has only aggravated these evils.

3. The third, and chief, cause of the demoralization of the negroes has been the comparative indifference of the white

---

* "The American Review of Reviews," March, 1898.

203

Christians of the South to the religious interests of these people since the civil war.

Under the regime of slavery, as we have seen, a great deal was done by the Southern whites for the evangelization of the negroes. Whilst no one will claim that all was done that might have been done, yet, admitting all shortcomings, it remains true that the history of the world furnishes no parallel case of so rapid an uplifting of a race from the lowest fetichism to Christian worship. Slavery, with all its drawbacks, was as Gen. Armstrong says, "the greatest missionary enterprise of the century."

Now, if the Southern whites had, after the war, not only continued but redoubled their direct efforts for the religious advancement of the negro, there would have been a very different state of affairs in the South today. But, unfortunately, since 1865 the mass of the white Christians of the South have taken no serious interest in the evangelization of the negroes. This indifference may be explained in part, but it can never be justified. When the negro and the Southern white man parted company politically, they also parted company ecclesiastically. When, as Booker Washington says, the negro got the idea that "every Southern white man was opposed by nature to his highest interests and advancement," it was inevitable that this should make it extremely difficult for the Southern white man to reach him with religious instruction. The negro, taught to believe that the whites of the South knew nothing of politics, drew the inference that they knew even less of religion. But the presence of a difficulty can never absolve from a duty. And it was the duty of the white Christians of the South to put forth more persistent efforts to help the negro religiously. We might not have been able to do all that was desirable, but this does not excuse us for doing little or nothing.

As to the Southern Presbyterian Church it is not too much to say that, except for sporadic efforts here and there, it has practically settled down to a policy of inactivity, if not of indifference, towards what in the minutes of our ecclesiastical courts we are pleased to call "Colored Evangelization."

In their report to the General Assembly of 1898, the Executive Committee of Colored Evangelization have this to say of

204

the difficulties met with: "Many of the obstacles that confront us are, perhaps, inherent in this particular work. But by far the most serious difficulty is the indifference of our people."

Rev. O. B. Wilson, who was appointed by the Assembly of 1897 to visit the churches in order to raise $10,000 for Stillman Institute, says in his report to the Assembly of 1898: "The task was not an enviable one, neither easy nor pleasant. It was encompassed with difficulties. The cause itself is unpopular; the times were stated to be 'very unsuitable for raising money'; the 'other calls were numerous,' etc. But a conviction of the crying needs of the work—a conviction that came from actual contact with it—converted the difficulties into a stimulus. I was deeply convinced that the very lethargy prevailing was a reason of unanswerable force demonstrating the need of vigorous work. . . . . . While I found much prejudice against the work in the minds of very many people, and a great indifference toward it, yet it was also noticeably true that in nearly every congregation there seemed to be a few persons, earnest souls, who took more than a mere passing interest in the subject, as if they had already felt that this part of our work was greatly neglected, and they stood ready to assist in it. Unless our professed belief in the value of souls is empty talk, how can it be otherwise?"

It will appear from all that has been said that the race problem in the South is, perhaps, the most difficult problem that God in His providence ever submitted to any people for solution. There is, after all, but one satisfactory solution to be found, the preaching to white and to black of the everlasting gospel, which is the wisdom of God and the power of God.

Dr. A. L. Phillips quotes a distinguished divine as saying, "Unless the gospel solve this matter, then it will be bang! bang!"*

VI. This paper will conclude with some reasons why the church, and especially the Southern Presbyterian branch of the church, should cast off indifference and gird herself for this work.

1. The welfare of our own posterity is at stake. Our children

---

* "Presbyterian Quarterly," October, 1891, p. 539.

and the children of our negro neighbors are to live side by side. Unless the white man elevates the negro, the negro will inevitably degrade the white man. Can our children live in contact with a race which, as has been shown, is making fearful strides in immorality and crime, and not be affected for the worse thereby?

It is said that Sir Robert Peel's daughter died of typhus fever of the most malignant type; and when inquiry was made as to how she had caught the infection, it was discovered that it was through a beautiful riding habit presented to her by her father. This riding habit, bought from a London tradesman, had been made in a miserable attic, where the husband of the seamstress was lying ill of fever, and it had been used by her to cover him in his shivering fits. The highest are not proof against infection that originates among the lowest.

Unless we meet this moral leprosy with Christ's word of power, "Be thou clean," it will pollute and destroy both races alike!

It is also to the interest of the coming generations that the South should be the negro's chief almoner. While we have no right to complain if others do what we leave undone, and while we are gratefully to welcome aid from without, the South cannot afford to relegate the evangelization of the negroes to others. What Gov. Vance said of the state and secular education applies equally to the church and religious instruction: "I regard it as an unmistakable policy to imbue these black people with a thorough North Carolina feeling, and make them cease to look abroad for the aids to their progress and civilization, and the protection of their rights as they have been taught to do, and teach them to look to their own state instead; to teach them that their welfare is indissolubly linked with ours."*

2. The Presbyterian church can do more than any other for the negro. In saying this, there is no intention to disparage the work done by other denominations. It is only claiming for the Presbyterian church what each denomination claims for itself without breach of true charity.

---

* "Message to the General Assembly of N. C.," 1877.

The Presbyterian church believes that it is peculiarly fitted to give the negro what he needs. The negro is, on the one hand, extravagantly emotional, and, on the other hand, extravagantly fond of uniform, whether military or ecclesiastical. The first of these characteristics has given the churches that emphasize emotionalism a strong hold on him in the past, and the second will give the churches that emphasize ritualism a firmer and firmer hold on him in the future, as his love of the showy blossoms into estheticism. These same characteristics will cause the work of the Presbyterian church for the negro to be slow; that is, if we are to give him what he needs rather than what he wants. His needs are, in our judgment, a soundly educated ministry, sober instruction, simple and quiet rather than ritualistic or emotional modes of worship, a simple and orderly system of church government and discipline, and a "home life in which the children will be carefully trained and instructed in the word of God and in the faith of the church."*

3. The work of the Southern Presbyterian church for the negro has reached the gravest crisis in its history. The few, feeble, and widely scattered negro churches, heretofore in organic union with the white churches, have been organized into an Independent African Presbyterian church. The charge has been brought against us that we have taken this action because of race prejudice, and with the purpose to rid ourselves of the burden of colored evangelization.

Those who bring the charge ignore the fact that it was at the request of the colored ministers and elders in convention assembled that this step was taken. †

Our critics, too, wherever they are brought into ecclesiastical proximity to the negroes, manifest the very race prejudice they charge against us.

These facts may serve as missiles to hurl at those who censure us; but they will not relieve us of odium in the sight of God and man, if we allow the new-born African Presbyterian church to perish for lack of sympathy and support. We shall be "made a spectacle unto the world, and to angels, and to men."

---

* Rev. D. Clay Lilly.
† Dr. A. L. Phillips, "The Independent," Feb. 24, 1898.

4. The Southern Presbyterian church should enter with fresh faith and enthusiasm into this work, because of the wide door that has been opened to us in Africa. The story of our Mission on the Congo may be classed among the wonders of modern missionary annals.

Our Secretary of Foreign Missions has said that if the work of colored evangelization had done nothing more than to raise up the colored missionaries now in the African field, the church would still be repaid a hundred-fold for all the money she has expended for the blacks. How are we to enlarge the work in Africa so signally blessed with God's favor except by enlarging the work for the negroes at home? And how absurdly inconsistent to send missionaries to Africa while we neglect the Africans at our doors!

5. This is a singularly opportune time to enlist the intelligent interest of the Christian people of every section of the Union in the race problem.

Events that have occurred in Ohio within the past two or three years, and more recent events in Illinois are calling attention to the race question as a national problem, whose difficulties develop wherever the two races are brought together, especially where there has been no prior period of gradual adjustment as in the South. What would be the result if half a million negroes could be suddenly injected into the population of one of these states?

The annexation of Hawaii and the proposed policy of expansion have brought the whole American people with startling suddenness face to face with a new race problem.

The Spanish-American war has done much to heal the breach made by the war between the states. When we see the grandson of General U. S. Grant serving on the staff of General Fitzhugh Lee, it looks as if North and South had indeed clasped hands.

We may expect from henceforth, with the blessing of God, a better understanding and a closer sympathy between the people of the two sections in regard to the race problem.

Much has been said of late years about the "New South," but out of the mists of ignorance and prejudice concerning the race problem, "there is emerging a New North."*

* "The North Carolina Presbyterian."

208

The New North and the New South, recognizing the common responsibility of the two sections for the existence of the race problem, and approaching this problem with mutual understanding and sympathy and an earnest desire for the best interests of white and black alike, can do more in five years towards a satisfactory settlement of the race question, than has been accomplished in thirty-five years of mistrust and contention.

Let the prayers of Christians, white and black, from one end of this land to the other, rise to God for wisdom and grace to solve this problem according to His righteous will!

"THE SACRIFICE OF A RACE"

By Dr. P. B. Barringer, M.D., LL.D.

An address delivered by him before the Race
Conference at Montgomery, Ala.,
May 10th, 1900.

Copies of this address may be had, for twenty cents each,
at Anderson Bros., Charlottesville, Va.

RALEIGH, N. C.
Edwards & Broughton, Printers and Binders

1900

PREFACE.

The history of the negro, as a race, is one of profound pathos. From time immemorial and in all places he has been the burden-bearer, the plaything, the tool and the discarded dupe of his more fortunate brothers. Where are the fifteen thousand negroes imported into Great Britain before the "trade" was abolished? Gone! Where are those taken to Portugal and Spain by pious (?) Prince Henry "in order that they might be made Christians?" Gone! Not a trace. Where are the thousands which Carthage, before the Punic wars, furnished Rome? An occasional suspicious excess in the richness of Neapolitan tint is seemingly the sole remainder. Yet he has always served well. He served us here in the South long and faithfully, but, in view of what is now seen, can it be claimed that we worked the negro harder or more effectually than the abolitionists unwittingly "worked" him? The effect of their working was seen in the war, the hardness of it in his present condition. Well may belated philanthropy pour out its gold, but if they paid till the very soil of the South could be worked as an ore, they could not atone to him. Can millions save him? I am afraid not—it is full late. Few appreciate how far he has already gone back to original racial tendencies. Here is an intelligent, upright, honest negro, and there another, but they, as a rule, were born slaves; few indeed are the men of promise under thirty

213

years of age and fewer under twenty; and so strong is the downward current that most of them who stand fast are destroyed by attrition.

If the young negro can be taught to work he can be saved. Will industrial training do this? It may if simplified or limited to agriculture. The present system of industrial education gives too little industry and too much education. We might as well, moreover, be frank and confess that the trades unions, fast coming into the South, will not let a negro work at a trade. Here, as well as North, when it comes to a fight, industrial or otherwise, between white and black, the whites are for the whites. What then? Compassion, charity and mercy; missionaries, churches and hospitals—i. e., euthanasia.

But there can be no euthanasia for him who knows the symptoms of his disease and the physiological effects of the anodyne. Educate then, henceforth, the soul and the hand—more than the mind.

"THE SACRIFICE OF A RACE."

In the summer of 1619 there sailed into Chesapeake Bay an English privateer, cruising under foreign letters of marque (Savoyan), which had on board what remained of a hundred negroes captured from a Spanish vessel in the West Indies. This privateer*, "The Treasurer," was commanded by Captain Daniel Elfrith, and leaving twenty of these negroes at Jamestown, he sailed for Bermuda, where he placed the remainder on the Earl of Warwick's plantation on that island. Of these twenty negroes two became the property of William Tucker ("gentleman"), of Elizabeth City County. These, a man and a woman, he named respectively, Anthony and Isabell, and to them was born a child, "baptized" William, seemingly the first American of African descent born on this continent. [Brown's "Genesis of the United States," Vol. II, pp. 886, 1034.] The birth of this child inaugurated a new race, and one whose history I am here to-day to recall and whose end I am here to predict.

The salient features of the history of this race up to the present are about as follows: A race of savage blacks, with one exception—the original tribes of Australia—the lowest of human kind, with fifty centuries of unbroken barbarism behind them, were torn from their native tropical land and transported to a republic founded as an asylum for those seeking to be free. But these blacks came not here for freedom; they were brought against their will, and to be slaves. It was not alone against their own will that they came. They came against the general wish of the Southern colonists, for while the pious clergy 'of New England were hailing the arrival of a slaver with prayer-

---

* Privateers at this time were called "Dutch men of war."

215

ful thanks, "because a gracious and over-ruling Providence had been pleased to bring to this land of freedom another cargo of benighted heathen to enjoy the blessing of a Gospel dispensation," [Curry's "Southern States of American Union," p. 163] the colonies of Virginia and South Carolina were petitioning the mother country to stop the slave trade. But the stock of the Guinea Company was owned in high places, [Brown's Genesis of the United States, p. 981,] and the colonists continued to be tempted, while the daily demonstrated fitness of the blacks for hard labor in this sunny clime caused a gradual change in the colonial sentiment. In a virgin land of incomparable fertility strong laborers were, of course, extremely useful, and hence much valued. Being valuable they were allowed to multiply, but this under a careful selective process of breeding that outstripped nature itself. Docility, decency, fealty and vigor were desired, and the slave man having these attributes, with his master's "pass," scorned the rural "paterroller" and roamed at will to replenish the earth. This selective propagation in which intelligence made use, in order, of animal desire, infant hygiene, race tendency to mimicry, the glamour of feudalism, and even religion itself, not only caused the negro to increase in numbers, but also to improve in kind. In a few generations the spindle-shanked and pot-bellied Ibo (Eboi) improved in shape as well as feature. The vigorous blue-black Wolof, the blackest but the finest of the West Coast negroes, and of whom not over a thousand a year were imported, became the type and the ideal. Mandingans, Ashantis, Fans, Yorubas, one and all, were made to conform, for the large were tempted with the small and the weak with the strong. The laws of breeding obtained through centuries of experience with the lower animals had here found a wider and a higher field. American slavery

7

has been described, and rightly, as "the greatest missionary effort in human history," but, in its early stages, it was more than this: it was the first and only application of intelligent hygiene to a special race, and that it should have been successful in improving it was natural, for the intelligence which was most potent in the upbuilding of this republic, then and afterwards, in fair measure divided its time with the abstruse problem of slave propagation. But under this intelligent stimulus the increase was so great that the plantations of the East were quickly stocked and the westward migration of younger sons with young families of slaves necessarily inaugurated that separation of families which was the first thing to influence the sentiment of the South against slavery. From this time on the multiplication of the negro steadily declined, for its necessary evils and dangers were now seen. But by this time, under artificial conditions, the vigor and prepotency of this race of exotics had been established. They increased so rapidly that it alarmed the whites and forced the transportation of slaves to more southern and western territories to avoid a dangerous local predominance.

The first stage of the slave problem now faced them. It must be clearly understood that the sentiment of the age favored slavery and any feeling against it in any quarter was influenced solely by local conditions. To-day there is not a State in New England that can maintain its negro population without importation,* and we can well imagine what must have been the state of affairs with the crude hygiene of colonial days. Being unprofitable in New England, slavery there naturally became unpopular, but

*Dr. Fisher, for many years registrar of vital statistics for Rhode Island says: "We must conclude, however reluctantly, that the race (negro) is not self-sustaining in this climate." The registrar of Massachusetts reluctantly admits the same thing.—*Hoffman's American Negro, p. 36.*

not until long after it had become a problem of danger in the South. In 1780, when Massachusetts, the first to act, freed her remaining handful of slaves, the four States of Virginia, North Carolina, South Carolina and Georgia, had almost a half million. It was then too late to let go; the South could only hold on and make the best of it.

It was soon seen that the American-bred negro was so much better than the "salt-water black" that this, coupled with the alarming increase in the Southern colonies, made the South demand the abolition of the trade. In this she was out-voted by the North, whose interests now lay in slave transport rather than in slave labor. This demand ultimately became so strong on the part of the South that the government was forced to stop the trade, but only after twenty years lease of life had been added, [As the result of what Washington called a "dirty bargain" South Carolina and Georgia voted with the North and permitted this. North Carolina met this by putting a tax of £5 on every negro imported after 1788,] carrying it to 1808. If the rate of negro increase for the first hundred years of slavery had been maintained to the present day, there would be nearly 26,000,000 negroes in the United States. [Darby's table, "View of the United States," p. 439.] But this was not to be, and it never will be; America will never see 26,000,000 negroes within its limits.

The reason that it was not to be was that there was early abroad in parts of this land, as one of its characteristic features, a spirit of sentimental altruism which was founded on the glittering generalities of the Declaration of Independence, a campaign document, rather than on the cold, logical and business-like statements of the constitution. This new cult placed itself above religion, above Christianity, and demanded a new Bible and a new Christ, because Christ and the old Bible [Exodus 21:6] both recognized slavery. It has been charged that this high and holy altruism was tinctured with the baser motives of policy, sectional jealousy, and even with the remains of an old Puritan-Cavalier hatred; but we of the South are of necessity biased judges. At any rate, the logical and inevitable result of such a spirit of universal brotherhood as then prevailed was the demand, sooner or later, on the part of the North, where this epidemic was prevalent, for the abolition of slavery.

The South, knowing that the negro could never be maintained within its borders as a freedman, refused. For years the fight went on, various compromises and plans being suggested, but none being satisfactory. From the beginning of this century up to 1860, the political history of this country consisted of a long parliamentary fight for and against slavery. The great men of the South and of the Union, Washington, Jefferson, Madison, Monroe, Randolph, Macon, Clay, Calhoun and others, were all slave owners, but all equally abhorred the evil practices of slavery. Not one of these ever dared urge general emancipation for the South where the negroes were numerous; and whenever any of them manumitted their own slaves they endeavored to send them out of the South. Randolph even bought land in Ohio and there set up his slaves in freedom, but they were not allowed to remain. [Mrs. A. Dixon's History of the Missouri Compromise, p. 249.] The reason of all this was that these men, as slave owners, knew the negro and knew that underneath his dusky skin the simple intelligence of a child was combined with the instincts of a veritable savage. They felt and knew that the negro as a freedman could not exist in America. They had seen and were familiar with the original cannibal African from which their loyal and affectionate slaves had sprung, and they knew that force, unobtrusive but steady

2

and persistent force, was necessary to the continuance in well-doing of this race of pagans but recently reclaimed. But in 1860 compromise failed, and though disguised in other forms,* the demand for the abolition of slavery became urgent; then came the war.

For our present purpose the most remarkable thing about that war was the fact that while its initial act consisted in the uprising of a few slaves on the border, under the influence of white persuasion, the slaves of the true South could not be induced to rise against their masters. Had the Southern man not known the negro, he would have thought as the North thought, that he was fighting with foes behind him as well as in front; but he knew, as he alone could know, that the negro was contented and happy in slavery. Had they been but let alone they would have remained contented. At all events when put to the test, the negro did not turn against the wife and children of his absent master, when everything possible favored an uprising. Negro regiments were organized, armed, and paraded up and down the border; brass bands were played, incendiary speeches made and altruism preached with a whoop, but the negroes did not rise. As Professor Shaler, of Harvard, well says: "If the accepted account of the negro had been true, if he had been for generations groaning in servitude while he passionately longed for liberty, the South should have flamed in insurrection at the first touch of war. We should have seen a repetition of the horrors of many a civil insurrection. It is a most notable fact that during the four years of the great contention

---

* After the war Senator Ingalls. of Kansas, said: "Waged ostensibly to maintain the integrity of the Union and in denial of the dogma of State sovereignty, the future historian will not fail to note that the three amendments" which he calls the "trophies of the victors," chiefly "relate to the freedom, citizenship and suffrage of the negro race."—*Curry's South, p. 219.*

when the blacks had every opportunity to rise, there was
no real mark of a disposition to turn upon their masters.
On thousands of Southern farms the fighting men left
their women and children in the keeping of their slaves
while they fought for a cause whose success meant that
those slaves could never be free." [Popular Science
Monthly, March, 1900, p. 520.] They were happy and
did not wish to be free. On this historic fact the South
takes her stand, and all the theories of the world will not
prevail against it.

To the people of the South the war of secession was practical annihilation. When that contest and its results are
compared with others of similar condition and circumstances, it will be seen that no people ever came nearer the
giving of their absolute all to a cause than did the people of
the South to the Southern Confederacy. Notwithstanding
this I have yet to meet the man of Southern lineage who
does not say with me that all the blood and all the treasure
given to that cause would have been well spent had it
effectually and for all time freed America from the negro.
But this it has not yet done as the people of the South well
know.

Accustomed as they were to the presence of the negro,
the people of the South were, after the war, slow to appreciate the fact that although the negro was gone as a slave,
he was in no sense removed as a burden. As they gathered around their broken hearthstones and desolate altars,
trying to keep alive and restore to flame the embers of a
civilization that they swore in their hearts should never
perish, they had little time for thought as to the future of
the negro as a freedman, for they looked beyond the negro
as the source of their then present evils.

As time passed on the Southern people began to see that
the war with all its losses had so far solved nothing, and

the white man's burden was still upon them and upon them alone. The savage, which their own insane folly had allowed them to buy and to breed, was, without other restraint than the law, henceforth to be their close associate and neighbor. Of necessity they tried to make the best of their condition, and they endeavored to explain to him the law, and then for the first time were reminded that for the negro there was neither the concept nor the word for law, as we know it. Could anything else have been expected? Where was the negro when our ancestors wrung from halting royalty Magna Charta? Where was he when the Petition of Right, Habeas Corpus and the Bill of Rights gave to us and to our children forever these benefits for which our fathers fought? Where was he? He was an unalloyed pagan in a tropical jungle, savage, brutal and ignorant—a cannibal and a trader in human flesh—two women for a "plug" hat, a man for a handkerchief and a child for a Jew's harp.

In his racial history from pagan to citizen he had never felt the emotions which called into existence our bulwarks of human right and liberty; stripes and shackles he had known, but neither the law nor the reason thereof; force, brutal force in his own land, and unobtrusive but unabating force in America. No appeal had ever been made to his sense of right, and the only appeal for which he had ear was the emphatic demand of power.

The people of the South next tried to instruct the negro in the economics; they tried to teach him how and to make him provide for the morrow, and again without a thought as to his racial history. They should have recalled the fact that for over fifty centuries [Erman in his "Ancient Egypt" puts the negro as a slave in Egypt as early as 2500-3500 B. C.,] of recorded history the negro had lived in tropical Africa where every law of nature conspired to make him improvident and thoughtless of the future. They should have recalled that as the slave of a slave master, who was, in turn, the slave of some petty chieftain whose only title to royalty was his superlative savagery, he had lived without guarantee of the morrow, feeling that his life might be demanded at any instant. He thus of necessity lived for the pleasures of the hour until it grew into a racial attribute, and the happy, thoughtless, goodnatured negro of days agone was true to his phylogeny. This was the alarming condition that faced the South at the close of the war. The old slave was, in the main, loyal and faithful, but as he was rapidly becoming a knave's dupe as a voter, what would the next generation be? In their perplexity the South thought that the education of the negro would solve their problem, so they divided in fair measure their own taxes with him (he had nothing) and began. For thirty years, ever increasing, never diminishing, they have poured out their hard-earned cash for him at the expense of the poor among their own people. What this has done for him, we shall see later, but first let us see what he and his friends did for the South.

For more than a decade after the war the South had what in popular speech is called "a hard time." A degraded and alien race, but recently slaves, had, by congressional enactment, been placed in control of eleven once sovereign Southern States. Men of this race whose grandfathers had decided between guilt and innocence through the chance of direct or reversed peristalsis with the "ordeal bean,"* sat in judgment over men whose forefathers had fought at Yorktown, Guilford, Kings Moun-

---

*Calabar bean (Physostigma venenosum) a poison of purgative-emetic properties, used on the Niger to determine guilt or innocence. If the accused vomits and recovers he is adjudged innocent, while if he does not vomit and dies, he is considered as having been guilty.

tain and New Orleans. Negro men who would turn back from any journey however needful if "a cat crossed the road behind them," boldly launched public enterprises that obligated the State for millions. I have myself heard the "Speaker" of a Southern Legislature addressed from the floor as "Marse Robert." Happy indeed in that day were those possessed of a sense of humor, for the explosions of mirth alone prevented the explosions of wrath. But these things passed. Amendments to the constitution count as naught when pitted against the inexorable laws of nature, and in time the white man came to his own. The Southern people now simply laugh at these episodes; they, as before stated, looked beyond the negro and were content to wait. But while they waited they worked.

For twenty long years they strained and yet it seemed the South would never move. It was not that their land was ravaged and laid bare—their people had reclaimed this same land when a primal wilderness. It was not the burden of negro education—they thought that a good investment; nor was it that temporary negro domination had imposed colossal financial burdens ($293,000,000)—they had faced greater odds. [It should not be forgotten that two and one-half thousand million dollars worth of property was wiped out of existence in the South by the proclamation of emancipation.] It was without lament, but rather with a grim pride in their handiwork that they paid their share of the Federal pensions and voluntarily supported, as best they could, their own veterans. But new evils came as old evils grew. The eternal vigilance required to keep down and repress the negro vote wore upon them, for this necessity always bore more harshly upon the conscience and morale of the white man than it did upon the hide of the black. They were weary, weary to the very core, but unbroken in spirit, when at last they began to feel that the burden moved—the South was rising.

It was not until the load was well lifted that the South began to see the burden that had held her down—an animate, living, growing burden, the negro—the negro to whom the South had hitherto always looked as a source of profit. It was their first intimation that the negro had changed, but he has changed, and the next generation will change more. This, however, I wish to recall—that when the "carpet bagger" had departed with the profits of the "Freedman's Bureau" in his pocket, the poor, wasted, stricken South, from a spirit of true altruism, spent hundreds of millions in an honest effort to improve the negro.

That slavery had inherent evils no man can deny, but under Southern slavery this much can be said—the negro improved both physically and morally, and, as a race, he was content. The Southern slave owner made a man of the savage; by intelligent and self-sacrificing care he overcame the natural tendency of a tropical race to decline in other climes, and he even, as we shall see later, reversed the law and made negro mortality in the South less than the white. (See table, page 23.) Slavery as it existed here was designed to shield and protect the negro at every point, and this it did, but of necessity the more it protected the more helpless it left him when its guardianship was withdrawn. And who withdrew this guardianship? The fine Italian hand which before the war bedecked the pagan with a "halo," and after the war mocked the ex-slave with the ballot, and which now black-balls the "coon" in the trades union, is the same which loosed him for the sacrifice. But God is not mocked, and when France recovers from the influence of the altruistic* cry of 1793, then may the aristocracy of culture and refinement in the Northern States of America see the dawn of deliverance. Their walking delegate of to-day with all that he implies is the mixed product of false altruism and the true anarchy born of it.

There is much use in this day and generation of the term "survival of the fittest," but few who use it ever stop to think of the complemental axiom, "the death of the unfit." Yet that truth has sounded the death knell of untold millions. Where is the Tasmanian, the Carib, the Hawaiian, the Iroquois and others of the American tribes that first met the white man? Their doom was sealed when "the fittest" first set foot on their shores. They perished as wild animals perish before man. But all wild animals do not so perish. If man needs them they survive. Here in the Sunny South my little boys have a dozen English rabbits which they breed to any demand, but if I were to force them to turn them loose in this land of orchards, shotguns, cur-dogs and cats not one of them would survive. No! Subjected to natural law they would go like snow before the sun, and so, in due time, will the negro go. He is living even now on the stamina and morality of slavery days.

Now it must be clearly understood that during slavery the negro, as a race, was not subjected to natural law; his existence here from the beginning, was absolutely artificial. Coming to us as an hereditary pagan, he was for over two centuries a slave in whom the functions of nutrition, muscular activity and reproduction were cultivated and given full play, and every function that tended to

---

* "Liberte, egalite, fraternite," was the cry of the Bastile. Such a cry could not appeal to the gentle and the respectable, but only to the slums. It was the cry of the proletariat for an assault upon aristocracy, as here.

make him inimical to the interests of his master, i. e., independent, was repressed. He was consequently fitted only for slavery.

With the proclamation of emancipation there began for the negro a new existence. For the first time since coming to America he was under the remorseless laws of nature, and being unfit to meet their demands here, he from that day, began to fall, and these are the signs of his fall.

(I will say before giving figures, that the simplest method of estimating the progress of a race or people is to compare that race with some other race under similar environment or with their own people at some other (earlier) period of time. The inherent diversity of the two races here compared, and the necessary difference in conditions in the times compared, render the problem difficult, but the results are so extremely one-sided as to banish doubt.)

First, we will consider material prosperity. There are but three States in the South that list white and colored property separately, these being Virginia, North Carolina and Georgia. [Hoffman's "Race Traits and Tendencies of the American Negro," p. 298.] In these the per capita wealth of the negroes was in 1891 as follows: Virginia, $18.90; North Carolina, $14.10; Georgia, $14.30; average per capita, $15.70 as compared with an average of $322.30 for the whites of the same three States. The relatively high per capita of $18.90 for the Virginia negroes demonstrates what all must have noticed—that the negroes there are physically and mentally superior to any in the South. Virginia was a slave-breeding State, and here naturally the best were kept and only the "culls" sold, but nevertheless throughout the South it is still a boast to be an "ole Virginny nigger." But if these are the best negroes what must be the wealth of the negroes of the general South when the taxable property of the Virginia negro is but 8.1 per cent of the whole? In Virginia moreover, the State expends on the negro annually [report of State Auditor, quoted by Hoffman, p. 301,]

For criminal expenses	$204,018
For education	324,364
For lunatics	80,000
Total negro expenses	608,882
Total negro taxes	103,565
Annual loss to Virginia, account of negro	504,817

It will be seen from the above that the annual net loss on the negro population of this State is over half a million dollars, and that the total negro taxes paid is even less by one hundred thousand dollars than the sum annually expended by the whites to repress negro crime. If this from the best, what of the "culls?" It must also be mentioned here that the larger part of the taxable property of the negroes throughout the South consists of small rural or suburban "patches" of real estate either given them by their old masters or else sold for a song, and that even the "unearned increment" of appreciation is due also to the whites who have built up the town and enhanced the value of the previous gift, pure or *quasi*.

Secondly, let us consider the negro from the standpoint of criminality. In Virginia (where I now live) there are now (census 1890) 1,020,000 whites to 635,000 blacks, but by the report of the superintendent of the Virginia penitentiary for 1899, there were among the State convicts only 404 whites as against 1,694 blacks, giving on the basis of population, negro criminality as 7.4 times greater than the white. The latest reports of the State penitentiaries from Maryland to Texas show about the same results, rising to 9.4 and 8.0 in Georgia, where progressive municipal administration draws the negro to town, and falling as low as 5.4 in Mississippi where the negroes live in the country and where white domination and negro disfranchisement are most complete. It will be understood that State convicts represent chiefly serious crime, but the jails and the chain gangs which, in the South, teem with additional thousands, are blacker still in proportion, for the Southern country negro as yet, thank God, figures chiefly in the minor crimes. In the cities he is, as a race, fast throwing off every vestige of moral restraint, as we see from the Washington Police Department report, quoted by the Baltimore *Sun* of March 30, last, which says of a city where the negro does not constitute one-third of the population, as follows: "According to one of the recent annual reports of the metropolitan police department there were, in the year, 10,587 arrests of whites and 11,975 of blacks. More than twice as many negroes as whites were arrested for carrying concealed weapons, more than twice as many for disorderly conduct, more than twice as many for assault and for assault and battery, more than twice as many for petty larceny and thirteen more for grand larceny, twice as many for profanity, seven times as many for criminal assault, and more than five times as many for housebreaking at night. Seven murders were committed by negroes to two by whites. In all the most heinous offenses known to criminology the negroes were largely in the excess. A very large proportion of all crimes were committed by young negro toughs under 25 years of age." And this from the "Mecca" where rather than repeal the fifteenth amendment and confess its folly, this government annually commits the outrage which brought on the revolution of '76.

But lest some "altruist" may think that his one-time

brother in black has suffered at Southern hands, I will quote elsewhere: In a recent paper on "Negro Criminality," [Address before American Social Science Association, September, 1899,] by Prof. Walter F. Wilcox, of Cornell University, a native of New England, and now statistician of the Census Office, we find that "in the Southern States there were six white prisoners to every 10,000 whites and twenty-nine negro prisoners to every 10,000 negroes." As Mr. Wilcox himself says, this difference might at first glance be ascribed to sectional prejudice, and he proceeds to combat this by making the declaration that "in the Northern States in 1890 there were twelve white prisoners to every 10,000 whites and 69 negro prisoners to every 10,000 negroes." In other words, if prejudice plays any part it is most pronounced at the North. This criminality of the negro, moreover, is not standing fast, for, as Mr. Wilcox further says, "The negro prisoners in the Southern States to 10,000 negroes increased between 1880 and 1890, 29 per cent, while the white prisoners to 10,000 whites increased only 8 per cent." In other words, crime among the American negro is, since the war, increasing with alarming rapidity because the negro, racially feeble in the power of conscience, is unable to meet the, to him, idealistic demands of the law. The short, quick shrift of the cowhide which he has always known, he can connect with the crime and abstain, but the slow procedure of Saxon jurisprudence makes the offense and the punishment as far apart in his mind as his religion and morality often are in fact.

But he is not only increasing in crime; he is developing what seems at first glance for him, a new form of crime. In a recent paper of rare candor and merit on the "Recent Erotic Tendency of the Southern Negro," [Carolina Medical Journal, March, 1900, p. 2,] Dr. S. C. Baker, of Sum-

21

ter, S. C., says, in speaking of this new crime for the negro: "Prior to their emancipation the crime of rape was almost unheard of. I have been able to learn of but one instance of even attempted rape, in this State (South Carolina), and that was unsuccessful." But speaking of the present he says: "The report of the Attorney-General of South Carolina for 1899 shows that there have been thirteen convictions for rape, and for assault with intent to ravish, twelve convictions during that year. All of them except one were cases of negro men against white women, the exception being the case of a negro man against a negro woman." Next, he confirms the views I have previously expressed in "The American Negro: His Past and Future," which were that it is the young negro of the South (the generation of negro with the one hundred million dollar education) that most shows the evidence of a reversion to barbarism and savagery, by the following: "The court stenographer of the third judicial circuit of this State furnished me the following information on the subject for the past ten years, as applying to his circuit: It may be remarked that the third circuit is about an average of the circuits of the State as to the density of population and its complexion, as to urban and rural inhabitants, intelligence and education of negroes, and so forth, and South Carolina is possibly about an average of the Southern States in these particulars. He says: "About twenty-five cases have come up for trial in this circuit during the past ten years, besides about five others which did not come up for trial because of the lynching of the accused. In all of these, with one exception, the negroes implicated were under thirty years of age. In the excepted case there were several negroes implicated, one being an older man who seemed to have been led on by the younger ones. For the crime of assault with intent to ravish I recall about ten cases, and all by negroes under thirty years of age. I am of opinion that 95 per cent of all crime in the third circuit is committed by the negro, and of this 95 per cent 90 per cent is committed by the free-born negro. It is very rare that you see an old slave charged with any crime. The majority of negro criminals are from fifteen to thirty years of age."

This, as figures go, seems to indicate a new form of crime for the negro, but I know, as you know, that it does not mean this. Did our prognathic, dolichocephalic cannibal come to us with brutal instincts moulded by centuries of crime on every lineament of his visage and yet clothed in the beatitude of sexual purity? No! When I see the leopard change his spots then will I believe it. It is a reversion pure and simple and these figures simply point again to the superb moral influence of slavery. In the hands of a gentle people the negro came quite near the gentleman, illiterate perhaps, but not ignorant, for mark you, there is a difference, as the history of some of our great men can testify.

But the question with us to-day is, can a race keep up this rapid criminal decline and live? Both the experience of the past and the present testify that it can not. Old as it is the saying "The wages of sin is death" might well have been taken from some modern work of hygiene.

Thirdly, I will take up the question of negro vital statistics, and here I must pay my respects to the work of Frederick L. Hoffman, from whose "Race Traits and Tendencies of the American Negro" [The MacMillan Company, New York,] most of these statistics are taken. An able, careful statistician, he brings an unbiased German mind to the solution of the greatest problem America has ever known. This book should be in the hands of every man who has at heart the future of his country.

These figures obtained from official reports are amply corroborated by private observation. Let me first take statistics bearing on the period before the war.

I have before spoken of the fact that in slavery the negro increased beyond measure. He was at that time really more prolific than the general white population of the South. This was owing chiefly to the fact that the negroes were owned by the wealthy and, being valuable, every care, hygienic and moral, was exercised, not only to see that they increased, but to rear them strong and healthy when born. The following statistics of four of the great cities of the South before and after the war will show, first, that there was a greater death rate among the whites before the war than among the negroes, and, secondly, that the mortality among the negroes since the war has largely increased:

ANNUAL MORTALITY PER THOUSAND.*

Charleston, S. C., from 1822–1894.

Before the War.		After the War.	
White	25.98	White	26.77
Negro	24.05	Negro	43.29

Savannah, Ga., from 1856–1894.

Before the War.		After the War.	
White	37.19	White	32.51
Negro	34.07	Negro	44.37

Mobile, Ala., from 1843–1894.

Before the War.		After the War.	
White	47.58	White	24.02
Negro	29.66	Negro	35.23

New Orleans, La., from 1849–1894.

Before the War.		After the War.	
White	59.60	White	26.71
Negro	52.10	Negro	42.56

Average of four Southern cities:

Before the War.		After the War.	
White	42.59	White	27.70
Negro	34.97	Negro	41.31

*Hoffman's "Race Traits and Tendencies of American Negro," pages 53–54.

(Parenthetically, observe that the whites are bestowing some care on their own health since relieved of the negro.)

The next stage of this subject will be the mortality of the negro since the war, and I will begin with the unborn child. It is known to everyone, especially to the physician, that children begotten out of wedlock are less apt to be reared than those begotten in legal matrimony. In approaching this subject I will first take a city where the negro is as favorably circumstanced as at any spot within the United States, viz: the capital city, Washington. The average for the sixteen years extending from 1879 to 1894, shows that while 2.9 per cent of the white children born were illegitimate, 22.5 per cent of all the negroes born in that city were out of wedlock. But that is far from being the worst of it. In the sixteen years extending from 1879 to 1894, the per cent of negro children born out of wedlock in this free city has risen from 17.6 per cent to the astounding figure of 26.5 per annum.

Next, let me consider death from still-birth in two cities of fairly representative type:

*DEATH FROM STILL-BIRTH PER 100,000 POPULATION UNDER ONE YEAR.

Washington, D. C.		Baltimore, Md.	
White	6,528	White	7,024
Negro	20,152	Negro	16,988

The negro certainly leads in not being born, but now let us see how the infants of this once strong and virile race are meeting the struggle for existence under natural law:

DEATH FROM DEBILITY, INANITION, ETC., PER 100,000 POPULATION UNDER ONE YEAR.

Washington, D. C.		Baltimore, Md.	
White	4,181	White	4,800
Negro	10,045	Negro	11,884

* "Race Traits and Tendencies of the American Negro," pages 65–66.

The rate of increase in licentiousness, etc., (for these figures point to syphilis) in these cities is fully borne out by the reports from other cities.

Next, I will consider the comparative (white and negro) mortality in childhood. For this I am able to present the statistics of three of the largest cities in the South for the year 1890: In the city of New Orleans for every thousand white children born, there died within the first year 269; of negro children born, there died 430. In the city of Charleston for every thousand white children born, there died the first year 200; of negro children 461. In the city of Richmond for every thousand white children born, there died the first year 187, and of negro children born, there died 530—over one-half. And yet they tell us there is no race problem! For the years after infancy the statistics are not so complete as regards age, and I must turn from the child statistics to those of general mortality.

In the five years extending from 1890 to 1894 inclusive, the general death rate in the population of the cities of Washington, Baltimore, Richmond, Memphis, Louisville, Atlanta, Savannah, Charleston, Mobile and New Orleans gave a general death rate for the whites of 20.12 per annum per thousand, and for the negroes, 32.61 per annum per thousand. [Hoffman's "Race Traits and Tendencies of the American Negro, p. 39.]

These figures speak for themselves. The negro, at least in the cities of the South, is already dying much more rapidly than the white. The question now to be asked is, is this true of the rural population? To that I answer, in less extent, yes. Moreover it must be understood there is a general drift of the negro to the cities and towns, and once there the negro seldom returns. The temptations of the cities appeal wonderfully to the negro; there is more excitement, more opportunity for "picking up a living," and the gregarious tendencies of this race, cultivated through ages in Africa, which is a land of small villages rather than of peasant homes, is gratified. It is a fact, however, that notwithstanding this high death rate, the negro population in the cities continues to increase. This is not because the negro birth rate exceeds the death rate, for it does not; it is because the negroes continue to flock to the cities and increase the population despite the terribly high death rate. No increase in the rural districts can ever offset this terrible annual drain. In the destruction of the race the city is to play a most important part and it is a thing which nothing in the negro's racial experience will enable him to meet.

In explanation of this terrible death rate, let us look and see what has caused it. From all that I can gather from the medical men of the South interested in this matter, the three great influencing diseases of the negro population are tuberculosis, syphilis and enteric (typhoid) fever. Of course cancer and everything else (except property) is on the increase with a markedly criminal race, but these are the great three.

With regard to tuberculosis the first thing I will show is that fourteen American cities, extending from Boston to New Orleans, but chiefly Southern, give for every 100,000 population, an annual death rate from tuberculosis of 280 for the whites and 591 for the negro population. These statistics are based upon the census of 1890 and the health reports of the cities. Now, for the sake of comparison with ante-bellum days, compare these figures with the statistics based upon the health reports for Charleston, S. C., from 1822 to 1894 inclusive, and we will find that from 1822 to 1848 the annual death rate for 100,000 population from tuberculosis among the whites was 347; among the negroes 342, that is, fewer negroes died from tuberculosis

than whites; but from 1865 to 1894 the annual death rate
from tuberculosis among the whites per 100,000 population was only 213, while for the negroes it had already
risen to 576. Now, let us turn to the next of the three
chief diseases from which this race is suffering—syphilis.
I will say here first, that syphilis rarely kills directly; it is
with the adult, rather a predisposing cause of death,
though a direct cause of foetal and infant death. (See
table, p. 24.) But if you have ever studied the cause of
the taking off of our American Indian, the Hawaiian, the
Maori, the Australian, the Tasmanian, etc., it will be seen
that syphilis has played the principal part. A most interesting table is found on page 325 of Hoffman's work,
comparing the Indian tribes of the United States, which
have held their own, with those which have decreased, between the years 1882 and 1895. Tribes which have been
isolated and thus held aloof from syphilitic infection have
held their own, while those which have broken up their
tribal relations, have accepted "squaw men" and have had
free intercourse with whites of a criminal class, have
almost perished. So it is with the negro. The breaking
up of the plantation home; migration to the city, the
crowding and temptations to vice incident to city life, are
all working to his detriment. An impure home is an
unusually unprolific home; copulation is not all that is
needful. If this alone were necessary to fecundity, the
French problem would long since have been solved, which
it is not.

Lastly, typhoid fever. Around nearly every city and
village in the South there is an irregular zone of negro
habitations. These usually are in the "hollows" and valleys and they are almost invariably supplied with drinking
water from shallow wells, whether the central village have
waterworks or not. The condition of this low-lying popu-

lation is, for typhoid fever, infinitely less favorable than that of the whites, who usually use "city water" or, if not, own better and more salubrious sites. The suburban spring and the low-lying well are the bane of this people. Within certain limits, the conditions here given apply in the country. A negro digs his well where he will reach water easiest, i. e., on low ground, while his shanty and "out-houses" are perched above. In slavery days the large negro quarters were, for the age, models of hygiene because an epidemic in the "quarters" was a financial crisis for the owner. But who now looks after the "ward of the nation?"

Beyond the facts here set forth I may state that as a Southerner and a physician, I am familiar with the physicians of the South, and it is the almost universal opinion of these men, who should and do know more of the negro than all other classes combined, that the negro, as a race, is steadily degenerating both morally and physically. The last census showed a decrease in gain as compared with the preceding and when the tide once turns the end will be in sight. [The Maori decreased from 142,000 in 1823 to 34,000 in 1890.]

In conclusion, all things point to the fact that the negro as a race is reverting to barbarism with the inordinate criminality and degradation of that state. It seems, moreover, that he is doomed at no distant day, to racial extinction. If reproduction ceases eight million will die out about as rapidly as eight hundred, as the outlook for this people is black indeed.

What brought about this condition? In my opinion emancipation—the negro feels that this was a *dies irae*. He has no enthusiasm for "Emancipation Day"—sounded the death knell of the negro, but it did not of necessity decree his speedy end. Something else was needed and fate supplied the need, the negro was duly crowned with the ballot and given control of the South. That settled it. Enmity was deliberately put between the son of the master, the only man who ever really loved the slave, and the son of the slave. The only sincerely friendly hand the negro ever knew was perforce turned against him, and without it he is falling. What will save him? Will education? The South has given him the best she had, and we see the result. Will industrial education prove a panacea? The report of the Bureau of Education [G. R. Stetson "The White Man's Problem," p. 6] for 1889-90, shows that of 1,243 graduates of seventeen colored industrial schools, three only pursued the trade for which educated, twelve were farming, 693 teaching academic schools, and the rest had joined the non-producing professions and pursuits. The wealth of the Indies could not give this entire race technical training any more than it could satiate the appetite of those thriving on the brokerage of philanthropy. Industrial training should be reserved for a more industrious people. In my opinion nothing is more certain than that the negro will go as the Tasmanian and the Carib have gone, but till then he is our problem. I say our because the New South, child of the Old, young, strong and undaunted, proposes to deal with this matter as she sees best. The future of the negro surely prompts compassion, charity and mercy—these he will get in full measure—but the white man of the South should not and will not re-enslave himself for the benefit of the black. Slavery is forever gone—and with it went the bonds which for two centuries fettered the master, and also every iota of his responsibility for this grand but ghastly tragedy— The Sacrifice of a Race.

BIBLIOGRAPHY.

" Report of Superintendent of Public Instruction of Virginia," 1900.
" Dietary Studies of Negroes in Eastern Virginia," Bulletin 71, United States Department of Agriculture.
"The Southern States of the American Union," J. L. M. Curry.
" Race Traits and Tendencies of the American Negro," Fred L. Hoffman.
" The Negro Population of the South," P. A. Bruce, Conservative Review, November, 1899.
" The Transplantation of a Race," Prof. N. S. Shaler, Popular Science Monthly. March, 1900.
" The Negro." Dr. J. H. Claiborne. Virginia Medical Semi-Monthly, April, 1900.
"The Earth and Its Inhabitants." Africa. Elisee Recluse, Vols. I and III.
"The White Man's Problem," George R. Stetson.
"Negro Criminality," Walter L. Wilcox.
"The Genesis of the United States," Alexander Brown, Vol. II.
" The Uncivilized Races of Men in All Countries of the World," Rev. J. G. Wood, Vol. I.
" The Negro in Maryland," Jeffrey R. Brockett.
" Carolina Medical Journal," March, 1900.

AN EX-SLAVEHOLDERS VIEW OF THE

NEGRO QUESTION IN

THE SOUTH.

By COLONEL ROBERT BINGHAM,

Superintendent of The Bingham School,

Asheville, N. C.

Reproduced by permission from the

European Edition of Harper's Monthly Magazine

For July, 1900.

241

PRESS OF
ASHEVILLE PRINTING CO.,
ASHEVILLE N. C.

An Ex-Slave Holder's View of the Negro Question in the South.

Heretofore the Race Question in the United States has been local, sectional and more or less sentimental. But now it is one of the most important National questions before us; and the necessity of dealing not only with the Black man and with the remnant of the Red man in continental America, but with the Hawaiian, the Japanese, the Chinaman and the Philippino in our new Pacific Islands and with the mixed races in our new West Indian Islands, makes it a highly important question.

That " History is philosophy teaching by example " is a saying as old as Cicero. Let us look at the history of our contact with other races dispassionately and take lessons calmly for our future from what has occurred in our past.

I suppose that Gail Hamilton's contention will be admitted that " If God made the white man white, the yellow man yellow, and the black man black, He intended for the white man to remain white, the yellow man yellow and the black man black." He prevents the loss of species in the lower animals by the infecundity of hybrids. He seems to have protected the integrity of race types among men by Race Antagonism. At any rate race antagonism is a patent and a potent factor which must be reckoned with in any philosophical study of history; and the effect of race antagonism, visible everywhere and always whenever different races come into contact, is no where more visible than in the contact of our race with other races.

What our race-history was in prehistoric times we can only guess at; but History teaches that the Roman, who subjugated and absorbed so many other races, failed in all his attempts on the Teuton, and Augustus on his death bed said with tears to Varus, who had been sent to subjugate Germany, " O Varus, my legions, my legions, where are my legions?" And History teaches very clearly that the race characteristics of the Angles and Saxons are more distinct and more permanent than those of any other of Teutonic tribes who overwhelmed the Roman Empire. The other Teutonic invaders of Southern and Western Europe lost their language and much of their race identity and were themselves absorbed, or were at least greatly modified, by their subjects. They failed to change the names even of the countries which they overran. Græcia remains Greece, Italia is Italy, Hispania is Spain; and though the Franks changed the name of Gallia to France, they lost their language and race identity so completely and were so thoroughly Latinized that the French are the head of the Latin races to-day. And the Latinized Franks who went to England with William the Norman lost their language and identity a second time at the hands of the English. But the Angles and Saxons who landed with Hengist and Horsa in 449 changed Britain to Angle-Land, and it has been England ever since. They touched the Celt, and in a hundred years there were no Celts except in the mountains of Wales and in the mountains of Scotland. The Norman touched them, and the Norman was absorbed and his identity disap-

3

peared. They came in contact with the Red man in America; and, as the Celt vanished away at the touch of the barbarian Angles and Saxons, so the Red man vanished away at the touch of their descendants, the Christianized Anglo-Americans. This same man touched the Frenchman from the mouth of the St. Lawrence to the mouth of the Mississippi, and the Frenchman's power in that vast region is with last year's snow, and what was once French America is now the heart of Anglo-American civilization and power. And during our Civil War the Frenchman undertook to establish himself on this Continent again; but just after the end of our war the Frenchman was ordered out of Mexico by the United States Government, and " stood not on the order of his going "—and the would-be Emperor Maximilian, no longer supported by French bayonets, was shot as a usurper in June 1867. The Yellow man touched the Anglo-American and has been excluded, more by the unwritten law of race hostility and race antagonism than by any formal acts of Congress. And the Anglo-American has just touched the Spaniard and the Spaniard has vanished from this Hemisphere.

So as a matter of simple fact, our contact with the Black man in the South is the only instance in the history of our race where any population of Anglo-Saxon blood has dealt successfully with another race on the same soil in about equal numbers. The English have dealt successfully with the Negro in the English West Indies. But the numbers involved are comparatively small and the disparity between whites and blacks is much greater than in the South. The English in Egypt and in India are the official class, the soil remaining in the hands of the subject races. In many of the English Colonies the Aborigines have met the fate of the Red man in North America, while in South Africa the English and the Dutch are in deadly conflict for the mastery.

Those who look at the matter only in a sentimental way may say that, although the negro in the South survived, he survived as a slave and that existence in slavery is scarcely existence at all. But early in the Century there was a deep and strong movement among the slave owners against holding slaves; and but for the agitation inaugurated by the abolitionists, some scheme for the gradual emancipation of the negro would in all probability have been worked out, and this might have settled the negro question peaceably. My father thought of going to Ohio in the '20s to be relieved of the burden and responsibility of slaves; but he found the condition of the African in the North West worse than in slavery. Everybody in the South knew that the condition of the ante-bellum free negro among us was worse than that of the slave, though the free negro had the right of suffrage in North Carolina till 1835. My father offered his nurse her freedom and support for a term of years in Liberia and she declined the offer. Many of the slaveholders in the South felt as my father did, and a bill for the gradual emancipation of the slaves failed to pass the Legislature of Virginia in the early '30s by only ONE VOTE.

It is safe to say that we of the South dealt more successfully with the negro up to '65, when he was taken from our hands, than our race has ever dealt with any other race on the same soil since the dawn of history. He came into our

4

hands from over seas, by the action of the people of New England chiefly, not by our own, as we did not own a single ship. He was a savage of a low type, and in some cases at least he was a cannibal. One of the most respectable and trustworthy negroes I know, a man of about 65, told me that his grandmother, who came direct from Africa, had told him as a boy that she had seen her people engaged in a cannibal feast before she was put on a ship and taken away from home.

Under our treatment this savage was so developed in the arts of civilization in a little more than a century that he was deemed worthy by the people of the North to share with them in the citizenship of the Great Republic; and this boon, which was given by law to every adult negro male in the South, is still denied to illiterates of our own race in New England; and in this year of grace 1900 it has been denied to illiterate Brown men and Yellow men in the new Territory of Hawaii by act of a Republican Congress, approved by a Republican President.

As the negro advanced so rapidly under our tutelage, it may be well for those whose ancestors united with ours in exterminating the Celt in England and the Red man in America, who have excluded the Yellow man, who have not succeeded with the Black man since they took charge of him in '65 as well as we had done before '65, and on whose success with the Brown man judgment must be suspended, it may be well for the people of the North to take our diagnosis of the case of the negro into careful consideration.

And it may be well for the people of the North to realize that in the nature of things we are better qualified to make a correct diagnosis of the negro's case and to treat it intelligently than they are. In the whole North only one-sixtieth (1-60) of the people are of African blood; and there are many people in the North who never saw a negro in their lives.

But in the South as a whole, one-third (⅓) of the people are of African blood; in several of the former slave states three-fifths (3-5) of the people are of African blood; and there are localities in all the former slave states where nine-tenths (9-10) of the people are of African blood, and it can hardly be denied that those who have dealt with only a very weak solution of a thing and who in many cases have never dealt with it at all, are less competent to judge it intelligently than those who have dealt with a saturated solution of it, so to speak, all their lives.

There is one proposition to which every intelligent man in the South, whether of Northern or Southern birth, will give hearty assent; and many Northern people who have never been in the South are being brought to the same conclusion by the logic of events. This proposition is that 'a great mistake was made against the negro by arming him with the ballot while he was still an intellectual, moral and political infant. We are Teutons, God's kings of men. But every step towards the highest freedom was won in the best blood of our race. We freed ourselves from feudal vassalage to the Plantagenets and established the principles of the *Magna Charta* in blood. We freed ourselves from ecclesiastical vassalage to a foreign potentate under the Tudors and established the Church of

5

England instead of the Church of Rome in blood. We freed ourselves from domestic ecclesiastical vassalage under the Stuarts and established the principles of the *Bill of Rights* in blood. We freed ourselves from the vassalage of taxation without representation under the house of Brunswick and established the principles of the *Declaration of Independence* in blood. We obtained manhood suffrage at great cost in moil and toil and blood and after many centuries of preparation for it.

Thomas Jefferson, the great apostle of Democracy, said " I am certain that the negroes will be free, and I am " "equally certain that they can never live on the same " " soil on terms of political equality with the whites."

Abraham Lincoln, the great apostle of Republicanism, in a speech delivered in Charleston, Illinois, on the 18th of September, 1858, said as follows :

" I will say that I am not nor ever have been in favor " " of bringing about in any way the social and political " " equality of the white and black races; that I am not nor " " ever have been in favor of making voters or jurors of " " negroes, nor of qualifying them to hold office nor to in- " " termarry with white people; and I will say in addition " " to this that there is a physical difference between the " " white and black races which will forever forbid the two " " races living together on terms of social and political " " equality. And inasmuch as they cannot so live, while " " they do remain together, there must be the position of " " superior and inferior; and I, as much as any other man, " " am in favor of having the superior position assigned to " " the white race."

And we of the South believe that some plan of gradual enfranchisement on the educational basis which is demanded of white men in Massachusetts, or on the combined educational and property basis which is demanded of white men in Rhode Island, would have been adopted if President Lincoln had been spared. And nothing could have stimulated the illiterate negro and the illiterate white man as much as making the right of suffrage a prize to be won by an educational qualification.

But this great opportunity was thrown away; and in the face of our own race's having attained manhood suffrage only after centuries of preparation for it and at great cost in moil and toil and blood, in face of the condemnation of such a course by our greatest political leaders, including Abraham Lincoln himself, in the face of the fact that manhood suffrage is still denied to illiterates of our own race in New England, in the face of all these facts this great boon was given to the negro without moil or toil on his part, without his having shed a drop of his own blood organized to attain it, and so, entirely without preparation for it. And it was done, not for the benefit of the negro, but as a move on the chess-board of party politics, and the party making the move has been checkmated in ten states ever since. And as suffrage has wrought evil and only evil to the negro ever since, and that continually, we believe that perhaps the best thing is to accompany it with the same sort of educational qualification which accompanies its enjoyment by our race in Massachusetts, Connecticut and Rhode Island, and which is demanded of brown men and of yellow men in our new

6

territory of Hawaii. In this way, if in any way, the evils
which threaten the negro may be averted.

The people of the United States seem to be only beginning
to realize that the War between the States was more a *Race
War* than anything else, not of Saxon against Saxon, but
of the free laborer of the North against the slave laborer of
the South, who, by a strange set of conditions, not of the
white man's own choosing, was protected by six million
men of Anglo Saxon blood. The contest began, not for the
purpose of freeing the negro, but for the purpose *of exclud-
ing slave labor from the Territories*, lest competition against
the white laborer in localities up to that time not occupied
at all should be inaugurated. It is well known that the negro is not tolerated by the farm laborer, mechanic, miner,
railroad employee, or by any other handi-craftsman in any
Northern or Western state as he is tolerated as yet every
where in the South to-day; and it was largely the handi-
craftsmen of the great North West who settled the question
at the point of the bayonet against slave labor, though protected by the men of the Anglo-Saxon blood in the South.
No laborer of any race, and least of all no negro laborer,
has ever been met on the border of a Southern state, as the
negro was met on the border of Illinois recently, with bul-
let and bayonet; nor has the Governor of any Southern state
threatened peaceable laborers with Gatling guns as
Governor Tanner, of President Lincoln's own state and a
member of President Lincoln's own political party, threatened
peaceable negro miners going from Alabama to seek work
in Illinois, nor to this day has a finger been raised to bring
these murderers of negro miners to justice. And this race
antagonism, which exists everywhere and among all races,
and no where perhaps more strongly than among the white
laborers of the North West againt the negro, must be met
successfully by the negro if he is to survive, and every
thing which tends to stimulate race antagonism must be
avoided.

But not only must race antagonism, existing everywhere,
be met by the negro, but as a free man he has become the
competitor of the white laborer in many fields of activity not
occupied by him on his own account as a slave. He has become
a carpenter, blacksmith, brick mason, shoe-makers, etc., on
his own account: he has become a contractor and builder, a
merchant, a livery stable keeper, a restaurant keeper,
a mail carrier and a mail contractor; he has in some
cases become a banker, a lawyer, a doctor; and in
all these occupations and in others not named, he
underbids the white man. This does not tend to
improve the relations between the races. And the
white laborer is taking the places vacated by the negro,
so that the competition is both upward and downward. In
these days of sharp competition between laborers of the
same race, leading sometimes to bloodshed, racial differences are greatly emphasized. And this industrial competition must be reckoned with by the negro, who, being
no longer protected by the Southern white man, must meet
it in his own name and by his own innate power. And can
the negro meet this competition successfully against a
race which has exterminated the Celt and the Red man,
which has excluded the Yellow man, and which has driven
the Frenchman and the Spaniard off the North American
Continent?

7

247

And not only must race antagonism and Industrial antagonism be met by the emancipated negro, but his being armed with the ballot has added *political antagonism* to his other difficulties; and this political antagonism is the more dangerous to him because it has weakened the feeling of the former slave-owner and his children toward him, and it is hardening the hearts of the non-slaveholding class against him more and more year by year. I believe that in the history of the whole world there never were as kindly relations existing between two races on the same soil as between the slave owner and the slave in the South before the Civil War, and nothing vindicates these kindly, and in many cases these tender relations so clearly, or falsifies the preconceived opinions of many Northern people on the subject so clearly as the confidence with which the white men of the South left their women and children to the protection of the negroes during the Civil War and the unexampled faithfulness with which the negroes discharged this trust; and we, who passed through these trying times can not forget this, their only redeeming feature, and we teach our children never to forget it. I have always loved the negro and I shall never cease to love him. My father and mother reared seven children in a slave woman's lap. She loved us better than her life. We loved her next to our parents, and I look with a sort of yearning pity on my grandchildren, because they can never know the love of a "black mammy." And I am sure that this kindly feeling between the out going generation of slave owners and of slaves is mutual. When the negro wants work, he comes to us for employment. When he is hungry, he comes to us still for food. When he is naked, he comes to us for clothing. When he is in trouble, he comes to us for counsel. When he wishes to buy a little piece of land so that he may own a home of his own, he comes to us to "stand for him." When his child is sick, he comes to us for medicine, and when it dies, he comes to us to help him buy its coffin. But when the election comes on, he does not come to us, but goes to our political opponent and his political master and gets his orders how to vote and a dollar or two perhaps in addition and often nothing but promises, accompanied by assurances that we want to put him back into slavery, and with this all connection between him and his political master ends till the next election.

Such persistent political hostility of employee against employer would hardly be tolerated by the property holders in any Northern state; it has become wearisome to the ex-slave holders, it is exasperating to their sons and grandsons, and it is intensifying the as yet suppressed race hostility of the non-slave holding class year by year.

So that friends of the negro must reckon with race antagonism, stimulated by industrial antagonism and inflamed by political antagonism.

Now when two races occupy the same soil, the voice of history is clear as to the three possible solutions of the race problem.

I. The races must amalgamate:

II. The stronger race must reduce the weaker race to slavery or at least to political subjection:

III. The weaker race must cease to exist.

8

248

(1.) In this case amalgamation cannot be thought of. The man of Anglo-Saxon blood has never amalgamated with inferior races as the Latin races have done in Central and South America for instance. He may mix his blood individually with that of an inferior race; but any offspring belongs distinctly to the mother's race and not to the sire's. And any female of Anglo Saxon blood forfeits her race identity even by a legal marriage with a man of an inferior race. There is no middle ground socially between the white man and the black man in the South, and there can be none unless the flood of years shall deposit a middle ground from its current as the Nile or the Mississippi deposits its delta from its own waters.

(2.) Slavery is a thing of the past. It lasted in the South as long perhaps as it was beneficial to the weaker race, and as long as the stronger race could stand it and remain strong; and as I know the slave-owning class no one of them would undertake to bear the white man's burden of the African again for any consideration.

(3.) The history of other races in general and of the English speaking race in particular makes it necessary for the friends of the negro to reckon distinctly with the question of his gradual extinction, if he is to avoid the fate which the Celt and the Indian have already met at the hands of our race, and towards which our dealings with the Yellow man on our own soil and with the Brown man on his own soil seem to point ominously.

Various solutions of the Negro question have been suggested, no one of which seems likely to be as successful as its advocates expect, though each will have its effect in the ultimate result, whatever that may be.

Education in books has been suggested, and has been on trial since '65. Many Northern people, who have looked at the negro only through a telescope or through the smoked glass of their own preconceived opinions, differ materially from us, who have seen him eye to eye and under the microscope, and seem to think that he is an Anglo-Saxon in a black skin and that he needs only some book learning to relieve him of his African disabilities; and we of the South, whether wisely or unwisely, determined to give this method a fair trial. And so, according to the Report of Dr. Harris, Commissioner of Education, 1896-'97, Vol. 2, p. 2296, the South, of its own volition, has spent a hundred million dollars of tax money on the education of the negro since 1870, and according to the estimate of the Rev. Dr. A. D. Mayo, in his address at Normal, Ala., of May 29, '99, p. 7, lines 25, 26, 27, the North and the Nation have expended an equal amount on him for the same purpose since 1861. But despite this vast expenditure of money on his education in books, he is only an African man still; and the criminal statistics hereinafter mentioned are unfavorable to any expectation of his rapid intellectual or moral development.

Industrial Training has been suggested and it is being pressed in some quarters as the most hopeful thing for the negro. But industrial training, though doubtless beneficial in many individual cases, will hardly do as much for the race as some of its advocates expect, for two reasons: 1st., the negro lacks mechanical talent, as is shown by the fact that while he has been working with tools for more than a century in the United States, there seems to be no record of

9

any successful mechanical device of his invention; and 2nd, because industrial training will only sharpen the already existing industrial competition and race antagonism.

Colonization in Africa or elsewhere has been suggested as a possible solution of the negro problem, and it may have some results. But our experiment in Liberia, and the experiment of the English in Sierra Leone, with small numbers and under favorable conditions, have not been successful. The colonization of eight million people is a physical and a financial impossibility, even if they wished to be colonized, and the negro has not the slightest notion of being colonized. Moreover, only the strongest races have colonized in the past. And, "Qua in terris"? To what country can his colonies go except to that undiscovered country from whose bourne no traveller returns!

The Distribution of the negroes among the Northern states has been suggested as a solution of the negro problem. But migrations have never occurred at the suggestion of philanthropists. The unhappy result of the migration of the southern negro farm laborers to Kansas some five years ago is discouraging to negro emigrants from the South to the North West; and the bloody issue of the migration of black miners from Alabama to Illinois has been already referred to. And those who dream the dream of the colonization or of the redistribution of the negro must reduce him to abject slavery before they can lead him about at their own sweet will.

Christianizing the negro is offered hopefully by some as a solution of the negro question. But to make this method successful it must regenerate the white man as well as the negro; and unless it prove more efficacious in the Anglo Saxon's dealing with the Black man than in his dealing with the Red man and with the Yellow man, his offering it to the Black man may not be very reassuring to him. And it is perfectly obvious to all who have learned the negro's characteristics by actual contact with him that in calculating the effect of Christianity on him the patent fact must not be lost sight of that in his mind religion and morals are severed more than in the Anglo-Saxon's.

With race antagonism, industrial antagonism and political antagonism to meet, it does not make the case of the negro more hopeful that his physical and mental and moral fibre have grown weaker since his freedom began. Insanity was almost unknown among the negroes in slavery. There must be insane asylums in every Southern State now for the colored insane and they are crowded with inmates. Smallpox and other contagious diseases were practically unknown among the negroes as slaves. They are very prevalent now. Drunkenness was practically unknown among the negroes as slaves. It is very common now. Venereal disease was almost unknown in slavery. The medical men say that it prevails among the negroes to a very alarming extent now. The sexual impurity of the negro is deplored by all who desire his uplifting, and most of all by such leaders of his own race as Booker Washington, Prof. DuBois, of Atlanta, and Prof. Eugene Harris of Fiske University, Nashville, Tenn. Prof. Harris' statement as to the Social and Physical condition of the Negro is given in the Report for 1896-'97 of the United States Government's Commissioner of Education, Vol. 2, pages 2310-11-12, where he says as follows: "The

10

250

constitutional diseases which are responsible for our unusual mortality are aften traceable to sexual immoralities. According to Hoffman, more than 25 per cent. of the negro children born in Washington City are admittedly illegitimate. In one county in Mississippi there were during twelve months 300 marriage licenses taken out in the County Clerk's office for white people. In proportion to population there should have been 1200 or more for negroes. There were actually taken out for colored people *just three.*" This is the testimony, prepared by this leader of his race, for the Government's Commissioner of Education. As a simple matter of fact wrong doing of this sort discounts a negro woman very little, the most respectable negro man marrying a woman with an illegitimate child as readily as any other to all appearance. I know a man well who has had five negro men in his employment for some years, no one of whom was more than ten years of age at the surrender. They are all faithful, industrious, respected and self-respecting men and all of them could vote in Massachusetts, and will remain voters in North Carolina whether the suffrage amendment passes or not. Four of them have money in the bank. The wives of four of these men had illigitimate children at marriage, all by black fathers, and there are very few exceptions to these conditions, as is admitted by the testimony of the negro against himself. Nor does it better the case that the negro brought this immorality with him from Africa, where it is still one of the most distinctive features of his savage kindred. That this race characteristic lost hold on the negro in slavery is certain. That it has regained its former hold on him in freedom is equally certain. Add to the low marriage rate and the necessarily low birth rate of legitimates the high death rate which is patent everywhere, and it is not surprising that, while the negro population increased nearly 36 per cent. from 1870 to 1880, the increase from 1880 to 1890 was only 13 per cent. which is about one half the increase among the whites during the same period. Such conditions as have only to continue long enough and the negro question will settle itself. And the bettering of these conditions calls for the best and the most united thought and action of both races.

But the most disquieting thing to the friends of the negro is his attitude toward crime and his consequent rapid increase in criminality. When a white man commits a crime, other white men combine to arrest and punish him, and he loses character and cast. When a negro commits a crime, other negroes combine to prevent his arrest and punishment and he becomes a sort of hero and martyr in the eyes of his race.

Dr. W. H. Wilcox, a native of Massachusetts, a Professor in Cornell University, and at present detailed in Washington City as chief statistician of the Census, delivered a striking address on Criminality before the American Social Science Association, at Saratoga, Sept. 6, '99. Dr. George T. Winston, born in North Carolina, then President of the University of Texas, and now President of the N. C. Agricultural and Mechanical College, delivered a striking address in December, '97, before the National Prison Association, at its meeting in Austin, Texas, on the Prevention of Crime. The conclusions of these two distinguished gentlemen, differing so widely in birth, rearing and environment, are practically

11

the same; they are very instructive, and they bear very strongly on the negro's chances to survive, now that he has been brought into direct competition with the man of Anglo-Saxon blood. I quote Dr. Winston's conclusions chiefly, as he gives the actual percentage more fully than Dr. Wilcox does. (1) "The negro element is much the most criminal of our population." (2) "The negro is much more criminal as a free man than he was as a slave." (3) "The negro is increasing in criminality with fearful rapidity, being one third more criminal in 1890 than in 1880." (4) "The negroes who can read and write are more criminal than the illiterate, which is true of no other element of our population." (5) "The negro is nearly three times as criminal in the North East, where he has not been a slave for a hundred years, and three and a half times as criminal in the North West, where he has never been a slave, than in the South vhere he was a slave till 1865." (6) "The negro is three times as criminal as the native white and once and a half times as criminal as the foreign white, consisting in many cases of the scum of Europe." (7) "More than *seven tenths* of the negro criminals are under thirty years of age."

These conclusions are strikingly verified by Prof. J. R. Straton, in the North American Review for June, 1900. According to the Census of 1890, as quoted by Prof. Straton, the minimum illiteracy of the negro, 21 7-10 per cent., is found in New England and his maximum illiteracy, 65 7-10 per cent., is in the so called "black belt," South Carolina, Mississippi and Louisiana. And yet the negro is four and a half (4½) times more criminal in New England, hundred for hundred, than he is in-the "black belt."

These facts, taken from the United States Census, show (1) that the educational method, as it has been applied thus far to the negro, lacks adjustment to his needs; and (2) that the North East, the North West and the Nation have not succeeded as well with the negro since '65 as the South did up to '65.

But the most fateful and fatal thing to be considered in the negro problem is the fact that the younger generation of negroes, already the most criminal class in our population, the United States Census says, have developed a mania —it can hardly be called any thing else—for assaulting white women. Those who live a thousand miles from the jungles of India may think that the reports that tigers come out from the jungles and devour hundreds of people every year are exaggerated. On the testimony of the tiger and of his kith and kin they may doubt or deny the facts and may express great sympathy for the downtrodden tigers when they are slain "flagrante delicto," or are tracked to their lairs and put to death. But those who live in the midst of the terrible facts feel a constant dread when the tiger is only in his lair, and they shudder when he is abroad with his appetite for human blood excited to such fury that he loses all sense of the consequences; and it need not be a matter of surprise if a very short shrift is allowed to the Indian tiger on the banks of the Ganges, or to the African tiger on the banks of the Altamaha. And it makes the assaults of the African tiger harder for the white man of the South to bear when even the women of his own race at the North express great sympathy for the death of the African tiger on the

12

banks of the Altamaha, but none for their Anglo-Saxon sister whom the African tiger has devoured, and when the negro editor of a paper in Wilmington, N. C., says that the Anglo-Saxon women are in collusion with the African tigers that devour them. And as long as the Anglo-Saxon is the Anglo-Saxon, this crime has only to touch *him* or *his* and his feeling is the same wherever God's sun shines on him.

[This view is strikingly verified by the recent murder of negroes in the race riots in New York City, and the more recent hangings and burnings of negroes by mobs in Colorado, in Illinois, President Lincoln's own state, in Indiana, President Harrison's own state, in Kansas, and in Ohio, President McKinley's own state, the lynchings in Urbana and Akron, Ohio, being attended with unusual violence.

Furthermore, in 1892 there were lynchings in twenty-seven (27) states of the Union, scattered from New York to California on the North, and from Virginia to Texas on the South. In 1897 there were lynchings in twenty-five (25) states, in all sections of the Union.]

And this assaulting of white women by negroes is a new crime. It was almost unheard of in slavery. The whole manhood of the South left their women in the hands of the negroes and went to the front during the Civil War with the feeling that the women were safe in the hands of the slaves. And they were safe, although on many plantations there were a hundred negro men and not a white man in a mile. No woman in the whole South was ever molested by a negro during the Civil War, nor for a number of years after the War. During the Spanish War I asked several old Confederates and ex-slave holders in several Southern States what the men of the South would do *now* if they were all called upon to repel an invasion which had advanced a hundred miles from the coast. Every one said it would be impossible to go. "But," I said, "it would be impossible not to obey the call of patriotism." "Then we would have to take all the adult negro males to the front with us and keep them there." "But," I said, "it would be impossible to take them all or to keep them all." "Then we would kill them all before we started," was the reply in every case. Such a contingency can not arise in any human probability; but this view of what it would necessitate if it should arise shows how the best people in the South and the negro's best friends feel about the African tiger who comes so often from his lair to devour our women. And in dealing with the black man this new factor must be reckoned with. One of the most influential Journals in New York * said nothing about the lynching of Sam Hose in Georgia for about three weeks; and then after an investigation at first hands, its conclusion was that the same thing would have occurred under similar circumstances in any state in the Union. And the Editor of one of the most influential religious weeklies in the Central West, † who had been very severe on the Southern people, went to Georgia in person to investigate; and, as reported by Rev. Dr. A. J. McKelway in the Presbyterian Standard, in answer to a question put to him by a clergyman of the Southern Methodist Church as to what he would do if a negro were to assault *his* wife or *his* daughter or *his* sister, he replied promptly, "I would kill him if I could," which statement he

* Harper's Weekly.
† The Interior, of Chicago.

13

modified several days later by saying, "I would try to kill him; but my neighbors ought not to let me do it."

It is entirely in accordance with the negro's fixed attitude towards crime that in all the deliverances of political and religious bodies of negroes, North and South, against lynching, I have never seen a word against the crime which has produced most of the lynching and which started it all. The same is true of deliverances of most organizations of white people at the North on the same subject. Great sympathy is expressed for the black man who pays the penalty for the crime; but very little sympathy is expressed, even by Northen women, for a white sister whom the African tiger has made his victim. All the best people of the South are entirely opposed to lynching. In practice it has failed as a remedy for the crime, and it has not only brutalized those engaged in it, but it has most seriously discounted the majesty of the law. It ought to be stopped. It must be stopped. But it will not stop till both races, North and South, unite in stopping the crime, which is confined almost exclusively to the negroes who were born after 1870.

When we consider that the freed negro must face the race antagonism of the man of Anglo Saxon blood, before which stronger races have fallen, that he must in addition face industrial and political antagonism intensified by his increasing lawlessness and criminality in all lines, but particularly in the special line referred to, which is straining the friendliness of his former friends towards him to the utmost and which is hardening the hearts of his racial and industrial opponents against him, when we consider all these things, it is well for the friends of the negro North and South to look these conditions squarely in the face if they would save him from the fate of the Celt, the Indian, the Frenchman and the Spaniard, as already enacted at the hands of our race.

And there is another factor which must be reckoned with. The negro has nothing to fear from the old slave owning class as yet, though the incoming generation have lost much of the kindly feeling which their fathers had for him. But the feeling of the non-slaveholding class against him, never good in the nature of things, is growing worse day by day, and a cloud, already "larger than a man's hand," has risen above the horizon, from which the lightning flashes angrily. To give a concrete illustration of this feeling, a negro assaulted a white girl near Asheville, N. C., about three years ago and was put to death by a mob, composed almost entirely of the *non-slaveholding class*, who turned out in great numbers, battered down the doors of the jail in order to get possession of the criminal, and overawed the local military company which was under arms to prevent violence.

I was not aware how strong the feeling of the non-slaveholding class against the negro is till I commanded them for four years in the Confederate Army, of which they formed the rank and file. This race feeling of the non-slaveholder and his children against the negro is held in abeyance as yet by the attitude of the slave-holding class, who have always controlled Southern sentiment. But the feeling is deep and strong, though latent and mostly quiescent as yet; it is

14

becoming less latent and less quiescent year by year, and it seems to be only a question of time when the attitude of the white laboring classes towards the negroes will be in the South what it has already become in the North.

It does not seem likely that any general outbreak or race war will occur. But it does seem more than probable, if the lawlessness of the negro continues to increase as it has been doing during the last two decades, that the non-slaveholding whites, under the stimulation of race, industrial and political antagonism, will take advantage of the fury caused by an assault of some white woman by a negro to settle their accumulated scores against the black man; and whenever and wherever such a thing occurs, the black man in that locality will join the Celt and the Indian.

In studying the Race problem in the South, these considerations must be reckoned with by those who would protect the negro from the direct competition with the man of Anglo-Saxon blood, which the negro's being freed has made inevitable.

But with some things in the negro problem which are ominous and with some things which are discouraging, there are at least two considerations which are helpful and hopeful.

(1) The lesser United States of the past has begun to be the Greater United States of the future; for the young Hercules of the West has aroused himself and has begun his labors, and these labors must extend through all the signs of the zodiac. In addition to the American born African, we have brought under our jurisdiction the colored races of our new West India Islands and of our new Pacific Islands. We have learned our lesson in the race question by our failure with the African man as a voter; and our mistake with the African man is correcting itself, and it will not be repeated with the other colored races for whom we have become responsible. The mistake made with the negro did not hurt the Southern white man. We are of perhaps the most unmixed Anglo-Saxon blood on the Continent. We have stood the strain of the illiterate voter of African blood, and have thriven on it politically. But will it ever do to give to the inhabitants of Spanish American countries, to Asiatics and to South Sea Islanders the opportunity to hold the balance of power in the Great Republic of the West?

(2) The Southern negro has this great advantage He is here, and he is here to stay. We know him. We like him except as a politician and a criminal. We need him. The native white laborer and handicraftsman of the South is accustomed to him, and as yet works kindly by his side in all forms of activity. He is excluded from employment on race grounds nowhere in the South. As a peaceful immigrant he has never

15

been slain on the borders of any Southern State. And while the negro holds the field as a laborer, other laborers come in very slowly from the outside to compete with him, as the statistics show very clearly. In the states of Virginia, North Carolina, South Carolina, Georgia, Alabama, Mississippi and Arkansas, as a whole the proportion of foreign born inhabitants to the native born is only one in one hundred and twenty-five, (1 in 125.) In the states of Ohio, Indiana, Illinois, Michigan, Wisconsin, Minnesota, Iowa, Missouri, North Dakota, South Dakota, Nebraska, and Kansas as a whole the proportion of foreign born inhabitants to the native born is about one in five (1 in 5.) It thus appears that practically no immigration to the South from the outside has occurred, which leaves the field clear to the negro if he can hold it.

We delivered the African man over to the nation in 1865 orderly, fairly industrious, without vices, without disease, without crime. In the hands of the nation he has become disorderly, idle, vicious, diseased; three times more criminal than the native white and one and a half times more criminal than the foreign white consisting largely of the scum of Europe; he was one third more criminal in 1890 than in 1880; and his maximum criminality and his minimum illiteracy concur in New England, according to the United States Census.

But if he goes out of politics entirely, so as to cease to antagonize his tried friends, and so as to cease to feel that some mysterious power in Washington will support him in idleness and protect him in crime; and if in this frame of mind he cultivates the friendship of those among whom he lives more kindly (except as a politician and as a criminal) than any where else in the United States, and with less competition than he would find any where else on the face of the earth, under these conditions he may become fit by degrees for full citizenship under the same educational and property qualifications required for white men in New England, and for brown men and yellow men in Hawaii. And when by intelligence and sobriety the African man has won without blood the boon which the Anglo-Saxon has taken centuries of moil and toil and blood to be prepared for, the right of suffrage should be made as inalienable to the black man as to the white man; for the white man cannot afford not to share his good things with the brother in black who lives on the same soil and is protected by the same flag. "There is that scattereth and yet increaseth; and there is that withholdeth more than is meet and it tendeth to poverty."

But if the New Race Question is to be met successfully, it must be met by a united New North, New South, New East, and New West.

16

THE
OLD SOUTH
A MONOGRAPH

By H. M. HAMILL, D.D.

SMITH & LAMAR, AGENTS
PUBLISHING HOUSE M. E. CHURCH, SOUTH
NASHVILLE, TENN.; DALLAS, TEX.

257

HE subject-matter of this little book first took form in an address before the students of Emory College, Oxford, Ga., in June, 1904. If apology be needed for putting it in type, the writer finds it in the request of an old woman, now eighty-six years of age, a true daughter of the Old South, whose lightest wish has been the law of his life for more than fifty years.

(3)

THE OLD SOUTH.

Y theme is "The Old South." I have no apology for those who may deem it time-worn or obsolete. I am handicapped in beginning by memories of other writers and speakers who have dealt more worthily than I can hope to do with my subject. The Old South has not been wanting in men to speak and write upon it. Friend and foe alike have exploited it. It has been the burden of poetry not always inspired, and of oratory not always inspiring. Not a few have been its critics who knew it only by hearsay. Indeed, much of current literature upon the Old South is from those who were born after it had passed away. I have no fault to find with any who have thus written or spoken, however worthily or unworthily, if only it was done in kindness. If over the dust of the Old South, while discoursing upon its virtues or its vices, any one has dealt generously with the one and

5

fairly with the other, I am content, though praise or blame may not always have been wisely bestowed.

I was born in and of the Old South. At sixteen, after a year under General Lee, I received my parole at Appomattox, and went home to look upon the ruin of the Old South. Whatever is good or evil in me I owe chiefly to that Old South. Habit, motive, ideal, ambition, passion and prejudice, love and hatred, were formed in it and by it. My life work as a man has been wrought under what is called the New South, but inspiration and aspiration to it came out of the Old South. The spell it cast upon my boyhood is strong upon me after more than a generation has gone. It is not the spell of enchantment. It has not blinded me to bad or good qualities, and after the lapse of a half century and despite the tenderness for it that grows with the passing years, I think I can see and judge the Old South and give account of it more impartially than one who received it at second-hand.

The Old South, in itself and apart from all other considerations, will always be a profitable study. It is the one unique page of our national

6

history. Indeed, it comprehends two hundred and fifty years of history with scarce a parallel. I think one will search in vain history, ancient or modern, to find a likeness to the Old South, socially, intellectually, politically, or religiously. I do not wonder that romancer, poet, historian, and philosopher have gathered from it material and inspiration. As a matter of fact, the past decade has brought forth more literature concerning the Old South than the entire generation which preceded it. Its body lies moldering in the ground, but its soul goes marching on. Wherein especially was it unique?

TO begin with, it was in the South rather than the North that the seed of American liberty was first planted. Jamestown, not Plymouth Rock, was the matrix of true Americanism. Poet and orator have made much of the rock-bound coast and savage wild to which the Puritan fathers came, and have had little to say of the Cavaliers who fought their way to conquest over savage beast and man. Winthrop, Standish, and Cotton

7

Mather are set forth by provincial and partisan writer and speaker as exclusive national types of pioneer courage, wisdom, and heroism. I have read more than one sneer in alleged national histories against "the gentlemen of Jamestown," of whom it was said that there were "eleven laboring men and thirty-five gentlemen." But the historians who sneer fail to note how these same gentlemen felled more trees and did more hard work than the men of the ax and pick. Long after Jamestown had become a memory, I had seen the descendants of those same derided gentlemen in the Army of Northern Virginia, possessors of inherited wealth and reared to luxury from their cradles, yet toiling in the trenches or tramping on the dusty highway or charging into the mouth of cannon with unfailing cheerfulness.

I do not disparage the stern integrity and high achievement of the Puritan sires. I gladly accord them a high place among the fathers and founders of the republic. But putting Puritan and Cavalier side by side, rating each fairly at his real worth and by what he did to fix permanently the qualities that have made us great, I am confident I could make good my proposi-

8

AUNT HANNAH.

tion that deeper down at the foundation of our greatness as a people than all other influences are the qualities and spirit that have marked the Cavalier in the Old World or the New.

Was it not in the Old South, for instance, that the first word was spoken that fired the colonial heart and pointed the way to freedom from the tyranny of Britain?   Later, when all hearts along the Atlantic seaboard were burning with hope of liberty, was it not one from the Old South who presided over the fateful Congress that finally broke with the mother country?   And did not another from the Old South frame the immortal declaration of national independence?   And when the hard struggle for liberty was begun, it was from the Old South that a general was called to lead the ragged Continentals to victory. Follow the progress of that war of the Revolution, and it will be seen how in its darkest days the light of hope and courage burned nowhere so bravely as in the Old South.

Seventy-two years and fifteen Presidents succeeded between the last gun of the Revolution and the first gun fired upon Sumter in 1861. Nine out of fifteen Presidents, and fifty of the seventy-

9

two years, are to be credited to the statesmanship of the Old South. What Washington did with the sword for the young republic, Chief Justice Marshall, of Virginia, made permanently secure by the wisdom of the great jurist. After him came a long line of worthy successors from the Old South, in the persons of judges, vice presidents, cabinet officers, officers of the army and navy, who were called to serve in the high places of the government. The fact is that whatever unique quality of greatness and fame came to the republic for more than a half century after it was begun was largely due to the wisdom of Southern statesmanship. It is hard, I know, to credit such a statement as to the dominating influence in our early national history, now that nearly fifty years have passed since a genuine son of the South has stood by the helm of the ship of State.

As with the statesmanship, so with the military leadership of the Old South. The genius for war has been one of the gifts of the sons of the South from the beginning, not only as fighters with a dash that would have charmed the heart of Ney, but as born commanders, tacticians, and

10

strategists. In the two great wars of the republic, Great Britain and Mexico were made to feel
the skill and courage of Southern general and
rifleman. In the Civil War—greatest of modern
times, and in some respects greatest of all time—
the greater generals who commanded, as well as
the Presidents who commissioned them, were
born on Southern soil, and carried into their high
places the spirit of the Old South. In the
extension of the republic from the seaboard to the
great central valley, and beyond to the mountains
and the Pacific, Southern generalship and statesmanship led the way. The purchase of Louisiana, the annexation of Texas and the Southwest,
were conceived and executed chiefly by Southern
men.

So for more than fifty formative years of our
history the Old South was the dominating power
in the nation, as it had been in the foundation
of the colonies out of which came the republic, and later in fighting its battles of independence and in framing its policies of government.
And I make bold to reaffirm that whatever
strength or symmetry the republic had acquired
at home, or reputation it had achieved abroad, in

11

those earlier crucial years of its history was largely due to the patriotism and ability of Southern statesmanship. Why that scepter of leadership has passed from its keeping, or why the New South is no longer at the front of national leadership, is a question that might well give pause to one who recalls the brave days when the Old South sat at the head of the table and directed the affairs of the nation.

SOCIALLY, the Old South, like "all Gaul," was divided into three parts—the slaveholding planters, the aristocrats of the social system, few relatively in numbers but mighty in wealth and authority; the negro slaves, who by the millions plowed and sowed its fields and reaped its harvests, and who for hundreds of years, both in slavery and freedom, have found contented homes in the South; and lastly the nonslaveholding whites, a distinctly third estate.

The nonslaveholding white of the Old South was essentially *sui generis*. He was really a vital part of a singular semifeudal system, yet, as far

12

as he could, he maintained his independence of it. He was between two social fires. His lack of culture and breeding, his rude speech and dress, barred him from the big house of the planter, except as a sort of political dependent or henchman. On the other hand, to the negro he was variously known as "poor folks," "poor white trash," and at best as "half-strainers." While there was not a little in common between him and the master of slaves, he had literally no dealings with the negro. Here and there, if one rose to ownership of land or slaves by dint of extraordinary industry or good fortune, his social position was scarcely improved. He became like the shoddy "New Riches" of our own time, in a class to himself.

There are not a few illusions as to these "cracker" whites, which fanciful magazine and dialect writers have helped to spread. A benevolently intended effort has been in progress for a generation on the part of certain sentimentalists, with more money than wisdom, to civilize and Christianize what they are pleased to call the "mountain whites." One would gather from the pleas made before religious conventions, and from the

13

facile writers who have made these whites their special care, that they have dwelt continually in religious darkness and destitution, and greatly needed the alien missionary to shed the effulgence of his superior civilization and Christianity upon them. I think I am in a position to say that this forlorn and destitute Southern mountaineer, true to his ancient characteristics, has received these effusive visitors and their benevolences with one eye partly closed and with continued cheerful expectoration at knot holes in the neighboring fence. I am reminded of one of Bishop Hoss's repertoire of anecdotes, all of which have pith and point. Of such a mountaineer as I am depicting, tall, lank, sinewy, frowzy, "a bunch of steel springs and chicken hawk," a tourist satirically inquired: "May I ask, my friend, if you are a member of the human species?" "No, by gum," said the mountaineer; "I'm an East Tennesseean."

As a matter of fact there are few people so thoroughly imbued with the religious spirit as these same "cracker" mountain whites, though it is a religion of the Old rather than of the New Testament, in the crude ethics and doctrines

14

which they commonly hold. Even the Kentucky feudist is after a sort an Old Testament religionist, who has not gone beyond the idea of the "blood avenger" of Mosaic permission. Rude, uncouth, ignorant of books as the poor whites of the Old South were and continue largely to be, I pay them the sincere personal tribute of admiration for the homespu.. virtues that have marked them as a peculiar people. For two years I lived in their wildest mountain fastnesses, went in and out of their rude cabins, taught their youth, broke bread at their tables, and worshiped God with them in their log meetinghouses. I have earned a right, therefore, by personal contact and knowledge to resent with warmth the imputations under which the cracker white, highland or lowland, is too often made to suffer. Even so distinguished an authority as the *New York Advocate,* in a recent article devoted to this class, permitted the usual distortion of fact in all things pertaining to Southern problems.

Of this rude figure of the Old South, it is enough to say that no hospitality of the plantation mansion ever eclipsed that of his humble home to the man who sought shelter beneath it.

15

If he never forgave a wrong, he never forgot to repay a kindness. His honesty was such that a man's pocketbook was commonly as safe in the trail of a mountaineer or lowlander as in the vault of a bank. If he had not books or learning, there was something quite as good for his uses which he had the knack of inheriting or acquiring—a home-grown wit and shrewdness of judgment of men and things. Religiously, he took his code and doctrines directly from the Bible, and too often patterned after both good and evil in that book. He saw no incongruity in dispensing homemade whisky and helping on a protracted meeting at the call of his circuit rider. As to his politics, he followed leaders only as he respected them, and was always a thorn in the flesh of the political trickster. If the master of slaves was an aspirant for office, and was possessor of both manhood and money, the cracker white easily became his supporter. Usually holding the balance of power, he taught many a sharp lesson to unworthy men who sought his political favor. Generally the poor white was hostile to slavery; yet singularly enough, true to the patriotism and loyalty strangely formed in him for

16

SAM DAVIS.

centuries in·his isolated condition, when the armies of the North began their invasions of the South, these same whites by the tens and hundreds of thousands put on the gray, and fell into line under the generalship of the owners of plantation and slave. If there was ever such a proverb current among them as "the rich man's war, but the poor man's fight," I did not hear it from the lips of the brave fellows from the log cabins who became the famous fighters of the Confederacy. Over their lowly and sometimes lonely and unkept graves I would lovingly inscribe that exquisitely pathetic epitaph which one may read upon a Confederate monument in South Carolina, dedicated especially to the men who had nothing to fight for or die for but patriotism and honor:

This monument perpetuates the memory of those who, true to the instincts of their birth, faithful to the teaching of their fathers, constant in their love for the State, died in the performance of their duty; who have glorified a fallen cause by the simple manhood of their lives, the patient endurance of suffering, and the heroism of death; and who, in the dark hours of imprisonment and the hopelessness of the hospital, in the short, sharp agony of the field, found support and consolation in the belief that at home they would not be forgotten.

2　　　17

BETWEEN the negro and his master there was ever in general a feeling of mutual respect and confidence. If I could gather from the Old South its most beautiful and quaint conceits and incidents, I would find none so full of pathos and interest as the long-continued and ever-deepening affection that often, indeed I might say commonly, bound together the white master and the black slave. Neither poverty nor ruin, nor changed conditions, nor disruption of every order, social and political, was effectual in breaking this bond of loyalty and love; and now, so long after the period of enfranchisement has come, if I wanted concrete evidence of the singular beauty of the social system of the Old South, I should summon as my witnesses those lingering relics of the ante-bellum order—the "old massa" and the old negro. Before the last of that era are gone I should be glad to contribute to some such monument as that proposed by ex-Governor Taylor—a trinity of figures to be carved from a single block of Southern marble, consisting of the courtly old planter, high-bred and gentle in face and manner; the plantation "uncle," the counterpart in ebony of the master so loyally served and

18

imitated; and the broad-bosomed black "mam-my," with varicolored turban, spotless apron, and beaming face, the friend and helper of every living thing in cabin or mansion.

I would that I had the power to put before you vividly and really the strange and beautiful social life of the Old South. It was Arcadian in its simplicity and well-nigh ideal in its conditions. It was a reproduction of the palmiest days and best features of feudalism, with little of the evil of that system. I know I am confronted by a host of critics and maligners of the so-called "slaveocracy" or "oligarchy" of the Old South. I have often read and heard of its despotism and cruelty from those who did not know or did not intend to be truthful or just. The war that swept slavery and the slaveholder out of existence was inspired and envenomed by such misrepresenta-tion. "Uncle Tom's Cabin" was a museum of barbarities set forth as the ordinary life of the Old South, a composite of brilliant and brutal falsehoods. I have no defense of feudalistic subjection of the many to the few, nor am I a friend to caste. Yet I have read history in vain and studied human progress to small account if

19

I have not, with others, discovered that a true development of society, the stability of government, the conservation of the rights of all classes, depend largely upon a social system in which one class, few in numbers, capable and conscientious, rules the other classes. A pure democracy is the dream of the idealist, and would be unprofitable even in the millennium. The men who own the lands of a country, its moneys, ships, and commerce, who maintain the traditions of the past, and trace their blood to the beginnings of a country's existence—these will inevitably become the leaders and rulers of a country. So the Old South had its aristocracy, whose leaders laughed at the doctrine of equality as proclaimed by sentimentalists at home and abroad.

This Old South aristocracy was of threefold structure—it was an aristocracy of wealth, of blood, and of honor. It was not the wealth of the shoddy aristocracy that here and there, even in the New South, has forced itself into notice and vulgarly flaunts its acquisitions. It came by inheritance of generations chiefly, as with the nobility of England and France. Only in the aristocracy of the Old World could there be found

20

a counterpart to the luxury, the ease and grace of inherited wealth, which characterized the ruling class of the Old South. There were no gigantic fortunes as now, and wealth was not increased or diminished by our latter-day methods of speculation or prodigal and nauseating display. The ownership of a broad plantation, stately country and city homes, of hundreds of slaves, of accumulations of money and bonds, passed from father to children for successive generations. Whatever cohesiveness the law could afford bound such great estates together, so that prodigality or change could least affect them. Here and there mansions of the old order of Southern aristocracy are standing in picturesque and melancholy ruin, as reminders of the splendor and luxury of the ante-bellum planter. A few months ago I looked upon the partly dismantled columns of a once noble home of the Old South, about which there clustered thickly the memories of a great name and family which for generations had received the homage of the South. As a child I had seen the spacious mansion in the day of its pride, as the Mecca of political leaders who came to counsel with its princely owner, or as the cen-

21

ter of a hospitality that never intermitted until the end of wealth came with the desolations of war. The glass of fashion and the mold of form made it famous as a social magnet. In those old days, its beautifully kept lawns, its ample shrubbery, its primeval park of giant oaks, its bewildering garden of flowers, its great orchards, its long rows of whitewashed negro cabins, its stables and .flashing equipages and blooded horses and dogs, the army of darkies in its fields, the native melody of their songs rising and falling in the distance, the grinding of cane or ginning of cotton, the soft-shod corps of trained servants about the mansion, the mingling of bright colors of innumerable visitors, the brilliancy of cut glass and silver, the lavishness of everything that could tempt the eye or palate— was like a picture from the scenes of Old-World splendor rather than of a young Western republic. As I looked and brooded over this ruin of a long-famous home, its glory all gone, its light and laughter dim and silent, I paid tribute to an aristocracy of wealth, pleasure-loving indeed, with the inherent weaknesses of transmitted estate, but one which, having freely received, freely

22

gave of its abundance in a hospitality eclipsing that of any people whom the world has known.

Porte Crayon, in *Harper's Magazine* long before the war, and Thomas Nelson Page, in these later days, have essayed by pencil and pen to set forth the charm of that wonderful hospitality and home life of the Old South. I saw the last of it. With my parole in my pocket, returning homeward through Virginia with other Confederates, hungry and foot-sore, we turned aside from our army-beaten road to a spacious plantation mansion on the crest of a hill, under whose porch sat a lonely old man, the one living creature we could discern. When we asked for bread, he excused himself for a moment on the plea that family and servants were gone, and that he must do our bidding. In a little while he returned with a huge platter of bread and meat, apologizing for a menu so little varied. When we had eaten as only Confederate soldiers could eat and were filled, we took pieces of money from our little store and tendered him in pay. I can never forget the big tears that welled up in the eyes of the old-time Virginian and the flush on his cheeks, as he said: "No, boys; it is the last morsel of food

23

that the enemy has left me.   There is not a living
creature or an atom of food remaining, but there
is not money enough in both armies to tempt my
poverty.   I've kept it up as long as I had it to
give."

Down under all this wealth of fertile field and
dusky laborer and palatial home, there was something in which the old-time Southerner took a
pride beyond that which he felt in material wealth.
His aristocracy of wealth was as nothing compared to his aristocracy of blood.   An old family name that had held its place in the social and
political annals of his State for generations was
a heritage vastly dearer to him than wealth. Back
to the gentle-blooded Cavaliers who came to
found this Western world, he delighted to trace
his ancestry.   There could be no higher honor to
him than to link his name with the men who had
planted the tree of liberty and made possible a
great republic.   Whatever honors his forbears
had won in field or forum, whatever positions of
public importance they had graced, he had at his
fingers' ends, and never grew weary of rehears-
ing.   I have nothing but tenderness for this old-
time weakness of the Southerner, if weakness

24

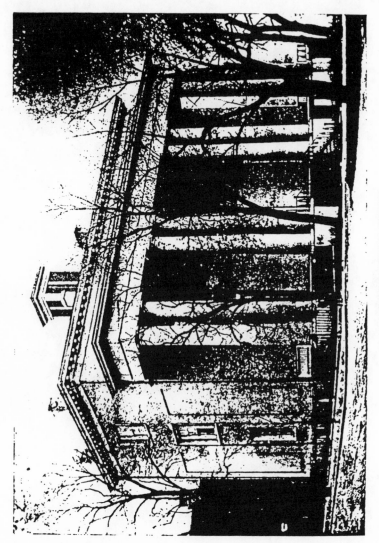

CONFEDERATE WHITE HOUSE.

it can be called. To glory in one's blood for centuries past, if only kept pure, to take pride in the linking of one's name and fame with the history of one's country, to grow gentler and truer and more self-respecting because of the virtues of a long line of ancestors who have lifted a family name to deserved eminence, to the writer has seemed a noble sentiment. I know how fools have made mock of it, and how silly people in the South have sometimes brought it into contempt; but I set forth in pride and gratitude for the Old South as one of its distinguishing characteristics this devotion to the memory and traditions of its ancestry. If here and there the course of transmitted blood lapsed into habit or deed of shame, it happened so rarely that it set the bolder in contrast the aristocracy of gentle blood. "Blood will tell." I remember as a boy watching admiringly and yet a little enviously the graceful and sometimes reckless military evolutions of a hundred or more young bloods, who were making holiday of the art of war. Trim, natty, elegant youngsters they were, in scarlet and gold, the scions of great families. I can remember wondering, as I watched them, if the

25

same dash and brilliancy that marked them as gala day soldiery would be maintained by them in the storm of battle which was making ready to break upon us. I had my answer. One day in Virginia the fortunes of war threw my regiment at elbows with theirs. Glitter and gold and scarlet were all bedimmed; but the gay laugh, the Cavalier dash, the courage that never quailed, were with them still as they swung into a desperate charge, singing one of their old cadet songs as lightly as a mocking bird's trill.

If any one should seek for the secret of that singular bravery, that supreme contempt of pain and privation and indifference to death that distinguished our Southern soldiery and won the admiration of its enemies, I think it will be found largely in the ambition of the younger generation to walk worthily after the steps of their fathers. Homogeneous in its citizenship, changing its customs little with passing years, slow to imbibe the spirit of other countries and of other sections of our own country, constant to its own ideals, and always a law unto itself, in no country on the face of the earth was a good name and family dis-

26

tinction more prized and potent than in the Old South.

Linked indissolubly with this aristocracy of wealth and of blood was one which, in my judgment, was stronger than either, and which extended beyond the lines of those who were born to the purple of wealth or the pride of a great name. I do not know better how to denominate it than this—the aristocracy of honor. Proud of their great homes and positions of leadership, and boastful of their high descent, the aristocrats of the Old South, true to the Cavalier traditions, erected an ethical system that defined and regulated personal and public matters and became the inflexible code of every Southern gentleman. Its foundation was laid in a man's "honor," and the honor of a gentleman was the supreme test and standard of every relation, public and private. The extremes of this old Southern ethical code were illustrated, on the one part, by the maxim that "a man's word is his bond," which meant that, the word of honor once passed between men, it must be as inviolable as life itself. Practically, it came to mean, as the present generation little knows or appreciates, that nine-

27

tenths of the business of the Old South was a mere promise to pay, and that its millions rested from year to year upon the faith and honor that underlay its vast credit system. A gentleman of the Old South might be guilty of not a few peccadillos. He might sin easily and often against himself, but woe to the man who sinned against other men by withholding what was due and had been promised "on honor." Personally I have known men of large business affairs whose whole fortunes depended on the passing of a word, and who on the instant would have surrendered their last dollar to make good that "word of honor." Nor was this exceptional. It was bred in the bone and flesh of every old-time Southern boy that upon this word of personal faith the gentleman must take his stand, and at whatever cost of comfort or convenience or self-denial or sacrifice, even to the death, he must make it good. Such was the code of honor upon its business side.

There was another illustration of the code of a more somber kind, now many years obsolete. It was by the crack of pistol and flash of sword that in the old time not infrequently were determined the fine points of honor. Long ago this

28

"code duello," with its Hotspur partisans, passed away, and I thank God for the gentler spirit that has come in its stead. With all of its blood and brutality, however, it had one merit which I am frank to allow it. It compelled one to circumspection in what he said and did, or it made him pay instant price for his wrongdoing. It differentiated the man of courage from the bully and the sneak, and it set in bold relief the marks of the gentleman. I am glad to say, too, that during the long and evil reign of the code duello satisfaction in money and by damage suits at law was not as popular as now. The Kentuckian whose bloody face provoked the inquiry, "What ails you?" answered by the code and card when he replied, "I called a gentleman a liar." The kind of gentleman who would salve the wounded honor of his person or family by a check was unknown or unrecognized before the war.

If one wishes to see the old-time planter at his best, he will find him as the pencils of Page, Harris, and Hopkinson Smith have drawn him—courtly, genial, warm-hearted, gracious, proud of his family, boastful of his ancestral line, a lover of gun and dog and horse and mint julep,

29

an incomparable mixer in the society of well-bred ladies and gentlemen, as unique and distinguished a figure as ever graced the ball or banquet room, the political forum, or the field of honor. His race will soon be extinct, and only the kindly voice and pen of those who knew him and loved him in spite of his weaknesses will truly perpetuate his memory. For two hundred years and more his was the conspicuous and unrivaled figure upon the social and political stage of our history. The good that he did lives after him; may the evil be interred with his bones!

SIDE by side with the aristocrat, waiting deferentially to do his bidding, with a grace and courtliness hardly surpassed by his master, I place the negro servant of the Old South. If one figure was unique, the other is not less so. Either figure in the passing throng would quickly arrest your attention. I am frank to confess to a tender feeling for those faithful black servitors of the Old South—the "Uncle Remuses"

30

and "Aunt Chloes" of picture and poetry. On the great plantations, in their picturesque colors, in constant laughter and good nature, well fed and clothed and generally well-kept and moderately worked, the negro of slavery lived his careless, heart-free life. The specter of hunger and want never disquieted him. His cabin, clothing, food, garden, pocket money, and holidays came without his concern./I think I state the truth when I say that for the millions of slaves of the Old South there were fewer heartaches than ever troubled a race of people. Freedom may be an inestimable boon. I know that poet and orator have so declared. But when I look upon the care-worn faces of the remnant of old-time negroes who have been testing freedom for a generation and have found it full of heartache and worry, I take exception to the much-vaunted doctrine of liberty as the panacea for all human ills. An old darky, with white head and shuffling feet and haunted look in his eyes, stopped the other day at the door of my office, and, after the manner of the old days, his cap in hand, asked "if massa could give the old nigger a dime?" Something in my voice or manner must

3i

have intimated to him that, like him, I belonged
to the old order, as he said: "It's all right for
some folks, dis thing they calls freedom; but
God knows I'd be glad to see the old days once
more before I die." Freedom to him, and to
others like him, had proven a cheat and a snare.
I have no word of apology or defense for slavery. Long ago I thanked God that it was no
longer lawful for one human being to hold
another in enforced servitude. But a generation or more of free negroes has been our most
familiar object-lesson, and the outcome is painful
at best. The negro who commands respect in
the South to-day, as a rule, is the negro who was
born and trained under slavery. The new generation, those who have known nothing but freedom, it is charity to say, are an unsatisfactory
body of people generally. Whenever you find a
negro whose education comes not from books
and college only, but from the example and home
teaching and training of his white master and
mistress, you will generally find one who speaks
the truth, is honest, self-respecting and self-re-
straining, docile and reverent, and always the
friend of the Southern white gentleman and lady.

32

CONFEDERATE MONUMENT.

Here and there in the homes of the New South these graduates from the school of slavery are to be found in the service of old families and their descendants, and the relationship is one of peculiar confidence and affection; and this old-time darky, wherever you find him in his integrity, pride, and industry, is in bold contrast with the post-bellum negro, despite his educational opportunity. Living as I do in a city famed for its negro schools, I have tried to observe fairly, and indeed with strong predilection in their favor, the processes and results of negro education. Son of an abolitionist of the Henry Clay school, I have sincerely wanted to see the negro succeed educationally and take his place with other men in skill and service. If any city of the South should be the first to confirm the negro's fitness for an education and his increase in value and in character as the subject of it, I thought it but fair to expect it of a city famous for its colored universities. But, with honorable exceptions to the rule, the negro of post-bellum birth and education in this city is usually a thorn in the flesh to one who seeks or uses his service, no matter what that service may be. "We don't have to work

3   33

any more," said one recently; "we are getting educated." Yet when one of the darky patriarchs of the Old South died the other day, a leading daily paper, in a tender and beautiful editorial, noted how this colored gentleman of the old school, after a long life of honor and trust, with hundreds of thousands of dollars passing through his hands as confidential messenger, had won the respect of all men by the sheer nobility of his life.

Perhaps the education of hand and foot and eye—the manual training schemes of Booker Washington and other like negro educators— may suffice to avert the degeneracy of the younger negro race. The trouble, however, is that many of these are not enamored of hard work and constant labor. They turn their backs upon ax and saw and plow which the white man offers them along with ample wages, and prefer the negro barroom and the crap table. After forty years have gone, and millions of money have been expended by both Northern and Southern whites in an effort to educate and train him for profitable service, the negro is found practically in two classes—the larger class massed in the

34

cities and towns, too often despising and shirk-
ing work except as compelled to it by sheer necessity; the other class consisting of those who
are not ashamed of any kind of work in field,
factory, or shop, the significant thing being that
those who want work and are doing it are commonly the negroes with little or no education,
while those who are shunning work are usually
of the so-called educated class.

I am not surprised at the failure of the negro's
secular education to make him a good and profitable citizen. It is only another illustration of
the folly of trying to sharpen the intellect and
leave untrained the heart and conscience. The
Old South, by contact, example, and precept,
put a conscience and a sense of right and honorable living into its slaves. The New South
is largely filling them with books. The negro
of the Old South was religious, genuinely so,
though by reason of his emotional nature his
religion was often a matter of feeling. But such
religion as he had he got from white teachers
and preachers, and it was real and scriptural.
It bound him to tell the truth, to lie not, to be
sober and honest, and to do no man wrong.

35

How well the negro learned and practiced this old-fashioned religion of slavery, let two facts attest. First, few negroes thus trained in the Old South, so far as the speaker knows, have suffered by rope or fagot for the unnamable crime that so often has marked the negro of the New South. If there be exceptions to this rule, certainly they are exceedingly rare. Secondly, at a time when every white man and even white boys were at the front fighting the battles of the Confederacy, the wives and mothers and children of the soldiers were cared for loyally and devotedly by the negro slaves to an extent unmatched in the history of the world. Such was the honor and conscience of the negro slaves that they watched over the helpless women and children of those who were engaged in a conflict involving their own slavery.

What the negro needs more than books and college curriculum is a conscience. He needs religion of the genuine, transforming kind that will stop his petty thieving, his street corner loafing, and his tendencies toward the barbarism from which in the Old South religion wrested his fathers. I think the time has come when our

36

Southern white churches should turn again toward the negro and help him as far as possible to a knowledge of pure and undefiled religion, after the example of such ministry as that of Capers and Andrew to the slaves. If I find any fault with ourselves in our relationships with the negro, it is that we too easily conceded that the negro's moral and religious interests should be taken out of our hands since the war by sentimentalists, or by those whose labors among the negroes were inspired by political rather than by genuinely benevolent motives. Once politics is no longer an ally to the negro, and White House favors are not permitted to turn his head, I have some hope that the Southern white and the negro may come together in peace and mutual affection under the power of the gospel of Jesus Christ, and after an alienation of more than a generation may take up again the old order of religious instruction and training, which the white fathers of the Old South were so zealous to give and which the black servants were so eager to receive. When a young pastor came to me a few weeks ago asking an opinion upon the fact that, in response

37

to a request from a score or more of families of negroes on his charge who were without church and other religious facilities, he and his wife had formed their children into a Sunday school and the teachers of his white school were giving them faithful and intelligent instruction every Sabbath, I saw in the incident an intimation of what the New South must do if it would restore the lost negro conscience of the Old South.

I cannot dismiss this passing glance at the social life of the Old South without a sense of abiding regret that it is gone forever. My last personal contact with it was the Christmas just preceding the war. Though the air was thick with rumors of impending strife, no gun as yet had broken the quiet of a land so full of peace and prosperity. I think the merriment of those last holidays of '61 was greater than ever before. I recall it all the more vividly because it was the last old-fashioned Christmas that came to my boyhood, as it was the last that came to the Old South. For weeks preceding it everything on the old plantation was full of stir and preparation. Holly and mistletoe and cedar were being put about the rooms of the big house

38

to welcome home the boys and girls from school. Secret councils were being held as to the Christmas gifts that were to be given religiously to every one, white and black. The back yard was piled up with loads of oak and hickory to make bright and warm the Christmas nights. The negro seamstresses were busy making new suits and dresses for all the servants. The master of the plantation was figuring up the accounts of the year and making ready for generous drafts upon his ready money. There was an increasing rustle of excitement and happiness that ran from the gray-haired grandfather and grandmother down to the smallest pickaninny in the remotest negro cabin. The peace and goodness of God seemed to brood over it all. The stately plantation home, with its lofty white columns, its big rooms, its great fireplaces, opened wide to all sons and daughters and grandchildren, uncles and aunts, nephews and nieces. We poured into it; and if ever heaven came close to earth and mingled with it, I think it was that Christmas Eve when the last wanderer and exile had come and the grace was said at the great table by a gray-haired patriarch of the Old South. There was

39

little sleep for small boys and girls, and long before daylight of Christmas shone in upon us we were scurrying from room to room crying, "Christmas gift!" to which, whenever first spoken by child or dependent, there could be but the one gracious response. Out on the back porches the negroes were waiting in grinning rows to follow our example, and many were the dusky faces that beamed with delight over their never-failing Christmas remembrances. Down in the cabins and up in the big halls of the mansion the lights and fires burned the entire week, and there was nothing that could eat that was not surfeited with the world of eatables made ready. I must beg pardon of the W. C. T. U., which had not then begun its beneficent prohibitory career, if I recall the big flowing bowl of eggnog, renewed daily and served generously to all. I know that this old-time Christmas beverage is growing into disrepute, for which I am sincerely glad, but I confess to a sort of carnal delight of memory when I recall how good it tasted to the average small boy on an early Christmas morning.

40

JEFFERSON DAVIS.

T HE Old South intellectually was a fitting complement to its unique social system. The charge has often been made against it that it produced few if any great writers and left no lasting impress upon the literature of the times. If this were true, it could be answered that the Old South was true to its distinctive mission. It needed to produce great thinkers, and it produced them, as the half-century of its dominating leadership attests. An Elizabethan age, with its coterie of great writers, comes to any nation only at long intervals, and under conditions which are of providential rather than of human ordering. The Southern man, by tradition, inheritance, and choice, and by virtue of a certain philosophic temper which seemed to inhere in his race, was trained to think and to speak clearly, and especially upon grave matters of public import. He was a born politician in the best sense of that much-abused term. Like Hannibal, he was led early in life to the altars of his country and dedicated to its service. He coveted the power and the authority of the rostrum rather than the pen. In the beauty of field and forest, of bright stream and blossoming flower,

41

of song and sunshine, or in the historic incidents of the Old South, he had ample inspiration and material for his pen, if he had cared to use it. But it was ever his ambition and delight to stand before his countrymen on some great public day, and set forth the length and breadth of some great argument, patiently studied and thought out in his library and now made luminous and inspiring to the listening multitude. If it were true that the South had no great writers, I could even content myself by recalling how, when one of its brilliant thinkers and orators cast his spell upon the culture of old Boston, the finest editorial writer of that city of writers placed over his leading editorial the next morning the question, "What could be finer?"

While it was true of the Old South that members of its learned professions commonly dallied with the Muses, there was no distinctive profession of letters. The professional poet, historian, and maker of fiction, and publisher and seller of books, were scarcely known. A rural people, a relatively sparse population of readers, the absence of great cities, the concentration of

42

306

thought and learning upon politics and plans of government, the entire lack of commercialism as a motive to literary production, were reasons why the Old South contributed comparatively little *per se* to the stock of permanent literature. There was another hindrance in the fact, which I do not like to recall, that the South, in mistaken largeness of heart or short-sightedness of vision, fell upon two ways that lowered its own self-respect and dwarfed the good it might have attained. It set up a fashion, on the one hand, of reading and patronizing alien books, and accounted these foreign literary products as better than its own. And along with this same mistaken fondness for foreign literary wares, it began to slight its own struggling colleges and schools, and to send its sons and daughters elsewhere for a culture not superior to that procurable at its own doors.

Yet with such admitted weaknesses, let no one suppose for an instant that the ability to write or think or speak worthy of the finest culture was in any wise wanting to the gentleman of the Old South. Enter his library, and you would find what is becoming rare in the New South, but

43

which was the mark of the gentleman of the Old South—the finest and completest array of costly books upon all subjects, ranging through science, art, literature, theology, biography, history, and politics. Nothing that money could buy or trained scholarship select was omitted. A man's books were his most intimate friends and comrades, and such were the wide range and patient study of the average gentleman of the Old South that wits and savants vied in paying tribute to his varied and scholarly attainments. In singular contrast, the other day one of our literary leaders, discussing the scanty sale of really valuable books, bemoaned the fact that the Southern gentleman's library is fast becoming extinct.

One feature of scholarship that was peculiar to the Old South was the general and thorough devotion to, and mastery of, the classics. I doubt if ever the youth of any country were so well grounded in the literature of Greek and Latin poet and historian, or caught so fully and finely the beauty of the old philosophies and mythologies. It was not an uncommon feat for a boy of fourteen, upon entrance as a freshman to a college of the old order, to read Virgil and

44

Horace *ore rotundo,* with a grace and finish that would do credit to a post-bellum alumnus. Latin, Greek, and the higher mathematics, with a modicum of the physical sciences, constituted the favored curriculum of the old-time academy and college. How much some of us owe to that ancient academy and that small college can never be rightly estimated. The standard of study was severe and thorough. The discipline was often rigorous and exacting. What, for instance, would our latter-day college boys think of a rule compelling their attendance, if within a mile of the chapel, upon sunrise prayer the year round? Or how would a shudder run through their ranks if I paused to tell them of how in our old Academy two score of us classical students, ranging in age from fifteen to thirty years, having been discovered demolishing the business signs of town merchants in an effort to fulfill the Scriptures which declared that they should seek a sign and none should be given unto them, were soundly thrashed with exceeding roughness and dispatch by the man who for many years has held the superintendency of public schools in the foremost city of the South! Alas

45

for the disappearance of those good old days and customs, of which the survivors have feeling and pathetic remembrance! For one, I am glad that free public education has come to the children, white and black, of the New South. Whether the hopes of the statesman and philanthropist shall be realized or not, I am also glad of the millions of money the New South has expended in the past generation upon the education of the masses. But the day of the ancient academy and college, as source and inspiration of an incomparable culture, will never be surpassed by latter-day educational systems, however widely extended and beneficent these may be. There was something intensely stimulating in the spirit and method of the old classical school; a sharp yet generous competition and rivalry of scholarship; a thoroughness that reached the foundation of every subject traversed; and above and through it all there was the sure development of a sense of honor and a pride of scholarship that lifted even the dull student into an ambition to succeed. Mixed with all was the example and influence of high-bred Christian gentlemen as professors and teachers, whose lives re-

46

enforced their teachings and molded us into the image of the gentleman of the Old South. The utilitarian in education was not yet in evidence. The bread-and-butter argument was reserved to a later generation. The cheap and tawdry "business college," recruited from guileless country youth ambitious to become merchant princes and railroad managers by a six months' course in double entry and lightning arithmetic, had not then entered upon its dazzling career. Boys were trained to read extensively, to think clearly, to analyze patiently, to judge critically, to debate accurately and fluently, and in short to master whatever subject one might come upon. Over that old-time educational method might be written the aphorism of Quintilian, that "not what one may remember constitutes knowledge, but what one cannot forget."

WE were not without noble intellectual exemplars in our Old South. The great thoughts of our home-born leaders, from Patrick Henry to Calhoun and Clay, were ever before us.

47

311

Our college debates, our commencement orations, were fashioned after the severely classical models these men had left us. From the rostrum, the party platform, the pulpit, whenever a man spoke in those days it was expected and demanded that his speech be chaste, his thought elevated, his purpose ennobling. We were old-fashioned, I admit, in theme and method. We did not aim so much to please and entertain as to convince and inspire. The forum was as sacred as in the palmiest days of Athens and Demosthenes. About it centered our chief ambitions. We had not come upon a degenerate age when a much-exploited college graduate, lyceum lecturer, and "D.D."—as I heard him before a great audience of university young gentlemen and ladies the other day—could descend to a contemptible buffoonery of delineation of the "American Girl" as his theme, and include in his printed repertoire such subjects as "The Tune the Old Cow Died of," which confirmed some of us who heard him in the conviction that Balaam's ass is yet lineally represented in ways of public speech and action.

Of the great writers and orators who left their

4ᵉ

ALEXANDER H. STEPHENS.

impress upon us in the last years of the Old South, I can speak from personal contact and experience, and with thankfulness that as a boy I was given to see most of them face to face and to touch, in spirit, the hem of their garments. The spell of the genius of Edgar Allan Poe, though the fitful fever of his life had ended, was upon the literature and literary men of the time. The weird beauty of the lines of this prince of the powers of harmony, contrasting so wonderfully with a strange analytical power that made him at once a foremost prose and poetical writer of his century, had set before us the measure of beauty and the test of genius. Then, in our own day, came Paul Hamilton Hayne, Henry Timrod, and Sidney Lanier. I cannot describe to you the feeling of ownership that we of the Old South felt in this trinity of noble singers; nor can I express the sense of tenderness that comes to me as I recall the pain and poverty that haunted them most of their days until the end came, to two of them at least, in utter destitution. It was my privilege early in life to fall under the spell of the minstrelsy of these three men. As long as the red hills of Georgia stand, and its over-

4   49

hanging pines are stirred by the south wind's sighing, let it recall to the honorable and grateful remembrance of Georgians the gentle yet proud-spirited poet who, having lost all but honor and genius in his native sea-girt city, came to his rude cabin home at Copse Hill as the weary pilgrim of whom he so tenderly sings:

> With broken staff and tattered shoon,
> I wander slow from dawn to noon—
> From arid noon till, dew-impearled,
> Pale twilight steals across the world.
> Yet sometimes through dim evening calms
> I catch the gleam of distant palms;
> And hear, far off, a mystic sea,
> Divine as waves on Galilee.
> Perchance through paths unknown, forlorn,
> I still may reach an Orient morn;
> To rest where Easter breezes stir
> Around the sacred sepulcher.

I know what a fashion it is to worship at the shrines of the "Lake poets," and how Wordsworth and Burns and Shelley and like singers of the Old World, with Longfellow, Whittier, and Lowell of the New, are set on high as the greater masters of poesy. But if genius is a thing of quality rather than quantity, I go back to the

50

dark days and memories of battle and take my stand lovingly beside the new-made grave of Timrod, the poet laureate of the Confederacy, and call to mind what I believe to be a poem that the greatest of English and American poets would be glad to claim as their own. Remember, as you read it, how in his dire want the poet wrote of the little book of which it is a part: "I would consign every line of it to oblivion for one hundred dollars in hand."

Spring, with that nameless pathos in the air
    Which dwells with all things fair;
Spring, with her golden suns and silver rains,
    Is with us once again.
. . . .

Still there's a sense of blossoms yet unborn
    In the sweet airs of morn;
One almost looks to see the very street
    Grow purple at his feet.
At times a fragrant breeze comes floating by,
    And brings—you know not why—
A feeling as when eager crowds await
    Before a palace gate
Some wondrous pageant; and you scarce would start,
    If from a beech's heart
A blue-eyed Dryad, stepping forth, should say:
    "Behold me! I am May!"

51

Sidney Lanier was of the Old South, though fame came to him from the New. It was fitting that the latest of the progeny of genius of the Old South should become the foremost of those who were to gild it with a fame imperishable. Born in Georgia, less than a score of years before the tragedy of the Old South began, writing his earliest poems as a boy in Confederate camp and Federal prison, his music tinged with the somberness of the time, Lanier's genius was like the last of the Southern flowers that burst into bloom just before the coming of chilling frost and wintry wind. It was like the bright-red flower of war which he describes: "The early spring of 1861 brought to bloom, besides innumerable violets and jessamines, a strange, enormous, and terrible flower, the blood-red flower of war, which grows amid the thunders." Why it is that the price of genius must always be paid in blood, I do not know; but not all the transmitted genius and culture and spirit of the Old South, which crystallized in this last and greatest of her literary children, could absolve Lanier from the pangs which Southern genius seems peculiarly called upon to suffer. As the holiest and brav-

52

est lives spring out of darkness and storm and sorrow, it may be that only such baptism of tears and blood which we as a people have received could fit our sons and daughters for their high vocation.

Lanier was easily the greatest of the poets of the South. Perhaps his final place is yet to be fixed among the greater singers of America, but it is comforting to know that the clear light of dispassionate judgment of the receding years dispels the first-formed prejudices, and lifts the singer into nobler and yet nobler place.

Broken with pain and poverty, yearning unutterably for the peace and quiet of an opportunity to pour out his divine genius in great and holy song, could anything be more utterly pitiful than this passionate cry for help, which lay among his papers after his death?

O Lord, if thou wert needy as I,
If thou shouldst come to my door as I to thine;
If thou hungered so much as I
For that which belongs to the spirit,
For that which is fine and good,
Ah, friend, for that which is fine and good,
I would give it to thee if I had power.

"A thousand songs are singing in my heart," he

53

declares, "that will certainly kill me if I do not utter them soon."

Lanier's genius was many-sided, and there is not a line he wrote of poetry or prose that one would care to blot. He had the exquisite sense of melody of Poe, but he had what Poe did not in the spirit of the maxim of his art which he often expressed in the words: "The beauty of holiness and the holiness of beauty." He had, too, the tenderness and pathos and lyrical beauty of Timrod and Hayne, yet the characteristic of his poems is that they call one to worship God. They usher us with bowed head and chastened spirit into the holy of holies. "A holy tune was in my soul when I fell asleep," he writes; "it was going when I awoke."

Just as in the ancient mythology, while one of divine descent might hold converse for a time with sons and daughters of men unmarked or unrecognized, yet by glance of eye or grace of motion would inevitably betray himself as of the progeny of the gods, so if ever for a moment I were in doubt as to the genius of Lanier my doubt would vanish as in the darkness, with bowed head and pitying heart of love, I sang

54

to myself his "Ballad of the Trees and the
Master:"

> Into the woods my Master went,
> Clean forspent, forspent.
> > Into the woods my Master came,
> > Forspent with love and shame.
> But the olives they were not blind to him,
> The little gray leaves were kind to him,
> The thorn tree had a mind to him,
> > When into the woods he came.
>
> Out of the woods my Master went,
> And he was well content.
> > Out of the woods my Master came,
> > Content with death and shame.
> When death and shame would woo him last,
> From under the trees they drew him—last;
> 'Twas on a tree they slew him—last,
> > When out of the woods he came.

ONE of the aphorisms of my youth was,
"Poeta nascitur, orator fit." That the poet
is "born," and ever bears upon himself the marks
of his divine enduement, I do not doubt; but that
the orator "becomes" or happens so by chance or
labor. I must strongly deny. A certain fluency

55

321

of speech, a certain gloss of oratory, may possibly be achieved by dint of elocutionary drill and practice. If one is minded, like orators of an elegant postprandial type, to stand before a mirror and practice the tricks of gesture and speech, he may hope to attain applause from those whose blood is kept well cooled by the ices of the banquet room. I have described it fittingly as "postprandial" oratory, for the reason that it is most appreciated when the stomach and not the brain is chiefly in operation.

But if any one as a boy had ever sat under the matchless spell of the real masters of the forum, those who were as fully "born" unto it as was Lanier to poetry or Blind Tom to music; if within a half score of years he had been permitted to hear in their prime Jefferson Davis, Robert Toombs, Ben Hill, Alexander Stephens, Judge Lamar, and William L. Yancey, the after-dinner elegancies of oratory of the class I have named would be tame and dispiriting. I would not underrate the men of later fame, but I am sure that it is not time and distance only that lend enchantment to the names of that galaxy of famous orators who closed the succession

56

of platform princes of the Old South. I would not detract an iota from whatever claim the New South may have to oratory, but I stand firmly upon the proposition, self-evident to survivors of the Old South, that the golden age of Southern oratory ended a generation ago. Compared with Yancey, the incarnate genius of oratory, any oration of that superb master of assemblies by the side of the best post-bellum oratory (always excepting Henry W. Grady) is as Hyperion to a satyr.

On a day that no one who was present will ever forget, while the war clouds were gathering and old political issues were giving place to the one dominant and terrible question of the hour, in a little Southern city, within the compass of twelve hours I heard the greatest of the orators of the last tragic era of the Old South. Whig and Democrat were words to conjure with, and the old-fashioned custom of joint debate was yet in honor. The crux of an intense and hard-fought campaign was at hand, and only the platform giants of the contending parties were in demand for the occasion. From fifty to a hundred miles around, towns, without railroad communication as now, poured their delegations in upon the crucial day of the campaign. For two days and nights in advance, processions with fife and drum and bands, cannon and cavalry, had held rival parade. The fires of a great barbecue, with its long lines of parallel trenches in which, under the unbroken vigilance of expert negro cooks, whole beeves and sheep and hogs and innumerable turkeys were roasting, sent forth a savor that would have tempted the dainty palate of an Epicurus. Floats were formed, and fair young women and rosy-cheeked children expressed in symbol the doctrines of their sires, and sang to us until our hearts were all aglow. To the small boy there were meat and drink, sights and sounds illimitable, and a tenseness of excitement that thrilled him with a thousand thrills, for in the presence and sound of the great men of his country the boy's heart must expand and his ambition take fire.

Not in a hundred years could I forget the speeches and speakers of that eventful day. Whole passages linger in memory now, fifty years after they were spoken. I recall the jubilant ring of Ben Hill as, lifting an old placard on

58

which was inscribed, "Buck, Breck, and Kansas," he said: "You got your Buck, you got your Breck, but where's your Kansas?" Or Brownlow, with the heavy thump of his fist on the table, declaring, "I would rather vote for the old clothes of Henry Clay, stuffed with straw, than for any man living." Or Toombs, with massive head and lordly pose, denouncing in blistering speech the unholy alliance of certain men of the Old South with the enemies of its most vital institution. Or Stephens, small and weazened, sallow and unkempt, with cigar stump in hand, his thin, metallic voice penetrating with strange power to the remotest part of the great open-air assemblage. All day, back and forth, the battle of the giants raged. Toward nightfall the Democrats were in dire distress over the seeming victory of the opposition. Yancey lay sick at home, sixty miles away, and the wires were kept hot with pleadings to bring him at any cost, if possible, to the scene. At nine o'clock that night I saw a strange tribute to the power of that orator, who, I doubt not, will stand unrivaled in the future as in the past. Pale and emaciated, taken from his sick room and hur-

59

ried by special train, upborne upon the shoulders of men whose idol he had been for twenty years, he was carried to the platform at the close of a day's great victory by the opposing party. With singularly musical voice and an indefinable magnetism which fell upon all of us, he began a speech of two hours' length. Within an hour, such was the magic of the man, he had turned the tide of defeat, rallied his party, and filled them with hope and courage. Within another hour he was receiving the tremendous applause of even his political enemies, and had undone all the mighty work of the giants of the opposition and sent them home with a chill at heart.

With such political leaders as these men, and with the finest intellect and character of the Old South devoted for generations to the study and exposition of the purest party politics, I am not surprised at the higher level of parties and platforms of the Old South. Politics was not a "graft," as the present-day political ringster defines it. The political and personal conscience were one and the same, and a man's politics was no small part of his religion. I am not saying that all political leaders were incorrupt-

60

ible statesmen, or that an unselfish patriotism was the invariable mark of its party politics.
The demagogue was not unknown, and the fine
Italian hand of the mercenary was sometimes in
evidence. But of one fact I am abundantly assured—the spoilsman and the grafter held no
recognized and official standing in that old-
time democracy. Men of ability and character
might aspire to political place and honor. They
might even go beyond the personal desire and
become open candidates for party favor. But
the service of the paid political manager, the
conciliation of the party "boss," the subsidizing
of the party "heelers," the utilization of the party
press in flaming, self-laudatory columns and even
pages of paid advertising matter, *ad nauseam* and
ad infinitum, as in recent Southern political contests—all these latter-day importations and in-
ventions of "peanut" politics would have merited
and received the unmeasured contempt of the
politicians of the Old South. There were certain old-fashioned political maxims that constituted the code of every man who would become
a candidate for office, as, for instance, "The office should seek the man, not the man the office."

61

I cannot find heart to censure the politician of the
New South for his smile at the verdancy and
guilelessness of such a maxim, but that which
provokes a smile was in my own remembered
years the working motto of the old-time Southern leaders of high rank. Another maxim was
that "the patriot may impoverish but not enrich
himself by office-holding." As a commentary
upon this maxim, it affords me infinite satisfaction, in a retrospect of the long line of men who
led the great political campaigns of the Old
South and held its positions of highest trust, that
most of them died poor, that none of them within my knowledge were charged with converting
public office into private gain, and that the highest ambition of the old-time politician was to
serve his country by some great deed of unselfish
patriotism, to live like a gentleman, and then to
die with uncorrupted heart and hands, and with
money enough to insure a decent burial. If he
left a few debts here and there, they were gratefully cherished as souvenirs by his host of friends.

Earlier in these pages I raised the question
as to why the South, once so potent in national
council and leadership, was now become the

62

mere servant of the national Democratic party, so much so that the recognized Sir Oracle of Republicanism and mouthpiece of his excellency the President is led to remind us, while a guest on Southern soil, of our pristine place and power, and to admonish us, in the frankness of an open and worthy foeman, to quit playing the rôle of lackey in national politics, and to put forth as of yore our own home-grown statesmen for national positions of highest honor and service, and to do all in our might again to restore the lost political prestige of the South. Come from whomsoever it may, Republican or Democrat, Grosvenor or Grant—for the latter before his death held like view with the former—the advice is well given and the point well taken. But when once the renaissance begins, I think the Augean stable of latter-day politics, even in the New South, will need another Hercules to purify it. Take, for instance, this statement from a recent issue of a great Southern newspaper: "The four candidates for railroad commissioner expended a total of $14,940.80 on their campaign expenses, Mr. ——, who was nominated, leading with $10,522.80. The twelve candidates

63

for the Supreme Court paid out $7,133.34. Sixteen Congressional candidates expended $15,-965.88."

In the *Independent* of recent date a leading Democratic manufacturer of New Jersey, under manifestly strong grievance, recites his experiences as a delegate in the State Democratic Convention, in which a vigorous effort was made, as in other Democratic Conventions, to force the indorsement of an unclean aspirant to the highest office of the republic. The article I cite is an evident instance of pot and kettle, but it sets in bold relief the straits and methods to which the dominating wing of the party of Jefferson and Jackson has been reduced, certainly in some of the Northern if not of the Southern States. I quote the closing paragraph of the article as a faithful picture of recent political happenings:

What are the means used by the bosses? First, corrupted judges at the primaries and bulldozing tactics there. Secondly, a brow-beating county and delegation chairman, with his attendant thugs. Thirdly, a properly managed credentials committee, with arrangements made beforehand, so that there will be con-

64

tests and the contests decided their way. Fourthly, a tactful chairman, who will have fine presence, be a hypocrite and pretend to fairness, but never recognize any but machine men. Fifthly, the presence of the boss, with his ever-ready check book and a fine knowledge of men to know what he must do to win his way with them.

In so far as this is a true picture of the dominant spirit and method of no small part of the Northern Democracy, and I firmly believe it so to be, I think it time for the South to first purge itself of the contamination that has come from thirty years of subserviency and emasculation, and then to assert and maintain the integrity and high principles of the Democracy of the fathers. If ever thieves and money changers were scourged from the ancient temple, it is high time that the lash of public scorn shall be laid upon the backs of all men, North or South, who have helped to disrupt and dishonor a once noble and victorious national party. When I remember, as a Confederate soldier, that William McKinley—peace to his dust—in the city of Atlanta, as Republican President, pleaded for equal recognition of Confederate with Federal dead; and that

5   65

---

one who has been honored by the Democratic party as standard bearer and occupant of a great office declined to vote for an ex-Confederate candidate in fear of the disfavor of his Western constituency; and when within recent months, in great cities of the South, I have personally seen the cunning handiwork of paid henchmen of a millionaire saffron newsmonger seeking most insistently and offensively to buy exalted position for their master, I am ready once more to secede, except that the second act of secession would be the sundering of all bonds that bind my party to corrupting methods and leadership, and the setting up again in the New South of the lofty political ideals and independency of the Democracy of the Old South.

THUS far I have tried to portray, in frankly admitted partiality, the social, intellectual, and political characteristics of the Old South. But I should be seriously derelict in my portraiture if I left unnoted that which was more to it than wealth or culture or learning or party. If the

66

Old South had one characteristic more than another, I think it was the reverent and religious life and atmosphere which diffused themselves among all classes of its people, whether cracker white or plantation prince or dusky slave. If I were asked to explain this atmosphere of religion, I should hardly know where to begin. Perhaps its largely rural population and its peaceful agricultural pursuits predisposed to religion the simple-minded people who made up the Old South. More than this, however, must have been due to the religious strain in the blood of the Cavalier, Huguenot, and God-fearing Scotch-Irish ancestry from which they sprang. Most of all, I think that the high examples of a godly profession and practice in the leaders of the Old South made it easy for each succeeding generation to learn the first and noblest of all lessons —reverence for God, his Word, and his Church. And until this day the reverence of the Old South is constant in the New South. While New England, once the citadel of an orthodox Bible and Church and Sabbath, is now the prey of isms and innovations innumerable, and while the great West is marked by the painful contrast

67

between its big secular enterprises and its diminutive churches and congregations, the South has continued largely to be not only the acknowledged home of the only pure Americanism, but the center also of conservatism and reverence in the worship of God and the maintenance of Christian institutions.

In no section of our country has the Christian Sabbath been so highly honored, Canada alone, with her reverently ordered day of rest, exceeding us in Sabbath observance. Here and there, however, is needed the cautionary signal of danger against the greed of railroad and other law-defying corporations, and the loose morality of aliens who come to us with money but without religious raising or conviction. In no other section is there such widely diffused catholicity of spirit and tolerance of differences among opposing religious beliefs. If the Roman Catholic has been freer from assault upon his religion in any country or time than in the South, I have failed to find it. If the Jew has as kindly treatment elsewhere under the sun, I should be glad to know it. And if there is as fine a courtesy and fraternity anywhere as among our Southern

6S

Protestant bodies, I have yet to discover it. A few months ago, though of another denomination, I was called to their platform by the great Southern Baptist Assembly. A month before that I was summoned by the Cumberland Presbyterian Seminary, of Lebanon, to instruct its young men. A month before that I was writing articles for the chief religious organ of the Southern Presbyterians. I have lived long enough and am familiar enough with other parts of the world to know that such practical catholicity chiefly obtains in the South.

Nowhere as in the South do men so generally honor the house of God by their attendance and support. I make bold to say that upon any Sabbath day by count more men may be found in churches in Richmond and Atlanta than in Chicago and New York, though the combined population of the latter cities is ten times that of the former. These same churchgoing men of the South, following in the footsteps of their God-fearing fathers, are the members and supporters of Southern Churches, and are quick to resent innovation or disturbance of the old order. No man is so reverent and courteous toward men

69

of the cloth as the men of the South, and wherever a minister of the gospel walks down the street of a Southern city or village, if worthy to wear the cloth of his sacred calling, he is the foremost man of his community in standing and influence.

Why this relative respect to the minister and the Church, and this clinging to religious forms and traditions, those of us who came up out of the Old South understand. Any reverent spirit of the New South in matters of religion is another of the heritages from the Old South. Then as now, even more than now, with our leaders and great men it was religion first, politics second, and money, or whatever money stood for, last and least. From my earliest recollection and reading, the governors, senators, congressmen, judges, great lawyers, physicians, merchants, and planters were commonly Christian men, both by profession and practice; and the man who was hostile or even indifferent to the Church and religion, however distinguished and brilliant he might be, was under ban of public opinion. As a commentary upon this significant religious affiliation of Southern leadership I

70

336

carefully noted a few years ago, in two contrasting lists taken at random of governors and congressmen, that while one list had five men out of twenty-five who were members of Christian Churches, the Southern list of twenty-five contained eighteen. While I share in the widespread regret that our Southern young men are not as reverent as were those of a generation ago, and are often conspicuous by absence upon Sabbath worship, yet in view of such facts as I am recounting I am more hopeful of the solution of the vexed problem of Christian young manhood in the South than in any other part of the land.

I HAVE paid tribute to the great political orators of the Old South. Let me pay higher tribute to its great preachers and pulpit orators, to whom, under God, more than to any other class or leadership, is due what the South has ever cherished as its best. There were giants in those days. If Yancey or Stephens could cast a spell upon a great political gathering, and play upon its

71

emotions as the harper plays upon the harp, George F. Pierce in his prime could stir men's hearts in a way that put to shame even the eloquence of the political rostrum. The last time I heard this greatest of all the orators of the Old South was not far from the time of his death. Marvin, fittingly called the "St. John of Methodism," sat in the pulpit behind him. To most of his audience Pierce and his preaching were known only by hearsay, and their firm belief was that Marvin was the real prince of the pulpit. I remember how Pierce battled against his bodily weakness and weariness, and how there came to his eye that wondrous flash as his old-time eloquence lifted him into heights and visions celestial. He was preaching of the pure faith once delivered unto the saints, and pleading for the old order of simple gospel truth and living. He had something to say of the new order of ministers who were substituting doubts and denials for the long-cherished doctrines of the Church. His opening sentence was: "A single meteor flashing athwart the heavens will arrest a larger measure of attention than the serene shining of a thousand planets." I think I know who the old

72

BISHOP GEORGE F. PIERCE.

man eloquent meant. A little while before, a dapper preacher, consumed by itch for popularity, had been dispensing a perfumed and smokeless theology that drew great crowds and tickled the ears of the groundlings. The theology of the Old South was too crude and barbarous and unscientific for such as he. Genesis was an allegory, creation an evolution, man was pre-Adamic, the deluge was only a local shower, the Pentateuch was polychromatic, Moses was largely mythical, there were two Isaiahs, all the ante-exilian history and writings were concocted by pious post-exilian experts, the incarnation and resurrection were touching legends but "quite unscientific," hell was "hades," and hades was a tolerably comfortable winter resort, and Bible inspiration, as a matter of fact, seldom inspired. Many times, in sight and sound of such dainty apostles of an emasculate Bible, have I longed for the ghosts of the stalwart preachers of my childhood—the Pierces, Thomas Sanford, Jefferson Hamilton, A. L. P. Green, P. P. Neely, Jesse Boring, McTyeire, Wightman, Summers, and the like—to rise up in their godly wrath and shake them over the flaming pit of a real old-

73

time, unabridged "hades" long enough to bring them to silence and repentance.

Down in the straw, at the mourners' bench of an Old South camp meeting, some of us got our theology and our religion. The Bible, in miracle and prophecy, was handled by reverent hands, and made most real to us as the infallible word of Almighty God. The law of Sinai, with unexpurgated cursings and blessings, was read to us amid the groanings of our troubled consciences. No ear so polite, no position so exalted, but a living and burning hell was denounced against its meannesses. As deep as the virus of sin in our souls sank the flashing, two-edged sword of the Spirit. The wound was made purposely deep and wide that the balm of Gilead might enter and heal the utmost roots of sin. By and by, when John the Baptists, like Boring and Lovick Pierce, had cut to the quick, and laid bare the wounded spirit, some gentler, wooing ministry, like that of Hamilton or Neely, came pointing the way to the cross. There was no lifting of the finger tip, daintily gloved and decorous, in token of a desire sometime or other to become a Christian. Cards, in colors, bear-

74

342

ing name and rates of the evangelist, agreeing to meet everybody in heaven, were not passed around for signatures. I never hear the old hymn of invitation, that lured many a hardened sinner of the Old South, as they sung it under the leafy arbor to flickering lights, after a weird, unearthly stirring of our hearts by the man in the pulpit, but I think of a great criminal lawyer, who for many years had led the bar of his State, and had made mock of God's Book and Church and ministers. He owned an old carriage driver who was one of God's saints in black, gray-haired and patient "Uncle Aleck," who had mourned and prayed over his unbelieving master. "Uncle Aleck," he said to him one day, "why do you believe in a book you can't read, and in a God you never saw? I have thousands of books in my library, yet I care nothing for religion." Uncle Aleck's only reply was to put his hand on his heart and say: "Marse John, I've been true and faithful to you all these years, ain't I, marster?" "Yes." "And I never lied to you or disobeyed you, has I, Marse John?" "No." "Then, marster, it's my religion that has made me what I am. I can't read, I can't see

75

God, but I know the Lord Jesus Christ here in my heart."

Drawn by some spell he could not resist, the great lawyer came to the old camp ground and heard the awfully solemn message of the preacher with bowed head and heart full of trouble. When the hymn was sung,

"Come, humble sinner, in whose breast
A thousand thoughts revolve;
Come, with your guilt and fear oppressed,
And make this last resolve,"

I shall never forget the startled look of preacher and people as straight to the mourners' bench sped the lawyer, crying in agony as he fell to the ground: "Send for Uncle Aleck!" And down in the straw white-haired old Aleck wrestled with God for Marse John, until a great shout went up from mourner and congregation as the master hugged the old darky and the darky hugged his master, saying: "I knew it was coming, Marse John." You will pardon a man whose head is growing gray if at times the heart grows hungry to turn back and see and hear the old sights and sounds of God's presence and

76

power as revealed especially at the ancient and now nearly extinct camp meeting.

ON a bright April day, 1861, books were closed in the old academy, there was the blare of bugle and roll of drum on the streets, people were hurrying together, and soon the roar of cannon shook the building, as they told us of the bombardment of Sumter by the batteries of the young Confederacy. For months the very air had been vibrant with sound of drum and fife, of rattling musket and martial command. The Old South was soon a great camp of shifting, drilling soldiery. Every departing train bore to the front the raw and ungainly troops of the country, the trim city companies of State guards, and the gayly dressed cadets of the military schools. There were tender partings and long good-bys, so long to many of them that not yet has word of home greeting come. It seemed a great thing to be a soldier in those brave days when the girls decked the parting ones in flowers and sang to them "The Girl I Left Behind Me," "Bonnie Blue

77

Flag," and "Maryland, My Maryland." The scarlet and gold and gray, the flashing sword and burnished musket, the gay flowers and parting song, marked the beginning of that mighty death struggle of the Old South. Soon the gay song deepened into the hush before a great battle, or rose into the cry of the stricken heart over the long lists of wounded and slain. War grew grim and fierce and relentless. There were hunger and wounds, pale faces in hospital and sharp death of men at the front; and sleeplessness and heartache and holy privation and unfailing courage and comfort of Southern womanhood at home. Fiercer and hotter came the storm of battle, as the thin gray lines of Lee and Johnston confronted the soldiery and the resources of the world. Manassas, Sharpsburg, Fredericksburg, Seven Pines, Chancellorsville, Vicksburg, Gettysburg, the Wilderness, Cold Harbor, Petersburg, Appomattox!—how these names, that wreathed with crape their thousands of hearts and homes, and marked the rise and fall of the battle tide, recall to us the passing of the Old South!

On another April day in 1865, as a boy in Mahone's Division, I looked my last into the face

78

346

of the Old South and its great commander, who came riding down the line of our stacked guns, and, halting his old gray war horse Traveler, tried to comfort our hearts by saying: "It's all over. Never mind, men; you have done your best. Go to your homes and be as brave and true as you have been with me."

In the great day of national assize, when empire, kingdom, and republic of earth shall be gathered to judgment, and the Muse of history shall unroll the record of their good and evil, the Old South, the "uncrowned queen" of the centuries, will be in their midst, her white vestment stained by the blood of her sons, her eyes dimmed by sorrow and suffering. No chaplet of laurel shall encircle her brow, and no noisy trump of fame shall hail her coming; but round her fair, proud head, as of yore, shall shine a halo of love, and Fame shall hang her head rebuked, and the trumpet fall from her nerveless hand, as the spirit of the Old South is passing by.

79

A Brief Synoptical Review of

SLAVERY

IN THE

UNITED STATES

BY

MRS. ANDREW M. SEA

née: SOPHIE IRVINE FOX

Historian, U. D. C.

Published by permission of the Author
by the
ALBERT SIDNEY JOHNSTON CHAPTER, U. D. C.
Louisville, Kentucky
1916

SLAVERY IN MASSACHUSETTS.

The papers concerning slavery in the United States contained in this pamphlet were prepared and read before the Albert Sidney Johnston Chapter of the U. D. C., at Louisville, Kentucky, not with any intent or purpose of reopening a discussion of a question long since settled by the arbitrament of the sword, and not even with the idea that they would ever be read elsewhere. They are now published in compliance with a resolution which was unanimously carried at the State Convention held in the City of Newport, Kentucky, October 8, 1902. I have consented to the publication only in the interests of the truths of history.

From the Northern press, pulpit and political arena have been thundered forth denunciations of slavery in the South and of the Southern slave holder. "Uncle Tom's Cabin," and books of similar import, have so industriously and persistently exaggerated and misrepresented conditions that wherever these books have been read the Southern slave holders are believed to have been veritable monsters of oppression and cruelty. I have undertaken to prove that Slavery in the South was a benign and blessed institution in comparison with Slavery as it existed in the "Confederated States of New England." In confirmation of this view I have freely quoted from a "History of Slavery in Massachusetts," by George H. Moore, Librarian of the New York Historical Society in 1862, and corresponding member of the Massachusetts Historical Society, and from historical facts and statistics gathered with almost infinite labor and pains by W. G. Brownlow, of Tennessee, and used by him in his celebrated debate with the Rev. Abram Pryne in Philadelphia, September, 1858.

It is remarkable that the researches of these two men, G. H. Moore and W. G. Brownlow, exponents each of the opposite sectional bias of environment and tradition, should trend along lines so similar that W. G. Brownlow's work, "Ought American Slavery to Be Perpetuated?" could answer as a sequel to G. H. Moore's "History of Slavery in Massachusetts."

G. H. Moore has arranged the result of his researches under two heads, namely: Facts and Theories. I will simply quote the Facts. The Theories were held in common by philanthropists in every State in this Union, notably among them Washington, Jefferson and Patrick Henry. But over the facts *peculiar* to the institution of slavery in New England the curtains have been drawn for considerably more than a century, and in the interest of truth and justice it is time they should be lifted and the light let in.

On G. H. Moore's opening page he says:

"The stains which slavery has left on the proud escutcheon of Massachusetts are quite as significant of its hideous character as the satanic defiance of God and humanity which accompanied the laying of the corner-stone of the slave holders' Confederacy," meaning the Southern Confederacy.

This statement reveals his Northern prejudice, in that he draws no distinction between the cupidity and inhumanity of the New England slave traders and the attitude of the Southern slave holders in defense of their Constitutional right to their slave property, and resenting the fanatical interference of the Northern anti-slavery men with their domestic affairs. But this is of small moment compared with his inestimable service to the truths of history.

From the volume of statistics compiled by G. H. Moore we find that the earliest records of slavery in Massachusetts are handed down from the period of the Pequod War, a few years after the Puritan settlement of the colony. The institution of slavery appears first distinctly and clearly defined in the enslaving of Indians captured in war.

"The Massachusetts Law of Slavery was based on the Mosaic Code. It is an absolute recognition of slavery as a legitimate status and of the right of one man to sell himself as well as that of another man to buy him. It sanctions the slave trade, and the perpetual bondage of negroes and Indians, their children and children's children, and entitles Massachusetts to precedence over any and all of the other Colonies in similar legislation. It anticipates by many years anything of the same sort to be found in the Statutes of Virginia, or Maryland, or South Carolina, and nothing like it is to be found in the contemporary codes of her sister Colonies in New England."

That great numbers of Indians, many thousands, were sold and transported out of the country the historical records of Massachusetts amply attest. At the time of King Philip's War the policy and practice of the Colony of Massachusetts with regard to slavery had already been long settled upon the basis of positive law. The accounts of the Colony of Massachusetts for receipts and expenditures during King Philip's War, from June 25, 1675, to September 16, 1676, give among the credits the following:

"By the following accounts received in or as silver, viz., captives; for 188 prisoners of war sold, $397.13."

They were "sent away" by the Treasurer, that is, sold into slavery. Captain Church's authority from the Plymouth Colony to superintend the selling of Indians into slavery is printed in Hough's Easton's King Philip's War, page 188. This same

Captain Church makes a report to the Plymouth Colony of one transaction alone by which eight score persons, meaning Indians, were carried away to Plymouth, there sold and transported out of the country, and that, too, in the face of promises that had been made them that, on their surrendering themselves, their lives should be spared and not one of them transported out of the country. Among the Indians sold into slavery and transported out of the country were the wife and son of King Philip, the boy being the grandson, the woman the daughter of good old King Massasoit, the best friend the English in America ever had.

The following extract is taken from Edward Everett's address at Bloody Creek, 1835: "An Indian Princess and her child, torn from the wild freedom of a New England forest to gasp under the lash beneath the blazing sun of the tropics."

African slavery was in full public force in Massachusetts from 1636, when the ship Desire, built at Marblehead, Massachusetts, one of the first slave ships built in the Colony, brought in a cargo of slaves, until 1788, when the Legislature passed a law prohibiting further importation of slaves. Graham, an authority much quoted, declares in Hist. U. S., Vol. 4, page 78, that it would be an "impudent absurdity" to regard this law against further importation of negroes as an expression of humane consideration for the negro. In 1638 a cargo of cannibal negroes was sent from New England to the Bermudas.

Sainsbury Calendar, 278, and Colonial Entry Book, Vol. IV., page 124. This first entrance into the slave trade in Massachusetts was not a private enterprise, but an enterprise of the authorities of Plymouth Colony. In 1639 the General Court passed a law regulating slavery.

The first Statute establishing perpetual slavery in America is to be found in the famous Code of Fundamentals or Body of Liberties of the Massachusetts Colony in New England, adopted in December, 1641. Under it slavery existed in Massachusetts for one century and a half without serious challenge. M. H. S., Coll. III., viii., 231. Said law reads as follows:

"It is ordered by this Court and authority thereof, that there shall never be any bond slavery, villenage, or captivity among us, unless it be lawful captives taken in war or such as shall willingly sell themselves, or be sold to us, and such shall have the liberties and Christian usage which the law of God established in Israel concerning such persons, doth morally require, provided this exempts none from servitude who shall be judged thereto by authority." Mass. Laws, Ed. 1660, page 5.

In 1780 the boasted Declaration of Rights appeared, and in 1783 the records of a church at Byfield, Massachusetts, contains a long account of a controversy between a Mr. Parsons and his zealous anti-slavery deacon, who had been suspended from communion because of his zeal against slavery. This shows that the abolition intention of the first clause in the Declaration of Rights had had no effect upon public opinion in Massachusetts.

In 1781 advertisements of slave property appear frequently in the newspapers, mixed up in the sales of wearing apparel, gold watches and other goods, such as New England rum, tobacco, etc. I will mention a few of the advertisements.

From the Continental Journal, March 1, 1781: "To be sold, an extraordinary likely negro wench, 17 years old, strong, healthy, with no notion of freedom, and not known to have any failing, but being with child, which is the cause of her being sold."

Competitors offer for sale:

"A choice parcel of negro boys and girls; just arrived."

"A likely negro wench, about 19 years old, with a child of six months of age; *to be sold together or apart.*"

"A likely negro man (taken by execution) to be sold at public auction at the Royal Exchange Tavern, in King Street, at 5 o'clock this afternoon."

Dr. Jeremy Belknap says: "Negro children were considered an encumbrance in a family, and when weaned were given away like puppies." M. H. S., Coll. I., V. 200. They were frequently publicly advertised "to be given away," sometimes with the additional inducement of a sum of money to any one who would take them off.

Negroes were rated as personal estate. The following extract from Judge Sewell's Diary is taken from the Original:

"1716. I essayed June 22 to prevent Indians and negroes from being rated with horses and hogs, but could not prevail."

The familiar phrase "treated worse than a negro" is historical in Massachusetts. Sewell's Diary, October, 1701.

Richard Baxter expressly recognized the lawfulness of the purchase and use of men as slaves, although in the same breath he condemns man stealing as piracy. The principal point of his work entitled "Christian Directory," was concerning the religious obligations growing out of the relation of master and slave.

Morgan Goodwyn, a clergyman of the Church of England, in his work, published in 1680, entitled "The Negroes and Indians Advocate," hardly intimates a doubt of the lawfulness of slavery, but pleads for the admission of slaves into the Church and for their humanity, against a very general opinion of that day, which denied them both.

It was in the power of masters in Massachusetts to deny the right of baptism to their slaves. I will quote from Matthias Plant to the Secretary of the Society for the Propagation of the Gospel, October 25, 1727:

"A slave woman is desirous of baptism but denied it by her

master. She is a woman of fine sense and excellent judgment far exceeding any of her race ever yet heard of, and equal knowledge of religion with any of her sex."

Dean Berkeley, in his famous sermon before the "Venerable Society," in 1731, speaks of the irrational contempt for the blacks in Massachusetts as creatures of another species, who had no right to be instructed or admitted to the Sacraments."

George Fox, in his work entitled "The Friend," says the Quakers were as greedy as anybody in trading in negroes," by this statement inducing the belief that they approved of slavery as a people with unanimous consent. Ralph Sandiford, another Quaker writer, in his work entitled "Brief Examination," published in 1729, declares that "the dark trade had crept in to the very ministry because of the profit by it." John Eliot seems to have been the first man in America to lift up his voice against the treatment of slaves in New England.

Toward the end of his life Cotton Mather states "he had long lamented with a bleeding burning passion that the New Englanders used their negroes as their horses, or their oxen, with so little care taken about their immortal souls; he looked upon it as a prodigy that any wearing the name of Christians should so much have the hearts of devils in them as to hinder or prevent the religious instruction of the poor blackamoores, and confine the souls of their miserable slaves to a destroying ignorance, merely from fear of losing the benefit of their vassalage."

There is ample proof that slavery flourished under the auspices of respectable Massachusetts merchants down through the entire Colonial period and long after the boasted Declaration of Rights in 1780: Felts, Salem, VII., 230, 261, 265, 288, 292 and 296. To gratify those who are curious to see what were the instructions given by respectable merchants in Massachusetts to the Captains of their slave vessels, I will quote from Felts, Salem, Vol. II., pages 289-290. It is said to be the only specimen extant:

"Novr. 12th, 1785, Captain ————:

"Our brig, of which you are in command, being cleared at the office and in other respects ready for sea, our orders are that you embrace the first fair wind, make the best of your way to the Coast of Africa, and there invest your cargo in slaves. * * * Male or female slaves, whether full grown or not, we cannot particularly instruct you about, and on this head only observe that prime male slaves generally sell best in any market. * * * You are to have four slaves upon every hundred and four at the place of sale, the privilege of eight hogsheads and two pounds eight shillings per month. This is all the compensation you are

to expect for this voyage. And conclude with committing you to the Almighty Disposer of all Events.
"Your friends and owners, ——————,"

The slaves purchased in Africa were sold chiefly in the West Indies and Southern Colonies. But when the markets were glutted and the prices low they were brought to Massachusetts. The Rev. Dr. Jeremy Belknap remembered personally a cargo of slaves brought to Massachusetts between 1755 and 1765 which consisted almost entirely of children. Sometimes the vessels of the neighboring Colony of Rhode Island, after having sold their prime slaves in the West Indies, brought the remnants of their cargoes to Boston for sale. M. H. S., Coll. I., IV., 197.

The nearest approach to an attempt to abolish slavery in all the Provincial and Colonial Legislation of Massachusetts was a bill of 1767, which reads thus:

"A bill to prevent the unlawful practice of enslaving mankind in this Province and the further importation of slaves into the same."

This bill was brought up in the House of Representatives a number of times, read and re-read there; finally it was duly "ordered that the matter subside," and a committee appointed to bring in another bill (a substitute in reality for the original bill) for laying an impost duty on slaves imported into the Province. Ibid., 393. Ten years later, in 1787, the original bill was again brought up, and again failed.

In 1706 an essay or "Computation that the importation of negroes is not so profitable as the importation of white servants" was published in Boston. It was attributed to Judge Sewall, one of the foremost writers of his day. As it shows so clearly why negro labor was considered unprofitable in Massachusetts, I will quote a few of its suggestions:

"By the last year's bill of mortality for the Town of Boston we are furnished with a list of forty-four negroes dead, which, being computed one with another at £30 per head, amounts to £1,320, a clear loss, not only to Boston, but to the country in general. On which we make this remark, that the importation of negroes into this or the neighboring Provinces is not so beneficial to the country as the importation of white servants would be.

"Negroes are eye-servants, great thieves, much addicted to stealing and lying.

"Negroes do not carry arms to defend the country, as whites do.

"By encouraging and importing white men servants most husbandmen in the country could be furnished with servants for £8, £9 or £10 per head, who are not able to pay £40 or £50, the common price for negroes.

"If necessity calls for it, that a husbandman must fit out a man against the enemy, if he has a negro he can not send him; if he has a white servant 'twill answer the end, and save his son at home.

"The bringing in of white servants would much enrich this Province, because husbandmen would not only be able to manure lands already under improvements, but improve more land that lies waste under woods, and enable this Province to set about raising naval stores, hemp to make sail cloth and cordage to furnish our own shipping, which would hinder the importing of same, and save a considerable sum, and in time we would be capacitated to furnish England with pitch, tar and other stores, which are now purchased in foreign nations. Negroes do not people our country as whites would do, whereby we should be strengthened against the enemy."

Governor Dudley, in his report to the Board of Trade in 1708, says: "Negroes have been found to be unprofitable investments, the planters prefer white servants."

Not one word of sympathy for the poor slaves dying by hundreds from disease caused by change from the tropics to the rigorous New England climate. It was simply a question of profit and loss. If negro labor had been as profitable in New England as it was on the sugar and cotton plantations of the South there never would have been the war between the States.

We have shown that the slaves in New England were denied the right to religion. And even the right to life itself was not clearly defined as belonging equally to the bond slave and freeman. For instance, Samuel Smith, of Sandwich, was called upon to answer before the Court for the offense of killing his slave. The record goes on to say:

"If Samuel Smith, of Sandwich, was hung for the murder of his slave in Massachusetts in the year 1719, it is due to the historic fame of the Province that the world should know it," adding the following significant words:

"It is greatly to be regretted that the trial, conviction and punishment of such an offender should be concealed among the neglected rubbish of a Massachusetts court room."

The original of the Fugitive Slave Law Provision in the Federal Constitution is to be traced to the Articles of Confederation of the United Colonies of New England, of which Massachusetts was the ruling Colony. The Commissioners of the United Colonies found occasion to complain to the Dutch Governor in the New Netherlands, in 1646, that the Dutch agent at Hartford had harbored a fugitive slave woman, of whom they say in their letter:

"Such woman is a part of her master's estate, and a more considerable part than a beast."

A provision for the rendition of fugitive slaves was afterward made by treaty between the Dutch and English. Plymouth Colony Records. Vol. IX., 6, 64, 190.

A case in Connecticut presents an illustration of this provision that is of great historic importance. It is that of a fugitive slave and attempted rescue in Hartford, in 1703, of which an account is given in Historical Notes, No. VI. This case laid before the Honorable General Assembly in October, 1704, after a statement of facts, etc., proceeds with reasons for the return of the fugitive, some of which we quote:

"According to the law and constant practice of this Colony, and all other plantations, as well as by the civil law, such persons as are born of negro bond women are themselves in like condition, that is, born in servitude. Nor can there be any precedent in this government or in any of Her Majesty's plantations, produced to the contrary. And though the law of this Colony doth not say that such persons as are born of Negro bond women shall be slaves (which was needless because of the constant practice by which they are held as such), yet it says expressly that no man shall put away, or make free, his negro or mulatto slave, which undeniably shows and declares approbation of such servitude, and that negroes or mulattoes may be held as slaves within this Government."

It is well to remember that the first entrance into the slave trade in Massachusetts was not a private individual speculation, but the enterprise of the authorities of Plymouth Colony, ordered by the General Court. Mass. Rec. I., p. 253, March 13, 1639, G. H. Moore, says:

"The humane efforts of Roger Williams and John Eliot to mitigate the horrors of slavery in Massachusetts hardly amounted to a protest against the institution. In their time there was no public opinion against slavery."

There are some things in connection with slavery in Massachusetts over which, but for the truths of history, the curtains should be drawn eternally. Barry's Hanover, page 175, and Josselin's account of two voyages to New England, published in London, 1664.

It will not be amiss to mention at this point G. H. Moore's estimate of the characters of the New England Colonists as portrayed in their handling of the Institutions of Slavery. He says a recent writer of English history, meaning Froude, has so clearly stated his (G. H. Moore's) views in regard to this matter that the language required very little change.

"It would be to misread history and to forget the change in the times to see in the Fathers of New England mere common-place slave-mongers. To themselves they appeared as the elect to whom God had given the heathen for an inheritançe. They were men of a stern intellect and fanatical faith who, believing themselves the favorites of Providence, imitated the example and assumed the privileges of the chosen people, and for their wildest and worst acts they could claim the sanction of religious convictions."

The same spirit actuated John Brown, assassin and blood-thirsty fanatic, to whom a monument has recently been erected by the Northern people, or, rather, by his admirers in the North.

Continuing, he says:

"In seizing and enslaving Indians and trading for negroes, they were but entering into possession of the herit-age of the Saints."

Compare Froude's History of England, Vol. 8, p. 480, with the above.

We have seen that on March 25, 1788, the Legislature of Massachusetts passed a law prohibiting the further importation of slaves. The following day another law was passed requiring all negroes in Massachusetts to depart out of the Commonwealth in two months on penalty of being apprehended and whipped and driven out.

In the Massachusetts Mercury, Boston, printed by Young & Minns. Printers to the Honorable the General Court, Sept. 16, 1800, the following notice occurs:

"The Officers of Police, having made return to the sub-scriber of the names of the following Africans or negroes, the same are hereby warned to depart out of this Common-wealth before the 10th day of October next, as they would avoid the pains and penalties of the law passed by the Legis-lature March 25, 1788."

To this notice was appended the names of negroes sent in by the police. G. H. Moore says in regard to this notice:

"We doubt if anything could be found in human legisla-.tion that comes nearer to branding color as a crime."

That the history of Colonial slavery may be clearly under-stood in all its bearings, and that the responsibility for the slave trade may be put where it belongs, I will state that Great Britain had aided her Colonial offspring to become slave owners. She had encouraged her merchants in tempting the Colonies to acquire slaves, she in fact excelling all of her competitors in slave steal-ing. From the reign of Queen Anne, the slave trade was among her most envied and cherished monopolies. The great "distinc-tion," as Queen Anne expressly called it, of the Treaty of Utrecht, was the contract granting Great Britain the exclusive right for thirty years of selling slaves to the West Indies and Coast of America. In 1775, the reply of the Earl of Dartmouth to the earnest remonstrance of the agent at Jamaica against the policy of the Government was as follows:

"We can not allow the Colonies to check or discourage in any manner a traffic so beneficial to the nation."

In conclusion, I will briefly sum up the result of G. H. Moore's exhaustive research among the historical records of Massachusetts in regard to the institution of slavery in that State:

"It is a stern historical fact that hereditary slavery existed in Massachusetts from the year 1641 by virtue and equity of an express law warranting the same, established by the General Court and sufficiently published; or, in case of the defect of a law in any particular case by the Word of God, to be judged by the General Court. * * * We express our regret that the Legislative Annals of Massachusetts record no attempt to repeal the local laws by which slavery had been established, regulated and maintained. * * * The fact is not to be disguised that the (abortive) efforts along these lines during the brief session of the General Court at Salem in 1774, were political movements against the Government, as much as anything else, the Colonists resenting bitterly the arbitrary decisions of the former (see Dartmouth's reply to the agent at Jamaica) concerning Colonial affairs. The honor of taking the lead against slavery and maintaining it, does not belong to Massachusetts, nor, indeed, to the separate action of any State. It was "considered abolished," "put aside and covered," but never having been formally abolished by legal enactment, it continued to exist, "in point of law," until 1866, when the Grand Constitutional amendment terminated it forever in the United States."

NOTE.—In an address delivered before the Edinburgh Philosophical Institution on November 1, 1911, on "The Scot in America and the Ulster Scot," Mr. Whitelaw Reid, the American Ambassador to Great Britain, said that in our war for independence the movement for equality for all men before the law began among the classes persecuted in their own country. The anti-slavery movement, which led to our last great war, began in the same way, but not in New England. That is a prevalent delusion, which their brilliant writers have not always discouraged. But the real anti-slavery movement began in the South, largely among the Scottish Covenanters of South Carolina and East Tennessee, twenty to thirty years before there was any organized opposition to slavery elsewhere, even in Massachusetts. The Covenanters, the Methodists and the Quakers of East Tennessee had eighteen emancipation societies by 1815. A few years later there were five or six in Kentucky. By 1826 there were 143 emancipation societies in the United States, of which 103 were in the South, and as yet, so far as known, not one in Massachusetts. As late as 1833 the gentlest and sweetest of American anti-slavery poets, John G. Whittier, was mobbed in Massachusetts for attempting to make an Abolition speech. John Rankin, the noted Covenanter and anti-slavery leader, said that it was safer in 1820 to make Abolition speeches in Kentucky or Tennessee than at the North, and William Lloyd Garrison said in 1833 that he was surrounded by contempt more bitter, prejudice more stubborn and apathy more frozen than among slaveholders themselves.

SLAVERY IN THE SOUTH.

African slavery was formally introduced into this country by the Dutch in 1619, at Jamestown, Va. In the month of August, of that year, a Dutch man-of-war brought a cargo of twenty slaves to Jamestown, Va., and they were offered in exchange for merchandise needed on the ship. They were regarded as indentured servants, with the exception that their servitude was to last for life, and they were employed by the planters to work the tobacco.

In 1711 there was a slave market or depot established in New York City, in what was known as Wall Street forty years ago, and slaves captured or kidnaped on the coast of Africa were landed there by New England trading vessels to supply the Southern market. About the same time another slave market was opened in Boston, near to where the Franklin House stood forty years ago. They kept but few of their captives among themselves, for it had been demonstrated that negro labor was unprofitable in the cold sterile regions of New England. The poor creatures, native to tropical skies, insufficiently clothed and fed, shivered through the rigorous Northern winters, homesick for the rice and cotton fields, the banana groves and scorching suns of Africa. Hundreds died from exposure and disease brought on by change from a tropical climate to the ice and sleet and chilling blasts of New England. When the Puritans from damp foggy England suffered so intensely from the bitter cold of their new country, think what the poor Africans must have endured, and Northern masters, fearful lest they should lose the entire profits of their venture, hurried the negroes south in sailing vessels and sold them into perpetual bondage to Southern masters. Merciful indeed were the dispensations of Providence that transplanted the Africans from New England to the Southern country, overruling the cupidity and inhumanity of their original owners, and settling them in a land where climate, soil and products resembled in some respects the climate, soil and products of their native tropics, and where the blacks took hold and thrived, the great majority of them happy and contented, because they were cared for and kindly treated, the ties that bound them to the soil and their white masters being more strongly cemented with each succeeding generation. Congress abolished the slave trade in this country by a law passed in 1800, which took effect in 1808. Twenty years before this, while the Constitution of our country was being formed, a committee of gentlemen, a majority of whom were from the slave states, reported a resolution or section authorizing Congress to abolish the slave trade in 1800. But this was defeated by the votes of New Hampshire, Massachusetts and Connecticut, and the period extended unto 1808, thus giving eight additional years to the inhuman traffic. Take notice that the New England conscience we have heard so much about was not sensitive in regard to the buying and selling of slaves, nor indeed to the institution in whatever form, until this law was passed. For hear what was done by Northern men, or rather New Englanders, in the slave trade, during the eight years of extended time, this extension of time secured by the votes of Northern men. The old saying, "make hay while the sun shines," was their motto. The bill became a law in 1808. From 1804 to 1807, a period of only three years, there were imported into the town of Bristol, Rhode Island, as many as 3,914 slaves from the coast of Africa. During the same period there were brought to Newport, now the famous watering place, 3,488 from Africa. Hartford, Connecticut, received 250 of these slaves, and begged for more. Providence, Rhode Island, received 500, and Boston 1,000, by consignment from agents in Africa.

Samuel Hopkinson, a prominent Rhode Island man, says in his "Reminiscences" that in 1770 Rhode Island had 150 vessels in the African slave trade, and eighty-seven years after they were still actively engaged in the slave trade. The foundations of some of the largest fortunes in New England were built upon the slave traffic, and I have the names of some of the men whose fortunes were made this way. A recent writer in the Courier-Journal, Louisville, a Kentuckian who has delved much among ancient records, declares that the foundations of New York, Boston and Newport, Rhode Island, were built upon the African slave trade. As late as 1857, just four years before the breaking out of hostilities between the States, there were seventy-five slave ships being fitted out to carry on the slave trade, and all of them being fitted out in Northern ports. This, too, in defiance of law, and in the face of the crusade against Southern slave owners by Northern politicians, preachers, writers and private citizens. For remember, it was about this time (in 1857) that John Brown was hanging slave owners in Missouri and Kansas for no other reason than that of their being slave owners, burning their houses over their heads, and committing other atrocities, and trying to incite the negroes of Virginia to arise and exterminate the entire white population of the State. I have heard the statement made, and gentlemen of the highest standing for scholarly attainments given as authority for it, that no Southern man ever owned a slave ship, and that no slave ship handled by a Southern man ever brought a cargo of slaves from Africa.

The slaves were brought to our doors by the English, Dutch and
New England slave vessels. The Southern people bought them,
made a home for the poor creatures, civilized them, Christianized
them, and trained them in the industrial arts. The farms and
plantations of the ante-bellum South were the finest schools of
technology in existence. The negro women were taught to card,
spin, weave, knit, sew, cook, wash, can and preserve. There are
many beautiful specimens of their handiwork at the loom preserved among old relics in my own State, and doubtless in every
Southern State. Their counterpanes, rag carpets, cottonade,
linsey, linen and jeans are justly celebrated. I remember an old
negress telling me with much pride, "My mistiss taught me to
carry seven shuttles." The men were taught many useful
trades, such as tanning, shoemaking, the blacksmith's trade, and
every industrial art that pertained to farming and gardening.
Montgomery Bell's large iron interests in Tennessee were conducted entirely by his slaves, some of them being so skillful in
the building and handling of furnaces, etc., that they were called
"furnace experts." I could multiply these instances a thousand
fold had I the requisite space. To-day the most valuable negro
servants in Kentucky are the ex-slaves.

And now we will touch upon the laws of the South in regard
to the protection of slaves against the abuse of power by unscrupulous masters. There was no such thing as "chattel" slavery
in the South, although Northern politicians and writers frequently have spoken of the slaves as chattels. Laws were in
force in all of the slave States for the protection of the slaves.
In some of them, Tennessee for instance, if a master failed to
provide decent clothes for his slaves, he was liable to indictment
by grand juries for this dereliction of duty, and for the killing
of slaves, unless proved by competent witnesses to have been in
self-defense, masters and overseers have been frequently hanged.
The laws of Louisiana, where the scenes of "Uncle Tom's Cabin"
were principally laid, were peculiarly sensitive in regard to the
protection of slaves against the abuse of power by unscrupulous
or unkind masters. I will quote from Bouvier's Law Dictionary,
a recognized authority on the matter:

"The laws of Louisiana expressly forbid the selling of slaves
in a manner to separate mother and child."

And for the transgression of this law a prominent citizen of
Louisiana, a Mr. Hunter, was fined $1,000 at New Orleans in
1856, and compelled to forfeit six slaves. This was much com-
mented on at the time by Northern newspapers, notably among
them the New York Herald of March 15, 1856. In one of the
books of reference I had recourse to in the preparation of this
article I came across a copy of the printed rules and regulations
that governed Mr. Joseph Acklan's plantations, situated in the

State of Louisiana, Parish of West Feliciana, opposite the mouth
of Red River, near about the same locality selected by Mrs.
Stowe for her sensational work of fiction. Mr. Acklan required
his overseers and agents to observe these rules to the letter.
They read this way:

"My negroes are all permitted to come to me with their complaints, and in no instance shall they be punished for so doing.
And in my absence I enjoin upon my agents to attend to their
complaints, and if they have been cruelly treated, the overseer
be at once discharged. Feel, and show that you feel, a kind regard for the negroes under your control. Never cruelly punish
them, nor overwork them, nor in any way abuse them, but seek
to render their situation as comfortable and contented as possible. See that their necessities are supplied, their food and
clothing good and sufficient, their homes comfortable, and be
kind and attentive to them in sickness and old age. See that they
keep themselves clean. At least once a week visit each of their
houses. See that they are swept out and thoroughly cleaned.
Examine their bedding, etc. See that things have been well aired,
their clothing mended and everything done to promote their comfort and happiness. If any of the negroes are reported to be sick
see without delay what ails them, and that proper attention be
given them. The regularly appointed preachers for my places
must preach during daylight. I want my people encouraged to
cultivate religious feelings and morality, and punished for inhumanity to their children and stock, for profanity, lying and
thieving."

This is the official record of the conduct of one plantation in
the South, by a humane, God-fearing slave owner. If the records
of the great majority of them could be gathered together, what
an interesting page of unwritten history it would furnish, and
how completely it would nullify multitudinous statements made
by ignorant, prejudiced persons against the slave owners of the
South and the institution of slavery as it existed among us. For
instance, Henry Ward Beecher, in a publication of his entitled
"Life Thoughts," declares "that if a colporteur should leave a
Bible in a negro cabin, he would be quickly ushered into Heaven
from the lowest limb of the nearest tree."

Carefully gathered statistics enforce the fact that there were
466,000 slaves connected with the different religious denominations in the South: With the Methodist Church, 200,000; the
Hardshell Baptists, 170,000; old and new school Presbyterians,
18,000; Cumberland Presbyterians, 20,000; Episcopalians, 7,000;
all other sects combined, 51,000, making in all 466,000.

It was the almost universal custom for planters to erect neat,
comfortable chapels on their own plantations, where the white
families and negroes worshipped in company. But in the large

cities there were a number of churches built, principally by contributions from the negroes themselves. One in Mobile costing $7,000, with a negro membership of 600. There were churches in Nashville and Memphis, Tennessee; in Huntsville, Alabama; in Charleston, South Carolina; in Savannah, Georgia; and in Richmond, Virginia, the Baptist colored church had a membership of 2,700. There were two colored churches in Petersburg, Virginia—one had 1,800 members, the other 1,400. The Baptists had 52,000 colored communicants in Western Virginia alone. No wonder the slaves in Virginia refused to follow John Brown's leadership. In Charleston, South Carolina, the Presbyterian Synod reported 5,000 slaves in connection with the Presbyterian Church in that State. Throughout Louisiana large congregations of slaves were found. In New Orleans, one African Methodist had a membership of 1,350, and supported six colored missionaries. A devoted Episcopal clergyman who labored among the people of eleven plantations in Louisiana, says thus:

"It has never been my privilege to declare the glorious truths of the Gospel of Jesus Christ to more orderly, quiet, serious congregations. Their hearts are unfeignedly thankful, and they show God's praise not only with their lips, but in their lives.

"The labors of pious missionaries among the slaves were gladly encouraged by the masters, even by those who were not themselves professors of religion."

This statement in regard to the labors of this devoted Episcopal clergyman, and of the encouragement given his labors by masters not themselves religious, is taken from the Philadelphia Christian Observer.

There were more slaves who were members of the different religious bodies in the South in proportion to their numbers than there were white people. That was the work God gave the slave owners of the Southern country to do, and in situations of unparalleled difficulties that was the work they did do, and the work that is still being done in the South for the benighted African, whose forefathers a few generations back were cannibals in the wilds of darkest Africa, and who had inherited the immoral propensities and lawless natures of their savage ancestors. John Wesley, after a two years' sojourn in Georgia, in his report made in 1739 to the Board of Missions in London that had sent him out, advised the purchase of more negroes for the use of American missions, for the reason that they were adapted to the climate, their labor valuable, and the missionaries were serviceable to them in a spiritual point of view. This report was made in 1739, and along about that time, in 1731, Dean Berkeley speaks of the "irrational contempt for the negroes in Massachusetts as creatures of another species who had no right to be instructed or admitted to the Sacraments." Millions of dollars have been spent and hundreds of valuable lives lost in the attempt to evangelize the negroes in Africa. Yet slavery in the South brought five times more negroes into the folds of the church than all the missionary operations of the whole world combined.

I have mentioned the fact that in the year 1800 negroes by hundreds were driven out of Massachusetts because of the prejudice against their color. About the same date, in 1801, one John Chavis, a full-blooded free negro, was riding as a missionary under the direction of Hanover Presbytery in North Carolina, universally beloved and respected. He studied at Princeton under Dr. Witherspoon, and was one of the foremost educators of North Carolina. Among his pupils were Archibald and John Henderson, sons of Chief Justice Henderson; Governor Charles Manly, Dr. James Wortham, the Edwards, Enlows and the Hargroves, besides many others. Many of his students became prominent as politicians, lawyers, preachers and teachers. Dr. Wortham writes:

"I have heard John Chavis read and explain the Scriptures to my father's family and slaves repeatedly. His English was remarkably pure, his sermons abounding in strong common sense, views and happy illustrations, without any efforts at oratory or sensational appeals to the passions of his hearers. He was a man without guile, seeking the good opinion of the public by the simplicity of his life and the integrity of his conduct."

After his death the Presbytery with which he was connected supported his widow. This extract is taken from a work published in 1888, and entitled "The History of Education in North Carolina," by Charles Lee Smith, Fellow in Johns Hopkins University, Baltimore, Maryland.

There are two aspects of slavery in the South that are without parallel in the history of slavery throughout the civilized world, namely: The religious instruction given to the slaves by their masters either personally or through the instrumentality of said masters; and the fidelity of the negroes during the war between the States, when every able-bodied man was at the seat of war and the women and children were entirely at the mercy of the negroes. There are no instances recorded of indignities offered Southern women by the negroes during that time, and thousands of them remained at home, even after they had been freed by the Government, and watched over and cared for the white families entrusted to their protection. This fidelity in the wake of the passing Institution of Slavery left a phenomenally beautiful light—a light which will never be seen again, for old things have passed away.

NOTE.—The Cyclopedia of Political Economy and United States History, volume 3, page 733, records the following, taken from the New York Evening Post:

"During the eighteen months of the years 1859-'60 eighty-five slave ships belonging to New York merchants, brought in cargoes, annually, of between thirty and sixty thousand African slaves, which were sold in Brazil, there being great demand for them in that country owing to new industries constantly springing up."

The names of the slave ships are given in the encyclopedia mentioned. During the period from 1808 when Congress passed a law making the slave trade a felony, until 1860 it was carried on in the North to a greater extent than even in the days of Wilberforce, and there is no record of any Northern slave-trader being prosecuted for violation of Federal laws. Old Peter Faneuil built Faneuil Hall in Boston with slave money. Georgia was the first State to abolish the slave trade.

SOURCES

THE "BENEFITS" OF SLAVERY

Civis. [Puryear, Bennett]. *The Public School in its Relations to the Negro.* Richmond: Clemmitt & Jones, 1877. [Published originally in the *Southern Planter and Farmer,* December, 1875; January, February, May, 1876.] (Courtesy of Yale University Library)

G.R.S. [Stetson, George R.] *The Southern Negro As He Is.* Boston: George H. Ellis, 1877. (Courtesy of Duke University Library)

Tucker, J.L. *The Relations of the Church to the Colored Race. Speech of the Rev. J.L. Tucker, D.D., of Jackson, Mississippi, Before the Church Congress, Held in Richmond, Va., on the 24-27 Oct., 1882.* Jackson: Charles Winkley, 1882. (Courtesy of Duke University Library)

Mayo, A[mory] D[wight]. *The Negro American Citizen in the New American Life.* [n.p., 1889] (Courtesy of the Library of Congress)

Campbell, Robert F. *Some Aspects of the Race Problem in the South.* Asheville: Asheville Printing Company, 1899. (Courtesy of the Library of Congress)

Barringer, P[aul] B. *"The Sacrifice of a Race."* Raleigh: Edwards & Broughton, 1900. (Courtesy of the University of Virginia Library)

Bingham, Robert. *An Ex-Slaveholder's View of the Negro Question in the South.* Asheville: Asheville Printing Company, 1900. [Originally published in *Harper's Monthly* (European Edition), July, 1900.] (Courtesy of Duke University Library)

Hamill, H.M. *The Old South: A Monograph.* Nashville: Publishing House of the M.E. Church, South, [1904]. (Courtesy of Duke University Library)

Sea, Mrs. Andrew M. [Sophie Irvine Fox]. *A Brief Synoptical Review of Slavery in the United States.* Louisville: Albert Sidney Johnston Chapter, U.D.C., 1916. (Courtesy of the University of Virginia Library)

CONTENTS OF SERIES

Other Books by John David Smith

Window on the War: Frances Dallam Peter's Lexington Civil War Diary, with William Cooper, Jr. (1976)

Black Slavery in the Americas: An Interdisciplinary Bibliography, 1865–1980 (2 vols., 1982)

An Old Creed for the New South: Proslavery Ideology and Historiography, 1865–1918 (1985; reprint edition, 1991)

Dictionary of Afro-American Slavery, with Randall M. Miller (1988)

Ulrich Bonnell Phillips: A Southern Historian and His Critics, with John C. Inscoe (1990)